Reading Chekhov's Text

Reading

Chekhov's

Text

EDITED BY ROBERT LOUIS JACKSON

Northwestern University Press / Evanston, Illinois

Northwestern University Press
Evanston, Illinois 60208-4210

Copyright © 1993 by Northwestern University Press
All rights reserved. Published 1993
Printed in the United States of America

ISBN 0-8101-1080-6

Library of Congress Cataloging-in-Publication Data

Reading Chekhov's text / edited by Robert Louis Jackson.
    p. cm. — (Series in Russian literature and theory)
   Includes bibliographical references.
   ISBN 0-8101-1080-6 (alk. paper)
   1. Chekhov, Anton Pavlovich, 1860–1904—Criticism and
interpretation. I. Jackson, Robert Louis. II. Series.
PG3458.Z8R4   1993
891.72'3—dc20   93-22840
                                               CIP

Contents

v

Contents

Robert Louis Jackson

Introduction

> Now here is a writer about whom it is
> pleasant to speak!
> —Leo Tolstoy, about Chekhov

"THERE ARE big dogs and little dogs, but the little ones need not be disheartened by the existence of the big ones: for we are all called upon to bark—and bark with the voice God has given each of us," Chekhov remarked to the Russian writer Ivan Bunin after praising the work of Guy de Maupassant. A curious strain of self-disparagement surfaces from time to time in Chekhov's remarks about himself. Was this modesty on his part? Was it a defense against a cultural milieu that did not and could not know his full worth? Or was it simply the reflex of a nature that made great demands upon itself and had no time for self-promotion? Whatever the answer, Chekhov turned out to be one of the "big dogs," and his bark grows louder and louder.

The antediluvian times have passed when one could say, as did Dmitry Merezhkovsky in 1914, that Chekhov knew nothing but the "contemporary Russian environment" and did not want to know anything more; that he was "in the highest degree national, but not universal"; that the Chekhovian environment was but "an inert, congealed moment, a dead point of Russian contemporaneity without any connection with world history and world culture." *Congealed* is a good word for Merezhkovsky's Chekhov criticism. Gone, too, are the days when one could say gracefully and emptily, like the Russian critic D. S. Mirsky in 1927, that "there is no distinctiveness in Chekhov's style and no color in the greyness of his world (beyond some slight shadings into a greyish-blue or yellow." *Grey* is a good word for Mirsky's Chekhov criticism.[1]

In the course of the twentieth century Chekhov has come to be recognized as one of the world's greatest writers and stylists. He is read everywhere. He is discussed. He is loved. No other nineteenth-century Russian writer, with the possible exception of Dostoevsky, has aroused so much interest in post-Soviet Russia as Chekhov. Russians have found in his work not only the anguish and uncertainties of a changing world

1

but also something tonic and restorative. His protean art continually breaks the mold of fashion and expectation, continually challenges critic and scholar, actor and director. Yet we know Chekhov far less than we admire him. We have only begun fully to discover the manifold complexity of his art, to perceive his organic unity of form and content, to plumb the depths, finally, of his artistic thought. For the painter of elusive moods, of fin de siècle anguish and melancholy, of mysterious noncommunication—as many early perceived Chekhov—was also a writer who explored the vast range of human life and experience, an artist-thinker with a complex worldview of his own that extended far beyond the thoughts and moods of his characters. We have only begun to validate Father Sergey N. Bulgakov's prescient observation in 1904 that after Tolstoy and Dostoevsky, writers who took as their chief theme "the basic questions of human life and spirit," Chekhov is "*the* writer of greatest philosophical significance." Thirty years later another critic, M. Kurdyumov, balked at the view that Chekhov raised no problems for himself and his reader beyond the familiar "Chekhovian themes" and observed: "We have simply not read Chekhov to the core."[2] That judgment still stands.

We know Chekhov's drama, certainly, far better than we do his prose. Our view of "Chekhov" is more often than not shaped by our perception of his plays. The classic works *Ivanov, The Sea Gull, Uncle Vanya, The Three Sisters,* and *The Cherry Orchard* are seen, heard, and read. A fairly extensive body of criticism and scholarship in Russia and the West deals with Chekhov's theater. Chekhov's prose has not been so fortunate. He did not write imposing novels like *Anna Karenina* or *The Brothers Karamazov,* works whose very magnitude commands respect. Chekhov preferred the less respected "small forms." Apart from his sixteen plays and farces, he wrote short stories—well over six hundred of them. The great masterpieces of Chekhov's prose fiction are numerous, and we are continually discovering new ones, even among the anecdotes, "scenes," and miniatures produced in the first years of his writing in the early 1880s.

Chekhov's genius in prose was to depict the sun in a drop of water. Yet the limpid simplicity of his stories is deceptive. The reader moves with ease and pleasure through these works. Only very gradually, when slowing down, does one ascertain their rich inner content. Whether because of expectations nourished in a nineteenth-century message-and-mission-minded Russian *intelligentsia* or because of a powerful Russian novelistic tradition that had established its artistic and intellectual hegemony toward the end of the century, Chekhov's deeper artistic thought and preoccupations eluded many of his early Russian critics. Only in relatively recent times have critics and scholars stopped and begun slowly to read the individual Chekhov prose and drama texts with the same care that has gone into the reading of Tolstoy or Dostoevsky.

The reader settles down and discovers that the Chekhov text is far from simple, that it has the density of all great poetry and prose, and that it moves in the same deep waters as does the work of Pushkin, Gogol, Turgenev, Tolstoy, and Dostoevsky. The word *poetry* is not out of place. "When I was still studying the history of literature," Chekhov wrote to the Russian poet Yakov P. Polonsky on January 18, 1888, "I was already familiar with one phenomenon which I elevated almost into a law: all great Russian poets manage splendidly with prose. You will not drive this conviction out of my head. . . . Perhaps I am wrong, but Lermontov's *Taman* and Pushkin's *Captain's Daughter*, not to speak of the prose of other poets, is direct evidence of the close affinity between full-bodied Russian verse and artistic prose."[3] Chekhov never wrote poetry—"Verse is not my element" (Stikhi—ne moja stikhija), he once noted—but his prose is profoundly poetic in character.[4] The multilayered meanings of a Chekhov text are inseparable from its poetic structure and dynamics. We read his prose as we would read a poem, seeking out its meanings in the complex interrelationship and interplay of language, image, structure, detail, and device. This is also true of our reading of Tolstoy and Dostoevsky, of course. Yet while Tolstoy and Dostoevsky can thunder out their concerns to the reader, Chekhov, as Merezhkovsky rightly observed, never speaks in a loud voice. For the most part he does not provide the reader with a visible superstructure of ideas or ideology to signal his deeper concerns ("Ward Six" is a notable exception).

In this respect Chekhov is closer to the great master of Russian prose Ivan Turgenev, who argued that a "poet"—by which he meant the writer in general—"must be a psychologist, but a secret one: he must know and feel the roots of phenomena but represent only the phenomena themselves in their flowering and fading." He also wrote: "Remember that however subtle and complex the inner structure of some tissue in the human body, the skin, for example, nonetheless its appearance is comprehensible and homogenous."[5] Chekhov certainly carried over this principle to the stage. "Let everything on the stage be just as complex and at the same time just as simple as in life," he once remarked. "People dine, merely dine, but at that moment their happiness is being made or their life is being smashed."[6] So too, on the stage of Chekhov's prose, everything is "just as complex and at the same time just as simple as in life."

Images of Chekhov vary. In the first two lines of his engaging little study of Chekhov, Korney Chukovsky projects the image of a jovial and gregarious Chekhov: "He was hospitable like a magnate. With him hospitality was a passion." Chukovsky goes on to document the "vital energy," the "passionate love of company," the "phenomenal sociability," the "bacchanalia of cheerfulness," of "this happiest of Russian great talents"—only to remind the reader some twelve pages into his work that Chekhov could burst into tears of "angry melancholy" over "cursed Russian reality."[7] Chukovsky clearly sought to counter the image of a gloomy Chekhov, one that all too often has confounded Chekhov with his fictional characters. Chukovsky captures very well essential characteristics of Chekhov. Yet the image of Chekhov as the "happiest of Russian great talents" is as one-sided as the image of a gloomy Chekhov. Who is this person whose extreme sociability and gregariousness engaged everybody and yet at the same time allowed no real intimacy? V. I. Nemirovich-Danchenko observed that Chekhov's "great inclination toward sociability went along with a great reserve." Olga Knipper, Chekhov's wife, experienced that reserve. She once wrote him that she felt "anguish, despair" when she felt that he was "distancing himself from her." "You never want to tell me anything, and you write as though from habit," she wrote in a letter. "What interests me is only you, your soul, your spiritual world. I want to know what is going on there, or is it too bold to ask this, and is entrance there forbidden?" A distinctly naive note echoes in these lines. Chekhov, it would seem, caught that note, for he replied: "You ask why I keep you at a distance from me. How silly, child!"[8]

Chekhov's own thumbnail sketch of his life in a letter written in 1892—the opening piece in this collection—serves as a good example of the way his spirited openness can both entertain and conceal. "If there are no facts, substitute something lyrical," Chekhov concludes his half-facetious survey of his life. And his strange reluctance to write about himself? "Autobiography? I have a disease: autobiographobia," he remarked some years later in a letter in which he again supplied a correspondent with information about his life: "Several dates, quite bare," as he put it. "But I can do no more." "It's a real torture for me to read any details about myself," Chekhov confessed, "not to speak of writing them up for publication."[9] A superabundance of material about Chekhov's day-to-day life and thoughts can be found in his rich correspondence and in the memoirs of many who knew him. Yet the inner person remains elusive, perhaps because that person is so directly and immediately and always the protean artist about whom there are no facts to fix the image into one mold. "Every individual existence revolves around mystery," one of Chekhov's characters observes.[10]

Among the immediate responses to Chekhov on the occasion of his death in 1904, those of the Russian writer Ivan Bunin stand out for their sensitive grasp of Chekhov's character. Bunin, of course, has his "idea," and he signals it through a pun in his brief résumé of Chekhov's life.[11] It was a "mistake," he writes, for Chekhov in early spring of 1890 to have undertaken his two-month odyssey to the island of Sakhalin by post chaise "despite the rain and the cold, with virtually no sleep and nothing to subsist on except the 'food of Saint Antony' [*Anthony* in English]." One may pass over Bunin's notion that Chekhov's trip was a mistake: this mistake was rooted deeply in the necessities of Chekhov's existence. Bunin's punning comparison of Anton Chekhov with the renowned "desert father" and ascetic Saint Anthony of Egypt (c. 250–355) is another matter. It provides the thematic clue to Bunin's portrait of Chekhov. Chekhov's day of baptism, his name day, January 17, falls on the feast day of Saint Anthony.[12]

The motif of Saint Anthony appears early in Bunin's memoir when he recalls Chekhov himself observing that "one must work 'indefatigably' and be truthful and simple in one's work to the point of asceticism." Bunin goes on in his recollections to underscore traits and habits of Chekhov's, some minor and some major, that point to patterns of restraint, reserve, and self-denial: Chekhov's habit of not eating until the end of the day ("otherwise on a full stomach one works badly," Bunin recalls Chekhov saying); the writer's "fortitude" in the face of the many trials of his life (economic need, illness, his role as supporter of his family); his restraint in the face of "trivial and vulgar abuse" of his writing; the laconic character of his discourse; his almost self-abnegating attitude toward his work; and his principled refusal to promote himself or to manipulate his image as a writer.[13] "It bears repeating," Bunin writes, "that Chekhov's self-control was formidable in his art and in his life."[14] In his notebook Chekhov summed up this motif of self-denial: "My motto is: I need nothing."[15]

Bunin's Chekhov is eminently human: a man of striking simplicity and nobility, reserved yet receptive, and full of humor and cheer; a man marked by an aristocratic delicateness and chasteness; a rarely independent and free man; and above all, an artist totally dedicated to his work. In a letter of October 4, 1899, responding to a "gloomy letter" from Olga Knipper on the failures of the Moscow Art Theater, Chekhov wrote characteristically: "Art, especially the stage, is a realm where it is impossible to go without stumbling. Ahead of you lie many unsuccessful days and wholly unsuccessful seasons; there will be great misunderstandings and deep disappointments—you must be prepared for all this. You must expect it and, in spite of everything, stubbornly, fanatically pursue your course."[16] Chekhov, too, stubbornly and fanatically pursued his course, though not without a counterpoint of self-questioning in the early years of his creative work.

One of the Chekhov's early correspondents, the poet Alexey N.

Pleshcheyev, remarked that reading Chekhov's letters was like "reading a talented literary work."[17] Here the man and writer emerges in all his vitality, wit, and protean genius. Though critics and biographers have drawn abundantly from Chekhov's correspondence (only a small part of his extant 4,400 letters has been translated into English, however), this vast "text" has yet to be intensively examined in its own terms. Marena Senderovich's essay, "Chekhov's Name Drama," is a first attempt at a close reading of Chekhov's epistolary text from a defined perspective: Chekhov's relation to his own creative process and his development as a writer. In her psychologically discerning essay, Senderovich shows how Chekhov's use of pseudonyms discloses his need for internal distancing— a reflex of what she calls his permanent inner duality. Chekhov's use of pseudonyms in the 1880s becomes a metaphor for Chekhov's nagging sense that he has not really given expression to his creative potential, to his most serious ideas. Chekhov speaks lightly of himself as "the most frivolous and least serious" of writers in a well-known letter to Vladimir Korolenko. He has "loved" his muse but has not "respected her." Chekhov had difficulty in facing his success in the late 1880s. Senderovich suggests the presence of deep fissures in Chekhov's artistic and psychological consciousness. These feelings of uncertainty and alienation find ultimate expression in the thematics of alienation and self-alienation in "A Boring Story." What ends tragically for the protagonist of that story finds a positive resolution in Chekhov, specifically, Senderovich argues, in Chekhov's journey to Sakhalin in 1890. The journey that for Bunin was a mistake for Senderovich was a logical occurrence in Chekhov's own artistic development.

Michael C. Finke's "'At Sea': A Psychoanalytic Approach to Chekhov's First Signed Work," centering on one of Chekhov's early short stories, takes its point of departure from the problem of pseudonym that is raised in Marena Senderovich's essay. Finke's main concern, however, lies in literary and psychoanalytic realms. "At Sea: A Sailor's Story," consisting of barely more than one thousand words, is a brilliant and psychologically intriguing miniature. Its first line—"Only the dimming lights of the receding harbor were visible in an ink-black sky"— sets the stage for the drama of the Fall.[18] "I do not know life," the narrator remarks at the outset. Yet the story of what happens when he and his father take their places at peepholes to spy on a newly wed English pastor and his young wife in the bridal suite belies his words. By the end of the tale both narrator and his father have "fallen" again, though we perceive them as having gained in moral stature, as Finke keenly observes in his analysis of the story. Finke's thoughtful article is double-barreled: he analyzes the literary subtexts of the story (Victor Hugo's *Toilers of the Sea* and Shakespeare's *Hamlet*) and, in this connection, explores the Oedipal situation that he finds at the story's center. He finds that Chekhov's alterations of these subtexts "directly parallel Freud's interpretation of Shakespeare's play: they superimpose direct conflict with the father onto an impossible erotic desire." Chekhov's relation to his "literary fathers" thus engages the Oedipal theme. Finke posits on Chekhov's part "an excessive degree of emotional, even unconscious, involvement" in the psychosexual Oedipal dynamics of this story. He concludes that "the definite antierotic strain in Chekhov's life and works may well bespeak an inadequate resolution of the issues glimpsed in 'At Sea.'" Not every reader will willingly follow Finke every step of his Freudian way, but as Dr. Dorn in *The Sea Gull* says of Konstantin Treplev's play-within-a-play, "There's something in it."

The next essay examines Chekhov's story "The Enemies," which involves a misunderstanding between a doctor, Kirilov, and an aristocrat, Abogin, that neither individual can resolve. Five minutes before Abogin appears, seeking assistance for his apparently ill wife, Kirilov and his wife have experienced the most extreme suffering: the loss of their only son. Their silent "music" of suffering is moving. Abogin, worried to despair about his wife, finally succeeds in convincing Kirilov to make a doctor's visit. It turns out, however, that she has absconded with a lover. Kirilov, stunned, falls into a blind rage in which he rails against the banal and comfortable world of Abogin. In the prestigious final lines of the story the narrator observes that "Kirilov's sorrow will pass," but his hatred and contempt for the well-to-do, "unjust and unworthy of the human heart, will not pass and will remain in the doctor's mind to the very grave." Both Kirilov and Abogin, each in his own way, fail to transcend a basic egoism. Yet the heavily laden message-oriented words of the conclusion, I argue, do not succeed in substantially modifying our initially sympathetic view of Kirilov—a person etched against the dark background of bitter struggle, fateful loss and interrupted grieving.

"In art, as also in life," Chekhov wrote shortly before his death, "nothing accidental takes place."[19] Indeed, in Chekhov's art no detail is without meaning. At the beginning of Chekhov's story "At Home," the governess informs Evgeny Petrovich, an attorney of the circuit court and father of seven-year-old Seryozha, that "somebody came from the Grigorievs to pick up a book, but I said you were not at home." This opening sentence seems irrelevant in contrast to the second and third lines in the story, where the governess informs Evgeny Petrovich that his seven-year-old son has been found smoking cigarettes. The drama of the story centers on the issue of smoking, while neither the Grigorievs nor the book they inquire about turn up again. Is this first line just background, decoration, filler? Vladimir Golstein's fine reading of Chekhov's story ultimately explains the opening line: the bookish Evgeny Petrovich, figuratively speaking, is not "at home," that is, he is initially incapable of communicating with his son on the issue at hand. By the end of the story he has "come home," at least, in the actions of his heart. As Golstein demonstrates, it is not pedagogy or morality or even art, finally, that is responsible for his final breakthrough to his son. "Evgeny Petrovich has captured his son's conscience, not by threatening to cancel his own love for the child . . . but by evoking Seryozha's own love and empathy." Emotional closeness and warmth provide a matrix for the action of the fairy tale. As any reader of Golstein's model analysis of "At Home" will confirm, the child's vision and Chekhov's art have two things in common: both break the frame of convention and both are marked by absolute honesty.

"In my childhood," Chekhov wrote I. L. Leontiev on March 9, 1892, "I had a religious education . . . with choir singing, readings in church from the Gospels and Psalter, with punctual attendance at matins, with the obligation to help on the altar and to ring the bells. And the result? When I recall my childhood it appears rather gloomy to me. I have no religion now."[20] Most critics and biographers have recorded the few but impressive facts about Chekhov's religious upbringing but have tended to let the matter rest with Chekhov's words "I have no religion." It is clear that Chekhov was not a believer in any conventional or, indeed, unconventional sense of that word. Not everything is clear and simple, however, about Chekhov's personal relation to religion. What did Chekhov mean when he predicted that "in the distant future mankind will know the truth of the real God, i.e., not guess at it, not seek it in Dostoevsky, but know clearly, as one knows that twice two is four"?[21]

"I am not a believer," Chekhov wrote to another correspondent.[22] There is no reason to doubt him. He left the Church, but he did not step out of the Judeo-Christian world or divest himself of the culture and traditions of Russian Orthodoxy that he imbibed as a child and lived with all his life. The real question is not so much Chekhov's personal religious beliefs (though this is not an isolated question) but the relation of Chekhov the artist to biblical and liturgical culture and tradition, to that "imaginative framework—a mythological universe," in Northrop Frye's words, "within which Western literature had operated down to the eighteenth century and is to a large extent still operating."[23] Russian nineteenth-century writers were steeped in the religious and spiritual heritage of Eastern Orthodox Christianity, and Chekhov was no exception. He was not a preacher or prophet. Unlike Gogol, Dostoevsky, and Tolstoy, he did not didactically invoke ethical or religious doctrine, and his art is not an arena for the kind of sharp

8

moral-religious crisis, conflict, or catastrophe one finds in their works (Chekhov's story "The Student" can be considered something of an exception). He was a secular writer and physician who drew from all currents in European and Russian literature, culture, and thought. Yet biblical and liturgical vision, imagery, and allusion permeate his art. The serious study of this religious subtext in Chekhov's work certainly is one of the major tasks of Chekhov criticism.[24] An in-depth analysis of the metaphorical function of religion in that subtext may well illuminate the great question of the nature and unity of Chekhov's artistic worldview. The essays of Nils Åke Nilsson, Willa Chamberlain Axelrod, Alexandar Mihailovic, Julie W. de Sherbinin, and Robert Louis Jackson in different ways approach the question of religious text and subtext in Chekhov's art and sensibility.

"It is interesting to note that the original plan [of 'The Bishop'], as described by S. N. Shchukin, explicitly stated that the bishop cried because, while reading the story of Christ's Passion, he applied it to the fate of every human being and to himself in particular, knowing that he was ill and that he was going to die. In the final version all these explanations were left out." Nilsson's point in his masterful discussion of Chekhov's great story "The Bishop" underscores a basic fact of Chekhov's art: explanations are left out. Chekhov "speaks" through the poetic materials of his text. Nilsson's treatment of the story richly documents Chekhov's poetry of word and image. A synopsis of the story, Nilsson observes, suggests a pessimistic view of life. In his analysis of the text—of the story's idea, imagery, language, style, and artistic devices—Nilsson shows that this judgment is not validated by the artistic texture and techniques of the story. Speaking of Chekhov's "bloc technique"—the juxtaposition of scenes of different character—Nilsson notes that this device is not used "just for the sake of effect." Behind this method is "a personal view on these questions" and one that is essential to the "whole idea" of "The Bishop." Facing illness and death, the aging bishop slowly, through recollection and time, comes to a recognition of what is essential in life. In the ending of the story, with its contrasts of scenes of death and the indifference of nature and general life, Chekhov gives expression to the "unsentimental agnostic's calm and simple view of death," a conception that "individual man is mortal, but life is eternal as mankind is eternal."

Merezhkovsky maintained that "Christianity was almost silenced in Chekhov's works" and that Chekhov "passed by Christ, not looking around, and then deliberately tried to look away from where Christ was to be found."[25] Rather, it appears, Merezhkovsky and his fellow intellectuals passed by Chekhov. They did not look deeply enough into Chekhov's texts to see where Christ and Christianity, where Blake's "Great Code of Art," the Bible, could be found. In reading "Holy Night," an artistic meditation on Christianity, faith, and the modern secular mind, we can gain deep insights into Chekhov's own complex relation to religion. Willa Chamberlain Axelrod's fine discussion of Chekhov's use of religious imagery, symbol, subtext, and allusion in her essay "Passage from Great Saturday to Easter Day in 'Holy Night'" shows us how deeply Chekhov had absorbed the legacy of Eastern Orthodoxy and empathized with its spirituality. The Church's liturgical passage from Lent to Easter is not "background" in the story. It is at the very center of the drama of the novice and ferryman Ieronim's lament over the death of his gentle friend, the monk-priest Nikolai, creator of religious hymns. "How beautiful," the narrator remarks to Ieronim apropos of the magnificent spectacle of Great Saturday. "You can't express the beauty," sighed Ieronim. "I cannot express to you how [Nikolai] used to write!" Ieronim exclaims. "Another time and we wouldn't even pay any attention to rockets, but tonight we rejoice at every vain thing. And where might you be from?" Clearly the narrator, who is a modern skeptic and rationalist who has lost faith, the mass of people who have come for the spectacle, and even the clergy who have "forgotten" Ieronim and Nikolai only marginally experience the deep pathos and joy of the liturgical "passover." The story's statement and the ambiguity of its ending are suggested in the ferryman's last call for passengers: "Christ is risen! Is there nobody else?" His Easter greeting, "Christ is risen!" is not answered by the traditional response, "Verily, he is risen!" At the same time his question "Is there nobody else?" has an ironic subtext. The question echoes Ieronim's anguish over the loss of Nikolai. Yet the narrator has not participated in the "passover" from the sorrow of death to the joy of Easter. "'Well, that's God's will!' said I [the narrator], affecting a monastic tone. 'We all must die. In my opinion you ought to be rejoicing . . . They say that he who dies at Easter, or during Eastertide, without fail will land in the kingdom of heaven.'" Ieronim replies, "That's true." Chekhov, of course, can in no way be identified with the banal, patronizing narrator in whom the "beautiful" has been sundered from the spiritual. "God needs only complete people," Chekhov once jested.[26] Something of Chekhov's completeness and the aloneness in his response to Christianity can be deduced from "Holy Night." "Between 'there is a God' and 'there is no God' lies a whole colossal field that the true wise man crosses with great difficulty," Chekhov wrote in his notebook. "Russian man only knows one of these two extremes, the middle between them is uninteresting to him, and he usually knows nothing or very little."[27] "Holy Night," among other stories, suggests that Chekhov crossed that field, if he ever crossed it, at least with humility.

Chekhov's "Ionych" is the story of the gradual moral, spiritual, and ultimately physical decay of a young provincial doctor, Dmitry Ionych Startsev. We do not usually associate the inner content of Chekhov's classic story with biblical or religious subtext. Yet as Alexandar Mihailovic shows in his essay, "Eschatology and Entombment in 'Ionych,'" "a network of Christological associations and references throughout the text throw into sharper relief Startsev's self-mortification, describing it in the metaphorical terms of the ossification and entombment of the self. The disturbing pathos of his fate is brought home by the reiterated suggestion in the imagery of the story that he rejects the possibility of salvation." Thus the spiritual corruption of the hero is perceived as a falling away from the Christian universe. Mihailovic's sensitive analysis of the symbolism and subtext of "Ionych" suggests the deep mythopoetic roots of the Chekhovian drama of life and consciousness.

Chekhov's "The Teacher of Literature" has been regarded as a satire on the vulgarity of provincial life: the story ends with the hero, "surrounded by banality," resolving to escape from that world. In her probing essay, "Life beyond Text: The Nature of Illusion in 'The Teacher of Literature,'" Julie W. de Sherbinin concerns herself with religious subtext. She explores in the story "a set of texts that derives from Russian religious culture," particularly examining the paradigm of the virgin and the harlot. As she points out, the parallels she observes serve to contrast rather than compare Chekhov's characters and situations with their biblical prototypes. Chekhov's satire of provincial life thus telescopes with a complex satiric play on the hero's unconscious romantic-religious expectations and his ultimate disillusionment. "The story's final paragraph is saturated with Marian signs that no longer exercise authority in Nikitin's life." In her discussion of the important literary subtext in the story, Pushkin's narrative poem "Count Nulin," de Sherbinin also traces Chekhov's ironic play with this theme. Central to her essay is the notion that the hero's "act of self-liberation moves him beyond the 'scripts' offered by the Russian literary and religiocultural traditions." Like Mihailovic, de Sherbinin provides striking evidence of the extraordinarily rich texture of religious and literary symbolism and allusion in Chekhov's writing. What is certain is that this subtext does not stand in isolation from the story's larger statement.

"The Student," Chekhov once insisted, was his "favorite story" and proof that he was not a pessimist. "Pessimist—that's a repellent word." The story certainly has been acclaimed by critics and readers as a supreme work of art. The Russian critic V. V. Rozanov saw in *The Brothers Karamazov* an embodiment of "a struggle that for thousands of years has been ravaging the human soul—the struggle between the negation of life and its affirmation."[28] Chekhov's profound and moving story "The Student" falls within this tradition: like Dostoevsky's great novel, it affirms life in the face of tragedy in human history. The Christian drama of death and resurrection, I suggest in my essay on Chekhov's story, informs the narrative. Central to the hero's renewal is the recollection of the tragedy of the Crucifixion and of Peter's denial. Ivan Velikopolsky's reaffirmation of faith is based on a rediscovery of an unbroken chain of events between the past and the present. These ethical connections find embodiment, finally, in transmitted narrative: the story of Christ and Peter that the Apostles tell, this same story that Ivan (Russian for "John") retells to several peasant women and men, and the story "The Student," in which Anton Chekhov reenacts that universal and eternal drama of despair and spiritual renewal.

It was inevitable that in its profound cultural, moral, and spiritual awakening in the late eighteenth and nineteenth centuries, Russian society—in thrall for centuries to an immobilizing serfdom and autocracy—should meditate profoundly in its literature and thought not only upon its congealed life and history but also upon chance and fate, of which that same society so often saw itself as victim. Central in this meditation embodied in its literature and philosophy is a historic emphasis on the primacy of freedom and responsibility in human culture. "All's nonsense on earth! . . . Nature is a ninny, fate is a henny, and life is a penny!" observes a character in Lermontov's *A Hero of Our Time*, citing an old Russian proverb.[29] However much tragic Russian life and history tended to validate the message of this proverb, the great giants of Russian literature and thought denied it all along the way. Pushkin, Gogol and Lermontov, Herzen, Turgenev, Dostoevsky, Tolstoy, and—last but not least in the nineteenth century—Chekhov insisted on man's freedom and its correlative, responsibility. The drama of "fate" saturates *The Sea Gull, The Three Sisters,* and *The Cherry Orchard.* Chekhov's profound story "A Woman's Kingdom" revolves around the complex notion that "a man's character is his fate."[30] Two other works that deal openly with the theme of freedom, fate, and responsibility are Chekhov's stories "In Exile," the focus of Richard Peace's fine essay, and "Ward Six," the subject of Liza Knapp's philosophically discriminating discussion. Not surprisingly, both of these stories bear the heavy trace of Chekhov's journey to the Sakhalin prison camps in 1890. Indeed, the central drama in both of these stories speaks of the grim triumph of congealed Russian life. What is more, two of the protagonists in these stories—the exiled ferryman Semyon in "In Exile" and Dr. Ragin in "Ward Six"—both embody the principle of passivity before Russian life. In this connection, Richard Peace signals the importance for Chekhov of Goncharov's *Oblomov* in the writing of "In Exile": "The elevation of the supine into an ideal may well have been one of the factors that so disconcerted Chekhov in his rereading of *Oblomov* the year before he undertook his Siberian journey." Reconciliation with reality is the essence of the preachment of the ferryman, Semyon. "The philosophical implications of the story," Peace writes, "are summed up in its concluding symbolism: 'Everyone lay down. The door opened because of the wind, and snow blew into the hut. Nobody wanted to get up and shut the door: it was cold and too much bother." Chekhov in his story, one might say, gets up and shuts the door. He shuts it in a way that does not deny tragic Russian reality but at the same time affirms a view—passionately held by Dostoevsky—that the essence of life is movement, striving, hope.

In "Ward Six" Chekhov again explores the philosophical theme of reconciliation with reality and again discloses the tragedy of a man, Dr. Ragin, trapped not by philosophy but by "philosophizing," a man who "loves reason and honesty intensely but has insufficient character and belief in his rights to build a reasonable and honest life around him." Like Oblomov and like the bloated and torpid peasant in Chekhov's story, Dr. Ragin, figuratively speaking, rolls over. His motto, we realize, is "It's all the same" (*vsë ravno*). In her excellent discussion, Liza Knapp shows how Dr. Ragin "elevates this colloquial verbal tick to the status of a general philosophical view that nothing matters." She discusses Chekhov's exploration of the "epistemology of suffering" in the context of Aristotelian discourse on fear and pity: "'Ward Six' is affective and effective largely because Chekhov makes proper, judicious, and artistic use of the very faculty that is impaired in his two heroes, Gromov and Ragin, the faculty for contemplating similarities. Their respective disorders, which are two extremes of the same continuum, prevent them from experiencing fear and pity in a healthy, moderate, cathartic fashion." The capacity to experience fear and pity in a way that is not debilitating or destructive is precisely the function of tragedy.

Joseph L. Conrad's comparison of Chekhov's "Volodya" with Turgenev's "First Love," Andrew R. Durkin's discussion of allusion and dialogue in "The Duel," Paul Debreczeny's consideration of "The Black Monk" as Chekhov's version of symbolism, and Svetlana Evdokimova's exploration of the mythopoetic roots of "The Darling" conclude the essays on Chekhov's prose. Our understanding of Chekhov's creative method, his way of overcoming his literary models, is enriched by Conrad's discussion. Conrad shows the closeness of Chekhov's ties with Turgenev. He also rightly speaks of Chekhov's "penetrating insight into adolescent psychology." Chekhov not only explored a "sensitive, naive teenager's confusion when confronted by awakening sexual urges, but as a doctor interested in then-new developments in psychiatry, he recognized and pointed to the need for positive human interaction." "Volodya" does not have the richness of Turgenev's masterpiece, "First Love," perhaps, in part, because it is too closely bound to its model. Yet in its focus on adolescent sexuality and suicide, it is a dark and compelling piece, worthy of the attention Conrad gives it. The writer and surgeon Richard Selzer, reviewing Chekhov's life and work, suggests "some impediment between [Chekhov's] romantic inclinations (for surely he loved women) and the reality of sex."[31] Whether or not Selzer is correct on this point, the two studies in this volume on "Volodya" and "At Sea" constitute an interesting introduction to the question of the erotic in Chekhov's work.[32]

Chekhov's "The Duel" has long been recognized as a work particularly responsive to and rooted in Russian literary tradition. One of its protagonists, Laevsky, has been seen as directly in the line of the Russian "superfluous man." The names of Pushkin, Lermontov, Turgenev, Tolstoy, Leskov, Byron, Schiller, and others have come up in discussion of this work, not to speak of such major nineteenth-century thinkers as Charles Darwin and Herbert Spencer. In his excellent discussion, "Allusion and Dialogue in 'The Duel,'" Andrew Durkin focuses on the writer Nikolai S. Leskov's impact on Chekhov's story. He demonstrates how Chekhov weaves a "popular," nonheroic element, linked primarily with the Russian writer Leskov's "Legend of the Conscience-Stricken Daniel," into the drama of Laevsky and von Koren. Durkin offers a particularly fine reading of the decisive closing episode of "The Duel." His discussion holds special interest for its focus on the deacon Pobedov and the moral-religious dimensions of "The Duel."

In a thoughtful and wide-ranging essay, "'The Black Monk': Chekhov's version of Symbolism," Paul Debreczeny examines Chekhov's enigmatic story in the context of early Russian modernism. He finds in Chekhov's story a fusion of symbolism and mysticism, yet at the same time he sees it as a work that resisted much of the rhetoric of symbolism. Debreczeny argues persuasively that Chekhov picked up and parodied in the figure of Kovrin ideas of Merezhkovsky and, in particular, elements of the mystical thought and personality of the philosopher and poet Vladimir Solovyov (a "likely prototype" for Chekhov's hero). Chekhov's stories, Debreczeny notes, drew the same kind of negative critical response that the symbolists did from critics. The essay concludes with the suggestion that Chekhov's links with the symbolists lie not in a sympathy with their outlook but with aspects of their artistic method. Chekhov "responded to every new trend, absorbing it into his own art."

Like "The Black Monk," Chekhov's "Darling" has been the object of intense discussion—though for different reasons. Touched by the devotion of the story's protagonist, Olenka, to her various husbands, Leo Tolstoy in his well-known afterword to Chekhov's story wrote: "In beginning to write 'Darling' [Chekhov] wanted to show what woman ought not to be. The Balak of public opinion invited Chekhov to curse the weak, submissive, undeveloped woman devoted to man. . . . But when he began to speak, the author blessed what he had meant to curse."[33] Renato Poggiolo suggests that a reading of the story convinces one that "the final esthetic outcome transcends the tale's original intent." He finds "no compelling reason to prefer [Tolstoy's] anti-feminism to Chekhov's feminism," however. Chekhov, he suggests, started out without any ideological pretensions, but unexpectedly a stock comic situation developed "into a vision of beauty and truth."[34] Poggioli concludes his discussion with an interpretation of the story as a new version of the myth of Psyche. In her essay, "'The Darling': Femininity Scorned and Desired," Svetlana Evdokimova, while acknowledging that elements in the story do suggest this parallel with the myth of Psyche, finds Olenka's love and character much more reminiscent of the Greek nymph Echo. In the relation of this myth and of an alternate version—the fable of Echo and Pan—to Chekhov's Olenka, Evdokimova finds the basis for two interweaving strands of interpretation—the satiric and the lyrical—that struggle for supremacy in criticism. Evdokimova validates both interpretations. She concludes her stimulating and incisive analysis of the mythopoetic dimensions of "Darling" with a fine critical reading of Tolstoy's afterword.

Two final essays shed light on Chekhov's drama from different angles: The first, Laurence Senelick's richly informed essay, "Offenbach and Chekhov; or, La Belle Elena," explores the important place Offenbach's work occupies in the development of Chekhov's dramatic art. It splendidly illustrates Chekhov's extraordinary capacity to integrate, transform, and energize art forms, light or serious, in his work. Chekhov from an early age "imbibed the Offenbachian perspective, which he found appealing." Unlike the Russian intellectual establishment that condemned Offenbach and operetta as immoral and alien, Chekhov, as Senelick points out, found the German composer's "anti-idealism," his irreverent treatment of gods and heroes, quite congenial. At the same time, Offenbach is shown in Chekhov's early stories to be "a Russian cliché for European culture." Senelick concludes with a discussion of Chekhov's appropriation and development of Offenbachian material and motifs—in particular, Offenbach's *opéra bouffe*, *La belle Hélène*—in his dramas *The Wood Demon* and *Uncle Vanya*.

"*Uncle Vanya* as Prosaic Metadrama," by Gary Saul Morson, approaches Chekhov and his play from a theoretical perspective. Morson is well known for his theory of "prosaics." The term, which he coined, has a double meaning: it denotes an approach to prose (as opposed to poetics) that takes prose on its own terms and a worldview that places special emphasis on unsystematic and everyday experience. In developing his theory of prosaics, Morson has focused especially on Tolstoy.[35] In his provocative essay Morson reiterates that for Tolstoy "it is not the dramatic events of life that matter, either for individuals or for societies, but the countless small, prosaic events of daily life." He argues that it was "above all this aspect of Tolstoy's thought that had the most profound influence on Chekhov." Morson sees both Chekhov and Tolstoy as embodying a "countertradition"—the kind he calls prosaics—opposed to the dominant tradition of the *intelligentsia*.[36]

"I believe in separate people," Chekhov wrote to I. I. Orlov on February 22, 1889. "I see salvation in separate individuals scattered throughout Russia here and there—whether they be intellectuals or peasants, there is strength in them, although they are few. . . . The separate individuals about whom I speak play an unnoticed role in society. They do not dominate, but their work is evident."[37] Chekhov is one of those individuals whose work is evident.

About Chekhov

Anton P. Chekhov

Do You Need My Biography?

DO YOU need my biography? Here it is. In 1860 I was born in Taganrog. In 1879 I finished my studies in the Taganrog school. In 1884 I finished my studies in the medical school of Moscow University. In 1888 I received the Pushkin Prize. In 1890 I made a trip to Sakhalin across Siberia and back by sea. In 1891 I toured Europe, where I drank splendid wine and ate oysters. In 1892 I strolled with V. A. Tikhonov at [Shcheglov's] name day party. I began to write in 1879 in *Strekoza*. My collections of stories are *Motley Stories, Twilight, Stories, Gloomy People,* and the novella "The Duel." I have also sinned in the realm of drama, although moderately. I have been translated into all languages with the exception of foreign ones. However, I was translated into German quite a while ago. The Czechs and Serbs also approve of me. And the French also relate to me. I grasped the secrets of love at the age of thirteen. I remain on excellent terms with friends, both physicians and writers. I am a bachelor. I would like a pension. I busy myself with medicine to such an extent even that this summer I am going to perform some autopsies, something I have not done for two or three years. Among writers I prefer Tolstoy, among physicians—Zakharin. However, this is all rubbish. Write what you want. If there are no facts, substitute something lyrical.

19

Ivan Bunin

In Memory of Chekhov

I BECAME acquainted with Chekhov at the end of 1895. We saw each other at that time only briefly, and I would not mention it if the meeting didn't call to mind several phrases that, in my opinion, are typical of Chekhov, even in tone.

"Do you write a lot?" he asked me, among other things.

I answered that I wrote little.

"Too bad," he said almost gloomily in his deep chesty baritone. "One has to work, you know, indefatigably your whole life." Then, after a silence, Chekhov added without any apparent connection: "In my opinion, after writing a short story one should strike out the beginning and the end. That's where we men of letters most often lie."

Then the conversation turned to poetry, and he suddenly asked with animation, "Tell me, do you like Aleksei Tolstoy's poems? In my opinion, he's an actor! As a child he tried on an opera costume and has never since taken it off."

After these fleeting encounters, chance conversations, from which I have cited several phrases only because they touch on favorite themes of Chekhov's—such as that one must work "indefatigably" and be truthful and simple in one's work to the point of asceticism—we did not meet again until the spring of 1899. In April of that year I went to Yalta for a few days, and one evening I chanced to meet Chekhov on the quay.

"Why don't you come to see me?" were his first words. "By all means come tomorrow."

"When?" I asked.

"In the morning around eight." And probably noticing a look of surprise on my face, he added: "We're early risers. And you?"

"I, too," I said.

"Well, then come as soon as you're up. We'll have coffee. You do drink coffee?"

"Occasionally I do."

"Drink it every day. It's a marvelous thing. When I'm at work I

20

have nothing but coffee and broth until evening. In the morning, coffee; at midday, broth. Otherwise on a full stomach one works badly."

I thanked Chekhov for his invitation and fell silent, pleased and excited. He too was silent, and we walked without a word the length of the quay and sat down on a bench in the square.

"Do you like the sea?" I asked, in order to say something.

"Yes," he replied. "But it's so empty."

"That's what's nice about it," I said.

"I don't know," he answered, gazing off somewhere into the distance through the lenses of his pince-nez, obviously busy with his own thoughts. "In my opinion, it's nice to be an officer, a young college student, to sit somewhere in a crowded place listening to cheerful music."

Then, as was his wont, he fell silent and, with no apparent connection, added: "It's very difficult to describe the sea. Do you know the description of the sea I recently read in a pupil's notebook? 'The sea was big.' Just that. In my opinion that's very good!"

The aforegoing phrases may strike some as strange or affected, but I don't hesitate to mention them; indeed I should like to emphasize that I regard them as typical of Chekhov. Chekhov and affectation! Only people who have no notion of Chekhov could juxtapose these two words. And who does not know that one of his most striking characteristics is precisely the absence of affectation, the complete absence of any kind of pose and of any kind of tricks—the sort we use to capture each other in our nets.

"I'll say right out," wrote one of Chekhov's memoirists, "I have met people no less sincere than Chekhov, but I cannot recall meeting anyone as simple and devoid of all stock phrases and pretentiousness as he was."

And that is the living truth. Chekhov passionately loved everything that was sincere, vital, and organic, provided there was nothing coarse or dull, and he positively could not bear phrasemongers, pedants, hypocrites, especially those who played their role so well that it became second nature to them. In his works he almost never speaks of himself, his tastes or opinions, for which, I might add, he was long considered an unprincipled man, not at all civic-minded. In real life he also never focused on his "I." He would seldom speak of his likes or dislikes, such as "I like this and that" or "I can't stand that." These are not Chekhovian phrases. His likes and dislikes, however, were remarkably clear-cut and well defined, and among the former, naturalness occupies a prominent place; and of course, only his endless thirst for the utmost in simplicity, his aversion to everything mannered, unnatural, or labored, explains his remark about the naive charm of a child's description of the sea. His words about the officer and music bring out another characteristic:

reserve. The unexpected shift from the sea to the officer was undoubtedly elicited by a concealed melancholy over health and youth. The sea is barren... yet he loved life, pleasures, and in recent years his thirst for joy, albeit the most simple and ordinary, would sometimes show itself in his conversations, but really do no more than show itself, for Chekhov never liked to dot his i's. . . .

In Moscow in 1895 I encountered a middle-aged man in pince-nez, simply but well dressed, rather tall, of slender build and lithe gait. He greeted me courteously, but with such simplicity that I—then still a youth and unaccustomed to such a tone on first meetings—mistook his courtly simplicity for coldness. I found him greatly changed in Yalta: he had grown thin, his face had darkened; his whole being, however, conveyed a sense of inborn elegance, the elegance of a man, however, no longer young, one who had experienced much and who had been ennobled by his experiences. His voice had a softer tone. But on the whole his manner was almost the same as it had been in Moscow: courteous but reserved, he would speak in a rather lively way, but more simply and briefly; during a conversation he would always be thinking something to himself, leaving it up to the other person to detect those transitions in the hidden currents of his thoughts, and he would always be looking at the sea through the lenses of his pince-nez, his face upturned just slightly.

The next morning, after the meeting at the quay, I went to his dacha. I vividly recall the cheerful, sunny morning that Chekhov and I spent in his little garden. He was very lively, joked a lot, and, incidentally, read me the only poem—so he said—that he had ever written: "Hares and Chinamen, a Fable for Children."

> Some Chinese betook themselves
>   to cross a bridge one day,
> While up ahead some hightailed hares
>   Scurried along the way.
> The fat men suddenly shouted out:
>   "Hey, hey! catch them, quick!"
> The hares cocked their tails still more,
>   And vanished in the thicket.
> The moral to this tale is clear:
>   He who wants to eat a hare
> Must, rising daily with the birds,
>   Ever obey his daddy's words.

From that day forth, I began visiting Chekhov more and more often and soon felt perfectly at ease in his house. In turn, Chekhov's attitude toward me also changed. Things became more lively and cordial. But his reserve remained, and it was manifested in his relations not only with me but also with those closest to him; it signified, as I later realized, not indifference, but something much deeper.

The white stone dacha in Autka, so elegant and beautiful in the bright southern sunshine under the dark blue sky; the little garden that Chekhov cultivated so caringly, for he was always fond of flowers, trees, and animals; his study, decorated only by two or three of Levitan's paintings and additionally containing a huge semicircular window opening out on the Uchan-Su River valley, overgrown with gardens, and on the blue triangle of the sea; the hours, days, and sometimes even months that I spent at this dacha; and the awareness of being close to a man who had captivated me not only by his mind and talent but also by his stern voice and his childlike smile—all these will forever remain among the fondest memories of my life.

Chekhov was well disposed toward me. This at least I felt in his letters, and in the cheerful smile with which he always greeted me. He responded very positively to the fact that I was writing. But the reserve that I have mentioned never left him, even in our most personal conversations. What he thought about my writings, however, I learned, as is proper, only after his death, from the newspapers; he himself hardly ever spoke to me about the matter. I might also add that he was a sterling family man: he loved his mother, sister, and brothers tenderly, but even with them he acted in ways that caused many people to think that he was indifferent to them. And so it was in everything.

He had a great sense of humor. Take a look, however, at his humorous works, even those over which the reader laughs hilariously: there is not a single pun, not a single rhetorical turn, no play for the audience. Chekhov loved laughter but only broke out in his charmingly infectious laugh when someone else said something funny. He himself would say the most amusing things with a totally straight face. He delighted in jokes, bizarre nicknames, nonsense, and mystification. Even toward the end of his life, in those moments when his health would improve slightly, he told a never-ending string of jokes. And with what refined comedy he would elicit irrepressible laughter! He would drop two or three words, slyly wink his eye over his pince-nez, and that would set us off. And his letters! Somebody—I believe it was Leo Tolstoy—said that well-written letters are the most difficult of all literary genres. Chekhov's letters were not only well written, but they were also remarkable in their spontaneity, precision, and beauty of style. And how much humor they contained, for all their extremely quiet form!

"Dear Ivan Alekseyevich, would you care to join us on Good Friday? We shall be expecting you. Come no matter what, without fail; we shall be serving a great many snacks, and what's more, the weather is wonderfully warm in Yalta just now, and there are flowers all over the place! Come, do us a favor! I've changed my mind about marriage; I don't want to marry, but nonetheless, if you feel I sound stuffy, well then, so be it, perhaps I may get married" (March 25, 1901).

Or again: "Dear Ivan Alekseyevich, tomorrow I shall be leaving for Yalta, where I beg you to address your congratulations to me on the occasion of my official marriage. . . . I wish you health and all the best. Yours, A. Chekhov, the bourgeois of Autka" (June 30, 1901).

But Chekhov's reserve was also manifested in many other and more important ways, and ones that really attested to his rare strength of character. Who, for instance, ever heard him complain, or who can tell how he suffered? There were certainly plenty of reasons for him to suffer. He began to work amid great material hardships. During Chekhov's boyhood, his family was in real need, and he worked to support his family to help make ends meet, in an environment, moreover, that could have extinguished even the most ardent inspiration: in a tiny apartment surrounded by chatter and confusion, often on the edge of a table around which sat not only the entire family but also a number of guests, many of whom were students. He was constantly facing material hardships, even after he became a well-known writer, and this state of affairs went on into his last years, in spite of illness and fame. All this time, I literally never once heard Chekhov lament over his fate—and not because of his enclosed nature and not because his needs were limited: he never made a secret of his permanent money problems; as for the so-called limited character of his needs—we know how limited—though nobly Spartan in his way of life, he hated what was mean and meagre.

For fifteen years Chekhov was wracked by an illness that inexorably led him toward his grave. But did the reader—the Russian reader accustomed to the anguished cries of so many writers—ever once hear a single complaint from Chekhov? Sick people are fond of their privileged position, and even the strongest among them appear to enjoy hectoring those around them with their whims, with their ceaseless conversations about their illness. The fortitude, however, with which Chekhov confronted illness and death was truly amazing! Even in moments of his most terrible sufferings almost nobody was aware of what he was experiencing. "You're not feeling well, Antosha?" Chekhov's mother or sister would ask him, after noticing how he had been seated all day long in his armchair with closed eyes. "Who, me?" he would reply quietly, opening his eyes which looked so gentle and mild without his pince-nez. "Oh, it's nothing, but I do have a slight headache." Then not another word.

He loved literature intensely and would speak of writers and their works, praising Maupassant, Flaubert, or Tolstoy, *The Cossacks* or *Anna*

Karenina. This was plainly a source of enjoyment for him. He would often speak highly of these writers as well as of Lermontov's *Taman*. "I can't understand," he would often say, "how Lermontov could have written this when he was little more than a boy! All I need to do is write something of that caliber, or even a decent vaudeville, and then I can die in peace!"

His conversations about literature, however, were quite unlike those typical professional discussions that are so unpleasant because of their cliquish narrow-mindedness, the pettiness of their exclusively practical and, more often than not, personal interests. As a man of letters, first and foremost, Chekhov differed so markedly from the bulk of writers that the words *man of letters* no more suited him than they do Tolstoy—for the simple reason that the majority of our Russian writers are motivated exclusively by the prospects of gain and advancement, are concerned solely with their own small world and literary intrigues. For this reason, Chekhov would strike up a conversation about literature only when he knew that his interlocutor above all else loved art in literature—free and disinterested art.

"You should not read your writing to other people before it is published," Chekhov often said. "And above all, you should never listen to the advice of others. If you have missed the mark, talked nonsense—you must be the one held accountable. After the high standards that Maupassant set by his superb art, it is difficult to work, but work we must, especially we Russians, and in work one must be bold. There are big dogs and little dogs, but the little ones need not be disheartened by the existence of the big ones: for we are all called upon to bark—and bark with the voice God has given each of us."

All that took place in the world of literature was, of course, close to the heart of Chekhov, and he experienced much aggravation in the face of the kind of falsehood, affectation, and charlatanry that thrives so hardily in literature today. But I never noticed any petty animosity in Chekhov's distress, nor did this agitation ever take on a personal character. It is usually said of most deceased writers that they rejoiced over the success of others, that they were immune to jealousy; therefore if I had suspected Chekhov of even the least jealousy, I would not have raised the subject. Yet Chekhov really did rejoice over any and all displays of true talent, and it could not have been otherwise, since the word *talentless* was possibly the most abusive word in his vocabulary. He always delighted in the deserved success of others, whereas he regarded his own successes and failures in a way that was possible only for a man as great as he was.

Chekhov worked as a writer for nearly twenty-five years, and how much trivial and vulgar abuse he had to put up with during this time!

25

He was a poet, one of the most sincere and princely of all Russian poets, always speaking of his ideals in the language of the poet, not the preacher. In depicting life, he remained above all what he was destined to be—an artist: never tendentious, overblown, or stooping to the expediencies of the moment! Given such a nature, could Chekhov have counted on the understanding or goodwill of criticism in Russia, a country where the majority of critics, particularly in recent times, have lacked even a smattering of artistic sense? Just consider—critics and purchasers of Levitan's paintings demanded that he "liven up" his landscapes, touch up his cows, geese, or female figures! For Chekhov, obviously, it was no bed of roses to have such critics, and they poured much that was bitter into his soul—a soul that was already poisoned by Russian life. And this bitterness would occasionally show itself, but, once again, only *show itself.*

"So, Anton Pavlovich, it looks as though we'll soon be celebrating your jubilee!"

"Oh yes. I know all about your jubilees. For twenty-five years they give it hot to a man; then they present him with an aluminum goose-quill pen, and for a whole day they dote over him in an exalted way with lachrymose kisses!"

Whenever the topic turned to his own fame or to what was being written about him, Chekhov would usually reciprocate with two or three words or a joke.

"Have you read it?" you would ask him, after noting some critical response to one of his works. At this point Chekhov would no more than peep over his pince-nez and, comically pulling a long face, would reply in his deep baritone: "My humble thanks! They write a thousand lines about someone or other, then add at the bottom: 'Oh yes, and then there's Chekhov: the whiner.'" On a rare occasion he would add seriously: "My dear sir, if you are criticized sometimes, it means you should remember us sinners more often: like seminary students, we are thrashed for every single slip we make. One critic prophesied that I would die under a fence: he depicted me as though I were a young man expelled from the gymnasium for drinking."

I never saw Chekhov lose his temper; he also seldom got irritated, but when he did he managed to control himself remarkably well. As I recall, he was once upset by the wording of a description of his talent in a very thick and dull book consisting of portraits of writers with notes about them. It was a pronouncement regarding Chekhov's "in-difference" toward moral and social issues as well as his alleged pessimism. Yet Chekhov's irritation showed itself in only two words spoken with severity and deliberation: "Utter idiot!"

I never saw Chekhov completely cold, either. He was cold, to hear him tell it, only at work, something he approached only after the thought and imagery of the upcoming work had become completely clear to him. Then he would set about working uninterruptedly, resolutely bringing the writing to a conclusion. "You should sit down to write only when you feel cold as ice," he once said. Of course, coldness here is of a special kind: it is the coldness of the artist, one that in no way interferes with what is called inspiration.

Could one say that there are many Russian authors whose spiritual sensitivity and aesthetic receptivity surpassed Chekhov's? One was constantly aware of his finely tuned responsiveness, his ability to grasp a thought at the slightest hint. It bears repeating, however, that his self-control was formidable in his art, as it was in his life.

For Russian society clearly to get a sense of the image of Chekhov, some great and versatile person would have to write a book that was devoted first and foremost to the entire creative work of Chekhov—of that "incomparable" artist, as Tolstoy put it. He would have to write about an author who bitterly suffered the miseries of Russian life, who depicted it with such directness and who said with such power that life for everyone ought to be buoyant and joyous, beautiful and refined in its every manifestation. As for myself, for the time being I can write no more than I have here, for as yet I have been unable to dig systematically into the thousands of small, but to me meaningful, memories about him, and, ultimately, because such reminiscences might be painful to Chekhov's family, to whom I am so attached. In place of recollections, I would like at this point to state one thing: in life Chekhov was all that he was in art, a man of lofty spirituality, cultivated and refined in the best sense of these words, a man who combined gentleness and delicacy with unusual sincerity and simplicity, sensitivity and tenderness with a rare truthfulness.

To be truthful and natural and yet retain nobility and charm implies a nature of exceptional beauty, integrity, and strength. And if I speak so often here about the composure of Chekhov, it is because his composure appears to be a token of his strength of character; it never abandoned him even on those days when he was full of the joy of life, and perhaps precisely this inner composure gave him in his youth the ability not to yield to any influences and to begin to work so unconstrainedly and yet with such boldness, "entering into no contracts with his conscience," and with such inimitable mastery.

Do you remember the words of the old professor in "A Boring Story"? "I would not venture to say that French books are clever, talented, or noble; but they are not so boring as Russian books, and it is no rarity to find in them the chief element of artistic creation: the feeling of personal freedom." Chekhov was distinguished by this feeling of personal freedom. He could not bear to see others deprived of it and would become even harsh and uncompromising if he thought others were encroaching upon it. "It's fine, just fine," I once heard a writer state concerning another, while in the presence of Chekhov, "provided it's all about love!"

"Whether it's about love or not about love is entirely irrelevant," rejoined Chekhov with a scowl. "The main thing is that it be talented."

It is a well-known fact that this "freedom" cost Chekhov a great deal, but he was not one of those authors with two souls, one for himself and the other for the public. The success Chekhov achieved was for a ridiculously long time much less than he deserved. But did he ever make the slightest effort throughout his whole life to increase his popularity? He literally experienced pain and revulsion as he contemplated those methods that people now frequently employ to achieve success. "Do you really think these people are writers! They's cab drivers!" he would state bitterly.

His unwillingness to put himself on display was at times excessive. "The Skorpion advertises its books badly," Chekhov wrote me following the appearance of his first book, *Northern Flowers*. "They have stuck my name at the very top, and having read this announcement in *Russkie vedomosti*, I swore never again to become involved with scorpions, crocodiles, or snakes." This was during the winter of 1900 when Chekhov first took an interest in several features offered by the newly founded publishing house Skorpion. At my request he submitted one of his early stories, "At Sea." Later on a number of occasions he was to regret this decision.

"No, all this new Moscow art is rubbish," he would say. "I remember seeing a sign in Taganrog: 'Arteficial Frukt Soda Business.' The new art is exactly the same: an artificial fruit soda business!"

Chekhov's reserve, I believe, was an outgrowth of his aristocracy of spirit, among other things, and his striving to be accurate in his every choice of word. The time will come when people will realize that Chekhov was not merely an "incomparable" artist, not only an amazing master of the word, but also an incomparable poet. But when will this time come? It will still take a long time for people to fully grasp the subtle and chaste poetry that always imbues Chekhov's bitter truth of life. He concealed the poetry of his soul even from those closest to him, just as he concealed his goodness and tenderness. And he was very tender. This was especially true in the final days of his life...

"Greetings, my dear Ivan Alekseyevich," he wrote me last winter in Nice. "I wish you a Happy New Year with all its new happiness! I received your letter. Thank you. Everything in Moscow is as fine and full as usual. There is no news (except for the New Year), and none is in sight. My play has not yet been produced, and I have no idea when it will be. February I will very likely be taking a trip to Nice and staying with N. I. Yurasov, from whom I recently received a letter. Give my regards to the lovely warm sun and quiet sea. Enjoy yourself fully, take comfort, don't think about illness, and write your friends a little more often. . . . Keep well, and stay cheerful, and be happy, and don't forget your old sallow northern countrymen who are suffering from indigestion and bad temper" (January 8, 1904).

"Give my regards to the lovely warm sun and quiet sea" are words one would seldom hear from Chekhov. But I often sensed that he was about to utter them, and at times like these my heart would ache. For instance, I recall how late one evening at the beginning of spring we were in the Crimea when suddenly these was a telephone call for me. I picked up the receiver and heard Chekhov's deep voice on the line: "Sir, take a cab and come at once. We shall be going for a ride."

"A ride? At this time of night?" I replied, astonished. "What's the matter, Anton Pavlovich?"

"I'm in love."

"That's great, but it's already ten o'clock. And besides, you might catch cold."

"Young man, this is no time for hairsplitting!"

I was delighed to comply, of course, and ten minutes later I was in Autka. The house where Chekhov lived in winter alone with his mother was, as always, dark and silent, except for a light that shone through the keyhole of his mother Yevgenya Yakovlevna's room, while two little candles, veiled in the gloom, burned in Chekhov's study. My heart shrank as always at the sight of that quiet study where Chekhov spent so many lonely winter evenings, filled perhaps with bitter thoughts of a fate that had so richly endowed him, disclosed to his gaze all the glories of our world, and then mocked him mercilessly.

"What a night!" Chekhov said to me, greeting me at the threshold of his study with unusual gentleness and a certain pensive joy. "Only it's so dull in this house! The only excitement is when the telephone rings and Sofya Pavlovna asks what I am doing, and I reply by saying: 'I'm chasing mice.' Come on, let's drive to Orianda. And who cares if I catch a cold!"

The night was truly marvelous, warm and silent with a bright moon and white billowing clouds with a few radiant stars in the deep blue sky. Our carriage rolled softly along the white road, and soothed by the quiet of the night, we sat silently gazing at the glittering golden dark expanse of the sea. Then came the forest, cobwebbed over with shadows, still bare, but always, as inspiring, tender, lovely, and pensive. Then giant troops of cypresses loomed darkly upward toward the stars. And when we left the carriage and strolled quietly beneath the heavens, we passed the pale blue ruins of a castle lit by the moonlight. Chekhov suddenly said to me: "Do you know for how many years I shall be read? Seven."

"Why seven?" I asked.

"Well, seven and a half, then."

"You are a poet, Anton Pavlovich," I said. "And the fact is that poetry has a long life span. The longer it lives the stronger it becomes—like vintage wine."

Chekhov made no reply, but when we sat down somewhere on a bench, once again with a vista on the luminous sea, he slipped off his pince-nez and, looking at me with those kind and tired eyes, said: "Poets, kind sir, are only those who use such phrases as 'the silvery expanse,' 'accord,' or 'to battle, to battle, take arms against the night!'"

"You are sad tonight, Anton Pavlovich," I said, looking at his kind, simple, and beautiful face, slightly pale in the light of the moon.

Lowering his eyes, Chekhov began thoughtfully stirring up some pebbles with the end of his stick. But when I said that he was sad, he cast a humorous sidelong glance at me. "It's you who are sad," he answered. "You are sad because you spent so much on the cab." Then Chekhov went on to say in earnest: "All the same, I'll be read for only seven years, and I have less time than that to live—perhaps six. But please don't go reporting this to the Odessa press." This time, however, he was wrong: he was to live a much shorter time.

Chekhov died peacefully, without suffering, amid the stillness and beauty of a summer's dawn, which he had always loved. And when he was dead, "an unusually contented, almost happy expression appeared on his suddenly youthful face"... Chekhov's death came to me as no great surprise, but as for his being read for only seven years, that, of course, was ludicrous. And yet the thought that he, whom I see so clearly seated beside me on a bench that unforgettable night in Orianda, now lies in the earth, somewhere just close by in a grave in the cemetery of Novo-Devichy monastery—to me this is indescribably absurd, preposterous, staggering...

Marena Senderovich

Chekhov's Name Drama

CHEKHOV, AFTER ALL, wrote his own artistic biography. In over four thousand letters and a large number of literary works he provided such a thorough and nuanced commentary on his artistic life that all that remains for us is to be attentive readers—the kind that Chekhov dreamed about his whole life long but never found. The search was, admittedly, a daunting one.

Chekhov's artistic biography lies concealed under thousands of details from everyday life. It is nonetheless couched in a clearly definable Chekhovian inner form: the form of a drama. The generic features of this drama are extremely interesting and may be compared with the generic complexity of Chekhov's dramaturgy. What begins as a comedy develops into a drama; in the final act we witness a tragedy. Owing to its basic content this drama may aptly be termed the *name drama*.

ACT I

What could be more natural for a comic writer, columnist, or feuilletonist than to sign his works with a pseudonym? That was the tradition. All of Chekhov's fellow writers in humorous papers signed their works in the same way. It was something of a professional convention, an adherence to a certain generic etiquette. Indeed, working for small journals required not just one but a whole series of pen names used alternatively in accordance with the particular type or genre of the publication and the kind of publishing concern. Pseudonyms were utilized as a kind of dress appropriate for various situations or just as a comic mask: "Keep [using] my Ulysses mask," Chekhov wrote in a letter to Nikolai Leykin, editor of *Oskolki*, on December 10, 1884. There were clear-cut distinctions in the use of pseudonyms that were guarded jealously by authors and editors alike. Chekhov pledged to Leykin in a letter of November 23, 1885: "I promise not to submit anything to humorous journals bearing the signature A. Chekhonte in December,

31

January, and the end of November or in general anything with the signature known to the readership of *Oskolki.*"

But this seemingly uncomplicated issue in the life of Chekhov was actually an exceedingly complex one. The drama consists not in the use of a psuedonym, but rather in the problems the author experienced. As early as 1883 this issue became an object of intense, exaggerated, even obsessive concern in Chekhov's letters. With the author's enhanced self-awareness, the pseudonym question became the object of an artistic game. Chekhov dramatized it. First, the issue was framed: "Conceal yourself under a pseudonym." The question of how to hide from the reader became a recurrent theme in Chekhov's correspondence with Leykin. The question arose at a time when he was becoming a rather well-known humorist—one who recognized the wit of his pen. "To hide or not to hide?" became a nagging question. Chekhov was upset because the editor signed his "trifle" with his full surname, rather than with a pseudonym, and he complained to Leykin about it at the end of December 1883. He could not be reconciled to having everyone know "who this Rover is . . . I have already swallowed insults from my closest friends on two separate occasions because of my notes," he wrote to Leykin in the same year. "Couldn't you print my feuilleton without a signature?" he wrote again on February 12 or 13, 1884. "By now everyone knows that I'm Rover. . . . Everybody knows, so I might as well throw away my pen!" It is noteworthy, however, that Chekhov still savored the opportunity of hiding under pseudonymity and quite willingly made use of it. In preparing to write a parody on B. M. Markevich's *Fumes of Life* (Chad zhizni), he wrote to Leykin on January 30, 1884: "I'll be able to engage in some gossiping while hidden under a pseudonym."

Pseudonymity liberated Chekhov by allowing him greater scope and openness. The reviews Chekhov wrote in *Oskolki* in 1884 bore the name Ulysses. By the year's end Chekhov suspected that his secret had been divulged and appealed to Leykin: "Keep [using] my Ulysses mask. . . . Write [Palmin] that it's not I writing." In a letter to his brother Aleksandr on May 13, 1883, he established this principle: One must write "without fail from afar and through a crack." He expressed his own intention: "If I write, it will without fail be from afar, through a crack." This is more than a mere generalization of his own position as author: Chekhov set his own experience as an example for his brother to follow. He succeeded in drawing his brother into this game and went on to instruct him in the matter. At the same time, the theme of "peeping" became an important and recurrent scenario in his short stories, including "At Sea," "The Malefactor," "The Night before the Trial," "The Joke," "Agafya," and "The Witch." In "Agafya" the theme of peeping was directly built in to the narrative device, whereas in the other texts its metaphoric character is more veiled.

Among his various pseudonyms, Chekhov most often used Antosha (A. or An.) Chekhonte. Here one is faced with another problem. It cannot seriously be argued that it is possible to hide under such a transparent pseudonym. Its use is more likely a final theatrical gesture of playful defense in the spirit of Chekhov's humorous texts. Thus Chekhov's relation to his texts is twofold: on the one hand, the pseudonym provides a means for concealment when it is unsuitable for Chekhov's authorship to be made manifest; on the other hand, the Russian author was playing hide-and-seek with himself, as children do when they close their eyes and say, "Come and find me." He does not try to avoid being found, but he avoids calling out his own name and at the same time hints at it. If one gives some thought to the question of this game, its meaning becomes clear: it establishes aesthetic distance between the writer and what he has written. Chekhov hides from himself just as he hides from his reader under a pseudonym—a typically Chekhovian correspondence (there are insufficient social and cultural motives otherwise to explain the use of the pseudonym); behind it one finds both shame for an action and fear of ridicule, which magically disappear under the enchanted hood of pseudonymity.

The need for internal distancing reveals an important facet of Chekhov's creative persona. The simple fact that Chekhov began his literary career by using a pseudonym tells us something. It is as though Chekhov came to accept the need for concealment, first as a literary device, and then as the very essence of the writer's profession or as a tenet of his authorial creed.

ACT II

Chekhov, who refused to take himself seriously and even indulged in humorous remarks about his role as a writer, traveled to Petersburg in December 1885. There, to his amazement, he was heralded as a serious writer in the literary ambience of the capital. "I was overwhelmed by the reception extended to me by the Petersburg literati," Chekhov wrote to his brother Aleksandr on January 4, 1886. "[Aleksei] Suvorin, [Dmitry] Grigorovich, [Victor] Burenin . . . the acclaim, the elation, all of this frightened me, for I knew I had been writing haphazardly, in a slipshod manner." But what was the matter? Why did Chekhov feel frightened? We are told that the writer, greeted with open arms in Petersburg, was dissatisfied with himself. "If I had known that I was being read this carefully, I would not have written like a hack," he continued in the same letter. In letters beginning in 1886, he reacted ambivalently to his situation: On the one hand, he made fun of it, turned it almost into a farce; he indulged in lighthearted, bantering self-elevation, which became a favorite leitmotiv in the letters up until 1889. On the other hand, still facetious, he seriously complained of his situation as a renowned writer; his complaints grew increasingly earnest and ultimately came to a climax in an anguished cry.

Returning from Petersburg on January 16, 1886, Chekhov wrote to Mikhail Dyukovsky on the eve of his birthday: "Tomorrow, a well-known writer by the will of fate is to be promoted to the rank of a hero of the day." Two days later, again jestingly, the Russian author complained to Victor Bilibin: "Earlier, when I didn't know I was being read and judged, I would write in a carefree way, as though I were just playing around. But now I'm afraid to take pen in hand." What was it that frightened Chekhov? When the time came to edit a collection of short stories, *Motley Tales*, Chekhov was faced with a Hamletian dilemma: "To sign or not to sign with my real name?" "In the book I'll be A. Chekhonte, not A. Chekhov," he wrote to Leykin on February 3, 1886. The question, however, remains: pseudonym or surname? Eleven days later Chekhov wrote to Bilibin: "For my book you advised me . . . not to use the pseudonym, but the surname... Why have you rejected the rationale behind your own advice? You may well be right, but I've thought it over and prefer the pseudonym—and with reason." He added two weeks later, again to Bilibin: "It's about the pseudonym and the surname again... You shouldn't drag the public into this matter... How is the public supposed to know that Chekhonte is a pseudonym? And who cares anyhow?"

Signing the book with his true surname appeared too serious an undertaking for Chekhov. Only truly famous writers should attach their own names to their works, and Chekhov felt that he was not among them. Moreover, the use of the comic pseudonym went along with the fact that Chekhov wanted to look ironically not only on the world but also on himself as an author. One should not misinterpret the earnestness of this pose. Like all of Chekhov's other serious resolves, it displays ambiguity. The pose provides self-defense against pretentiousness, but also justification for his position as a humorist: if I regard myself with irony, then I am entitled to treat you ironically as well. At this time Chekhov had no objection to being well known; on the contrary, he relished the thought. Yet the need to ridicule himself in the role of a celebrity was an integral part of his enjoyment. The author had to reflect a bit and felt the need for "dualism." Again on February 3, 1886, Chekhov wrote to Aleksandr: "I am sending you a contemptuous smile for having named your son Anton. Such audacity! You might just as well have called him Shakespeare! There are but two Antons in this world: myself and Rubinstein. I recognize no others." Two weeks later, on February 17, 1886, he wrote mockingly to Dyukovsky: "I'm writing you so you'll have one more autograph of a great writer... In 10–20 years you'll be able to sell this letter for 500–1,000 rubles. How I envy you."

The attention of Suvorin and the elation of Grigorovich and the other literati overwhelmed Chekhov and also delighted him. The response made him pause and take himself more seriously as a writer. And what did Chekhov find? He found that he was unwilling to portray himself as a serious writer, that he failed to respect his own gifts as an author. Another revelation was Chekhov's unwillingness to reveal himself fully. "I would write and try my best not to squander on a story those images and scenes that were dear to me and that—God knows why—I cherished and jealously hid," he acknowledged in a famous letter to Grigorovich on March 26, 1886. In this same letter, by the way, Chekhov returned to the question of whether or not he should place his own name on *Motley Tales*. The book was on its way to print, thought Chekhov, and therefore nothing could be done "because it is too late." He nonetheless chose not to sign his real name, "probably out of vanity. I do not like my book at all. . . . Had I known that people were reading me and that you were watching me, I would not have published this book." Grigorovich, however, succeeded in convincing Chekhov. Five days later, on March 31, 1886, Chekhov gave the following instruction to Leykin: "If it's not too late, then put 'A. P. Chekhov' in brackets beside 'A. Chekhonte' on the second title page of my book. . . . Just think, I received a letter from Grigorovich, who insists that I drop the pseudonym." Grigorovich is known to have convinced Chekhov of other things as well. Beginning to take himself seriously, Chekhov wrote to Bilibin on April 4, 1886: "[Grigorovich] is proving to me that I have *real* talent. . . . I'm pleased, of course, although I feel that [Grigorovich] is exaggerating."

Earlier, on February 15, 1886, Chekhov had sent the short story "The Requiem," bearing his real name, to the journal *Novoe vremia*. It should be noted that Chekhov had already signed his real name on three previous occasions, but only casually. From now on it became standard practice for Chekhov's real name to be attached to the short stories submitted to *Novoe vremia;* pseudonyms, however, continued to be used in lesser journals. We must therefore further clarify Chekhov's ambivalence with respect to himself, his work, and his name.

The very fact of being a writer seems to have made Chekhov regard himself and the world ambivalently. On the other hand, one may cite relatives, friends, and acquaintances of his who did not value his activity as a writer or simply did not read him. On March 26, 1886, Chekhov wrote to Grigorovich: "All those close to me have always regarded my writing with condescension and persistently advised me, in a friendly way, not to give up real work for scribbling. I have in Moscow hundreds of acquaintances, a score of writing fellows among them, and I cannot think of a single one who would read me or see an artist in me." In the same letter, Chekhov is convinced of his "literary insignificance." In another letter of April 11, 1886, to Mikhail Chekhov, he wrote of his writing as "subsidiary work."

On the other hand, all his relatives recognized, valued, and enjoyed the benefits of his medical profession. Chekhov was fully cognizant of the dualism in his existence and at this time could not easily reconcile himself to it. "I am a physician and as such am up to my ears in my medicine, so that no one could be more bothered than I by the saying about catching two hares," he wrote in the letter to Grigorovich. "Besides my wife—medicine—I also have literature—my mistress," he wrote to his brother Aleksandr on his birthday in 1887. He subsequently elaborated on this flippant remark and turned it into serious reflection. In one of his revelations to Suvorin on September 11, 1888, Chekhov justified the fundamental need for this dualism:

> You advise me not to hunt after two hares at once and not to think of practicing medicine. I do not know why one should not hunt two hares even in the literal sense. If there are hounds, then why not hunt? In all probability it's the hounds (in the figurative sense now) that I haven't got, but I feel bolder and more contented when I remember that I have two professions and not one. . . . Medicine is my lawful wife, and literature—my mistress. When I am bored with one, I spend the night with the other. Though this behavior is disorderly, at least it's not boring, and what is more, neither really loses anything through my treachery.

The joke about medicine as wife and literature as mistress is widely known and is quite in accord with the facts of Chekhov's life. Yet it denotes more than the empirical facts that Chekhov was simultaneously busy with medicine and literature and that a great writer deemed medicine his major activity. Chekhov was saying something more. He was saying: "I feel bolder and more contented when I remember that I have two professions." Here the author was speaking of his inner need for ambivalence.

Chekhov was divided, moreover, even in respect to his literary work, and again his name is involved. Having begun regularly to sign his real name, Chekhov nonetheless continued—quite as regularly—to publish under pseudonyms, as though serving notice that in literature as well he was equally "treacherous." Leykin and Suvorin considered themselves Chekhov's wife and mistress; more precisely, each of them thought himself to be the wife, while suspecting the other of being the mistress.

In 1889, however, Chekhov changed both wife and lover but remained faithful to duality. At once swept away and disillusioned by the theater, exhausted by the staging of *Ivanov*, Chekhov wrote to Nikolai Pleshcheyev on January 15, 1889: "Belles lettres is a restful and sacred thing. The narrative form is one's lawful wife, while the dramatic form is a showy, noisy, impertinent, and tiresome mistress."

The dualism of Chekhov's world outlook now assumed the nature of an opposition between the sacred and the profane. Narrowly viewed, this opposition represents a division between the serious short stories to which Chekhov attached his name and the "trifles" that he continued to sign with pseudonyms (as Chekhov became more widely known, this habit increasingly took on the character of a convention). In a different Chekhovian vein, however, it implied a distinction between the serious and the "trivial": "The serious within me endlessly alternates with the trivial. Such seems to be my fate," he wrote to Yakov Polonsky on February 22, 1888. Such a state, indeed, was a matter of fully conscious principle. True to his dualism, Chekhov counseled his brother Aleksandr in late December 1886: "Never sign any trifles with your full name. . . . What for? Surely you don't want to bring shame upon yourself?" There is a more important aspect to consider, however. The sacred is identified with that which is hidden within, the still unuttered and unwritten, while the profane is associated with everything that has been written. Thus Chekhov wrote to Suvorin on October 27, 1888:

> The themes sitting around in my head are annoyed by and jealous of those already on paper; it's disgraceful that the rubbish is out, while the good material is lying about in the warehouse, like useless junk. . . . What do I call good? Those images which seem best to me, which I love and jealously guard lest I waste or mutilate them for some hastily written "Name Day Party." . . . All that is now being written displeases and bores me, whereas everything that sits in my head interests, moves, and excites me.

The division between high and low is invariably present in all of Chekhov's value judgments. In 1886 Chekhov contrasted his "trifles" and humorous stories with the short stories of *Novoe vremia*; subsequently, when he was overtaken by a passion for the novel, Chekhov would speak ironically of the *Novoe vremia* tales of this period, opposing everything that he had written to the novel that had been mentally conceived but never completed. Chekhov was aware of the contradiction between high and low in his authorial nature and joked about it with frank delight in a letter of October 17, 1887, to the writer Vladimir Korolenko: "Among all the Russians who are happily engaged in writing today, I am the most frivolous and least serious; I am infamous for this sort of thing. Speaking in the language of the poets, I have loved my pure muse but have not respected her. I have been unfaithful to her and more than once taken her to places that did not befit her."

Chekhov expressed the same thought, now in a serious vein, but with a Chekhovian mixture of irony, facetiousness, and regret, in a letter of February 22, 1888, to Polonsky: "Oh, if they knew at the *Severny vestnik* that I write vaudevilles, I would be declared anathema! But what is to be done if my hands itch and feel like breaking out into tra-la-las? As hard as I try to be serious, nothing comes of it, for within me there is a never-ending alteration of the serious and the trivial. Evidently such is my fate."

It looked as though destiny had brought Chekhov into a situation that he had neither foreseen nor sought. He had begun his humorous writing for the sake of money; counting on an undemanding public, he was not looking for empty fame. When that fame came to him unexpectedly, self-respect would not let him accept the fact that it was undeserved; he knew himself. Serious writers, moreover, who believed in his talent insisted that he take himself seriously.

Chekhov sketched out and wrote *Ivanov* with lightning speed in October 1887. He was in a buoyant, sparkling mood. His letters at this time were full of exhilaration, a jocular enjoyment of success, hilarious jokes and puns. Chekhov wrote to his brother Aleksandr that "the plot was unprecedented" (October 6–8, 1887), that he "wanted to be original" but was not sure whether he would succeed (October 24, 1887). Chekhov's passion for the theater had taken hold. With trepidation Chekhov awaited the staging of *Ivanov*; he prepared for the opening "as though for a wedding" (letter to Aleksandr Lazarev, November 15, 1887). The first performance took place in an atmosphere of particular excitement in which there was both "outright hissing" and "solid success," all of which induced in the author "fatigue and vexation" (to Aleksandr Chekhov, November 20 and 24, 1887). In his letters about *Ivanov* Chekhov superbly dramatizes all the peripeteia relating to the staging and performance of the play; he produced, indeed, the raw material for a backstage drama in which the author himself is both actor and director. *Ivanov* created a great stir in both capitals. "People keep inviting me and singing my praises," wrote Chekhov from Petersburg to his brother Mikhail on December 3, 1887. "Everyone is positively wild about my play, although they scold me for carelessness." Chekhov was received in Petersburg as a renowned writer. In general, the end of 1887 may be said to mark the high point of Chekhov's sensational renown; in contrast, the period of his southern trip and his work on "The Steppe" represented a time of real repose.

The period of preparation for and work on "The Steppe" seems to me, in fact, the one in which Chekhov was least at odds with himself. Chekhov had just taken a trip to the south, to the places where he had spent his childhood. His turn to childhood in "The Steppe" should most likely be understood as a reexamination of his life, a return to beginnings. It is as though Chekhov was removing himself from his immediate concerns. Everyday life was placed in a broader perspective. Chekhov freed himself of the burdens of being an author and allowed questions of reputation and name to retreat into the background. "As you may well imagine, a traveling man hardly has any time for writing," Chekhov observed to Leykin in a letter of May 22, 1887, but he added: "True, I did write for a Petersburg paper . . . in order to prevent my family [*familiia*] from living at others' expense. I wrote abominably, clumsily, all the while cursing paper and pen." It is difficult to avoid the impression that Chekhov is playing with words. Instead of the more common *sem'ia* for family, he uses the word *familiia*, the first meaning of which is "surname"; but he undoes the effect immediately by implying something totally different between the lines. Chekhov "hardly has any time for writing" and does so "abominably, clumsily, all the while cursing paper and pen," or else his name (*familiia*) will be obliged to live "at others' expense." In other words, Chekhov is to live at the expense of his name. We are faced with a full-fledged Chekhovian inversion.

Chekhov achieved an unprecedented freedom and harmony in the course of his work on "The Steppe." From the beginning he directed the story to a select readership and assumed that it would not meet with the approval of either the general public or the critics. "The writer . . . will understand me, but the reader will grow bored and become fed up," Chekhov wrote to Korolenko in January 1888. The same idea was repeated in a letter to Polonsky on January 18, 1888: "There are many passages that will be understood by neither the critic nor the public. Both will find it vacuous and thoroughly unremarkable, but I will be satisfied if even two or three literary gourmets understand and value these very passages. That will be enough for me."

Chekhov, however, set his sights even higher—above the heads of his select readers. On January 19, 1888, he wrote to Pleshcheyev: "The theme is a poetic one, and if I do not break away from the tone I began with, I may well conceive something 'out of the ordinary.' I feel there are some passages in my little narrative with which I shall please you, dear poet, but on the whole, I will most likely not meet your expectations." This passage already contains the seed of new discontent.

ACT III

The closer Chekhov came to completing "The Steppe," the more contradictory his attitude toward it became. He wavered over whether he had accomplished what he had intended and had a premonition that he would be misunderstood, while he also expressed some awareness of the poetic, original quality of his new narrative, his feeling that in "The Steppe" he had fully expressed himself, achieved real perfection. On January 23, 1888, he wrote to Pleshcheyev: "You expect from me something special, something particularly good—what a field for disappointment! I'm afraid and fear that my 'Steppe' will turn out to be inconsequential. . . . To be frank, I squeeze, strain, huff and puff, but still it does not satisfy me, although in places there are 'poems in prose.'" After he finished the work he wrote to Aleksandra Kiseleva on February 3, 1888: "My 'Steppe' does not resemble a novella—rather an encyclopedia of the steppe."

Once "The Steppe" was completed, Chekhov complained of having overexerted himself. On February 4, 1888, he wrote to Lazarev: "I have put too much juice, energy, and phosphorous into my 'Steppe'; I have strained and exerted myself in the writing process, squeezed it out of myself, and taxed myself to the breaking point. Whether or not I have succeeded I do not know, but in any case 'The Steppe' is my masterpiece. I can do no better. . . . I am experiencing a crisis. If I don't get a prize now, then I'll start going downhill." Chekhov's crisis is an unmistakable feature of this period. But the crisis, brought on by overexertion, was merely a physical manifestation of a deeper discontent. Chekhov wrote in the letter to Kiseleva: "There have been no such narratives for a long time even in our prestigious thick literary journals. I am coming forth in an original way, but I'll catch it for my originality as I did for *Ivanov*. There will be much talk."

"The Steppe" was enthusiastically received, but all the same, personal responses and commentary in the press were full of misunderstandings and complaints. In a letter of March 6, 1888, to Pleshcheyev, an irritated Chekhov wrote sarcastically:

Tomorrow I am going to see P. N. [Ostrovsky], and I have a proposal for him. I shall remind him of 1812 and the partisan warfare, when anyone who desired could attack the French without donning a uniform. Perhaps he will go for the idea that in our day and age, when literature has been taken captive by 20,000 false teachings, a nonofficial partisan criticism would be far from superfluous. Perhaps he would like to bypass journals and papers, escape ambush, and stage a surprise Cossack raid. This idea could surely be implemented with the aid of the pamphlet. Pamphlets are currently in vogue, inexpensive, and very readable. The

40

Orthodox priests are aware of this and are daily bombarding the public with their pharisaical eructations.

Chekhov wrote to Suvorin on December 23 of the same year: "There is no criticism. The hackneyed Tatishchev, the ass Mikhnevich, and the indifferent Burenin—there's the full range of our criticism. To write for this crowd makes no more sense than offering a person with a cold flowers to sniff."

A temporary lapse in creativity following "The Steppe" aggravated Chekhov's crisis. In a letter of February 22, 1888, he complained to Polonsky: "After 'The Steppe' I have done virtually nothing. . . . Out of boredom I wrote a frivolous little French farce called 'The Bear' . . . 'The Steppe' consumed so much of my lifeblood and energy that it will still take me a long time to take up something serious."

Dissatisfaction with himself and with his writing kept troubling Chekhov: he came to an awareness of the fundamental dualism of his nature—that of the sacred and the profane in his artistic life (in his own words, "the sacred" and "the commonplace"). In this period Chekhov had finally allowed himself to write seriously and freely, in accordance with his own inner criteria. The Pushkin Prize brought him universal acclaim. Yet precisely in this period his sense of dissatisfaction with his position in literature, or, rather, his life in literature, reached crisis proportions. In a typically Chekhovian way, this crisis had a dualistic character, as did the very character of his fame. The paradox of simultaneous recognition and misunderstanding forced Chekhov once again to look at himself from without and to peer more deeply into himself. Assessing his status in Russian literature, Chekhov came to the conclusion that his fame was a transient one. The paradox of recognition without understanding led him to the bitter conclusion he drew in his letter of October 10, 1888, to Suvorin: "The second- and third-rate writers of newspaper fiction ought to erect a monument to me, or at least present me with a silver cigar case. I have blazed a trail for them to the prestigious thick journals, and to laurels and to the hearts of all decent people. As yet this is my only merit, whereas all I have written and for which I earned an award will not live in people's memories for even a decade."

Why would Chekhov's work "not live in people's memories for even a decade"? Does this remark testify to Chekhov's underestimation of himself, or does it point to the "objective" fleeting character of fame? Chekhov viewed the transitory nature of life—and therefore the fleeting memory of himself—as a saving grace, since he was displeased by what he had written. On April 18, 1888, Chekhov wrote to Ivan Shcheglov about his story "The Lights": "When I review the works I have written

41

I feel a sense of nausea: how repulsive! Well, what of it... The hell with it. No matter what inanities we write at the present time, no matter how much our brainless critics subtilize over us, in ten years all of this will be irrelevant. And therefore, *capitaine*, forward without fear or doubt!"

The transience of fame, however, was merely an external gauge of the artist's worth, an outer framework for evaluation. Chekhov did not limit himself to the external but looked deeply into himself. He experienced a deep dissatisfaction with what he had written and, finally, arrived at an assessment tragic to a celebrated writer. On October 27, 1888, Chekhov wrote to Suvorin: "If I am to speak in all conscience, then I must say that I have not begun my literary activity, even though I have been awarded a prize. . . . Everything that I have written to date is rubbish compared with what I would like to write and would passionately love to write."

The gesture is not one of modesty, but rather of despair—a sincere reaction to the opinions of people Chekhov respected in his literary entourage. "In Petersburg I have for some odd reason been nicknamed Potemkin, although I have no Catherine," he wrote to Kiseleva on March 25, 1888. "I am obviously considered a favorite of the muses." Chekhov returned to this issue on a number of occasions. He was deeply wounded by being called Potemkin, and in a letter of November 16, 1888, to Shcheglov defended himself in a tone of complaint and self-denigration: "Why do you tease me with the name 'Potemkin'? So far I can see nothing of Potemkin in myself except industriousness, weariness, lack of money, and boredom of colossal dimensions. I am ashamed of my 'Bears'; my prize, too, I'm ashamed of; I dislike the theater, have grown accustomed to literature and my family. There are no interesting people around, and the weather is miserable... What is there to envy here?"

Oddly enough, however, Chekhov began to adapt himself to the role of Potemkin. "To begin with," he wrote to Lazarev on October 20, 1888, "I am a 'favorite child of fortune' in literature—a Potemkin, sprung from the bowels of *Entertainment* and *The Wave*; I am a petty bourgeois among the gentry, and such people don't last long, just as a hastily tightened string is also short-lived." Chekhov's accommodation to this painful role came about quite naturally, for it was produced by his permanent inner dualism, the division into sacred and profane that required his denying a part of himself and led to his justifying his external diagnosis. While in Petersburg, Chekhov wrote to Kiseleva on February 17, 1889, about the success of *Ivanov:* "There are now two heroes in Petersburg: Semiradsky's naked Frina and the clothed Chekhov. Both are a sensation. Despite all this I am bored and would gladly flee to my beloved Babkino." "Semiradsky's naked Frina and the clothed Chekhov" are scandalously short-lived topics.

A leitmotiv in Chekhov's letters in 1888 is his complaint of weariness, that literature had become a kind of "forced labor," *lege necessitatis*. Whereas he had formerly termed literature his mistress, he now had to "drive himself to work," he wrote Shcheglov on September 14, 1888. He suffered from overwriting and in addition felt that writing was unnecessary and fruitless, since one gets "five grains of gold" out of "one hundred poods" of sand (to Pleshcheyev, September 15, 1888). And precisely because he felt that so little of genuine quality was being extracted from his pen in spite of all he wrote, Chekhov experienced a feeling of inadequacy in his position as a distinguished writer. He looked at the future grimly also because he felt the frailty of his gift as writer. In a letter to Lazarev on October 20, 1888, Chekhov observed ironically: "Even great writers run the risk of burning themselves out, annoying the public, losing touch with reality, and finally being forced to throw in the sponge. Personally, I am exposed to this risk to the utmost degree . . . the train most likely to derail is that which travels nonstop daily regardless of weather and the amount of fuel."

Never had Chekhov's complaints of the burdens of authorship echoed so painfully as at the end of 1888. The letters from this period convey a profound feeling of alienation and emptiness. On December 23, 1888, a troubled Chekhov wrote to Suvorin:

> There are moments when I positively lose heart. Why and for whom am I writing? For the public? But I do not see it and believe in it less than I do in ghosts. The public is uneducated, ill bred, and even the best among them deal with us unfairly and insincerely. Does this public need me or not—I cannot make it out. Burenin says I am not needed and that I am busying myself with trifles; but the Academy gives me an award. The devil himself couldn't make anything of it. . . . If we had real criticism, then I would know that I was shaping real material— whether good or bad is of no matter—that to people who devote themselves to the study of life I am as necessary as a star is to an astronomer.

Oddly enough, the external and internal contradictions do not clash but in a strange way rather harmonize, even enhance one another. To Chekhov's malaise, however, must be added still another element: Chekhov complained that his celebrity as a writer constituted an obstacle between himself and other people. On November 24 or 25, 1888, Chekhov wrote to Suvorin:

> You say that writers are God's chosen people. I shall not argue. Shcheglov calls me the Potemkin of literature, and therefore it is not for me to

speak of the thorny path, of disappointments, etc. I do not know whether I have ever suffered more than shoemakers, mathematicians, or conductors do; I do not know who speaks through my lips, God or someone else who is worse. I'll allow myself to mention only one unpleasantness that I have experienced, one that is probably familiar to you also from experience. Here's the rub of the matter. You and I love ordinary people; but others love us because they see something extraordinary in us. For example, people are always inviting me to their houses, everywhere wining and dining me like a general at a wedding party. My sister is indignant because she is always invited out as a writer's sister. Nobody wants to love the ordinary people in us.

Chekhov gives full and profound expression to this phenomenon in "A Boring Story" (Skuchnaia istoriia), written in the late summer of 1889. The story is existential in character, exploring the alienation of a name that acquires existence independent of its bearer, a name that not only no longer has anything in common with the bearer but also keeps him from living; it stands between him and the world and plunges him into inauthenticity. Chekhov later denied any personal connection with his hero, but is it possible to read the beginning of "A Boring Story" and not see a connection here with Chekhov's letter to Suvorin?

There is in Russia an eminent professor, a certain Nikolai Stepanovich, a privy councillor and knight of many orders; he possesses so many medals, both Russian and foreign, that when he wears them the students refer to him as an iconostasis. He has acquaintances in the highest aristocratic circles. . . . And so on, and so forth. All this—and much more that could be said—constitutes what is called my name.

This name of mine is a celebrated one. In Russia it is known to every educated person, and in university halls abroad they preface it with "distinguished" and "honored." It is one of those few fortunate names that it would be considered a sign of bad taste to abuse or speak of lightly. And that is as it should be. After all, my name is closely connected with the idea of a celebrated, richly endowed, and indisputably useful man. . . . The bearer of this name—that is, I myself—I conceive to be a man of sixty-two years, bald, with false teeth and an incurable tic. I am as lackluster and ugly as my name is brilliant and beautiful.

"A Boring Story" gives a full embodiment to the theme of name alienation. We witness a gradual separation between the fate of the name and the fate of the bearer. The plot comes to a climax with the professor sitting "all alone in a strange town" and meditating: "I am famous, my name is pronounced with reverence, my portrait has appeared in *Niva* and *Vsemirnaia illiustratsia*, I have even read my own biography in a German magazine. And the end result? I'm sitting all alone in a strange town, on a strange bed. . . . I do not love this celebrated name of mine. I feel as if it has betrayed me." As he awaits death, the professor conjures up in his imagination an image that verges on the grotesque: "Clearly great names are created to live their own lives independently of those who bear them. My name is now serenely strolling about Kharkov." The existential crisis, finally, reaches its peak in the professor's conception of the final irreversible divergence of his own fate from the fate of his own name: "In another three months [my name] will be painted on my tombstone in gold letters brilliant as the very sun, by which time I myself shall already be under the sod." Here a familiar, even hackneyed situation, taking on the extreme form of an existential crisis, ceases to be a commonplace, and the primal tragic meaning of the event is disclosed to us.

In "A Boring Story" Chekhov gives heightened expression to the crisis he himself experienced in 1888 and 1889. It is no accident that the writer-physician makes his hero a physician who says of himself that he will not make his way into literature. The concept of name, whereby Chekhov expresses his attitude toward his own name, serves to bring into focus the contradictions of his own fate as a man and writer. Only "A Boring Story" fully confirms that Chekhov was not only obsessed with the problem of name but consciously gave attention to it, recognized its deep significance. In "A Boring Story" Chekhov's development of the motif of alienation of the name becomes a means of deeply analyzing the creative personality.

Though it represents an expression of crisis, "A Boring Story" did not provide a solution. On the contrary, the letters from the end of 1889 attest to a deepening of that crisis. In a letter written around December 20, 1889—only a fragment of the letter remains—Chekhov said to Suvorin: "Essays, feuilletons, foolish pieces, vaudevilles, boring stories, a great many mistakes and absurdities, reams of paper written on, an academic prize, the life of Potemkin—and with all this not a single line that in my eyes could have any serious literary significance. There was a mass of work done under pressure, but there was not a single moment of serious labor." The situation did not lend itself to an intellectual literary remedy; it called for a vital answer. Chekhov went on in the same letter: "I have a passionate desire to hide somewhere for about five years and to busy myself with some painstaking, serious work. I need to learn everything from the very beginning, because as a man of letters I am a sheer ignoramus." The vital answer was Chekhov's journey to the island of Sakhalin. He made that journey so he could escape from an inauthentic existence into which his famous name had plunged him. The trip constituted a flight from the name, paradoxical as it may seem, that Chekhov no longer felt was his own and that deprived his life of authenticity.

To pursue further the analogy with "A Boring Story," it might be argued that Chekhov undertook his journey to Sakhalin in order to avoid the fate of Nikolai Stepanovich. In spite of differences between the circumstances of the old professor and Anton Chekhov, their complaints have much in common: boredom, a suffocating life, stagnation— the attributes of aging. Chekhov wrote to Suvorin on May 4, 1889, three months before he began to write "A Boring Story": "There's a kind of stagnation in my soul. I explain this by the stagnation in my personal life. I am not disenchanted, not tired out, not in the doldrums, but suddenly everything has simply become somehow less interesting to me. I'll have to put some gunpowder under myself."

Nikolai Stepanovich and the author of "A Boring Story" are linked also by a regret that life has not been lived the way it should be and by the thought that it would be a good thing to set it straight. Here is another one of Chekhov's confessions (April 8, 1889) to Suvorin, a person with whom he unburdened himself more freely and fully than with anybody else: "I think if I could live another forty years and in all these forty years read, read, and read and learn how to write in a talented way, i.e., concisely—then at the end of that time I would fire on you all with so huge a cannon that the heavens would shake. But now I am just a Lilliputian, like the rest."

There are many well-known instances in the history of Russian literature when authors commit fatal acts resembling those of their protagonists. In this case, however, Chekhov preferred a reversal: he found a way out that allowed him to avert the tragic outcome that overtook the hero of "A Boring Story." Once Chekhov conceived the idea of a journey to Sakhalin, he became unusually animated. His gloomy mood, depression, and boredom faded away. Chekhov single-mindedly prepared for his trip, was impatient to set out as quickly as possible, and looked forward to unusual impressions. "All day long I sit and read and make extracts. I have nothing in my head or on paper except Sakhalin. Mental derangement. Mania Sachalinosa," he confessed to Pleshcheyev on February 15, 1890. Two days later he wrote to Suvorin: "Spring is in the air, and I am vexed that I have not yet left for Sakhalin." He wrote humorously to Kiseleva on January 28, 1890, of his upcoming trip: "Will my Indian gift be acceptable to my future spouse from whom I am running away to the island of Sakhalin?" This bit of jest, however, alluded to his true motives; Chekhov wrote seriously about them on February 2, 1890, to S. N. Filippov: "Indeed I am going to the island of Sakhalin, not for the sake of the convicts, but for no particular reason... I'd like to strike out a year or a year and a half from my life." Responding in a letter of March 9, 1890, to Suvorin's doubts about the wisdom of his journey, Chekhov enumerated all the rational motives for his trip to Sakhalin, but added, as though sensing that his arguments were unconvincing: "Granted that the journey may result in absolutely nothing, still won't there be two or three days I shall remember all my life with rapture or with bitterness?"

On March 22 of the same year, Chekhov confessed to Shcheglov: "Please, don't place any literary hopes on my Sakhalin trip. I am not going for the purpose of observations and not for impressions, but purely and simply because I wish to live for six months in a way I haven't lived until now." Social concern is evidently an inadequate explanation for this trip. The final letter written just prior to his departure confirms the seriousness of his reasons for this trip—reasons stated and reiterated in his correspondence before his trip at the beginning of 1890. In this letter Chekhov remains strikingly true to himself, to his original intention. What is confirmed in his letter to Shcheglov is not only why he is going to Sakhalin but, more important, what he is fleeing from:

> If criticism, the authority of which you cite, knows what you and I do not know, then why has it been silent until now, why is it not revealing to us truths and immutable laws? If it knew, then believe me, it would long ago have pointed out the path to us, and we should know what there is for us to do, and [Konstantin] Fofanov would not be sitting in an insane asylum, [Vsevolod] Garshin would be alive at this time, [Kazimir] Barantsevich would not be sulking, and we should not be bored and dull as we are now, and you would not feel drawn to the theater nor I to Sakhalin.

Chekhov's impressions of the trip—they abound in his letters and are conveyed with power—provide further evidence that the chief reason for the trip was to overcome his crisis. The letters suggest a state of deep satisfaction, a richness of experience and fullness of life such as Chekhov, apparently, had never had before. "Really, I have seen such riches and have had so much pleasure, that even dying now does not frighten me," Chekhov wrote to Suvorin from Blagoveshchensk on June 27, 1890. On his return to Moscow on December 10 of that year, he wrote to Shcheglov: "I am up to my chin in contentment; I have had my fill and am so enchanted that I want nothing more and would not be offended if I were struck down by paralysis or carried off to the other world by dysentery . . . . I have been in hell . . . and in heaven." A week later, on December 17, he wrote Suvorin: "How wrong you were when you advised me not to go to Sakhalin! I have a paunch now, and . . . my dear, there are myriads of midges in my head now, a world of plans, no end of things. And what a sourpuss I would be if I had sat at home. Before my trip, 'The Kreutzer Sonata' was an event for me, but now it seems ridiculous and addleheaded. Perhaps the trip matured me, or perhaps it made me lose my mind—the devil knows."

It was in this way that Chekhov resolved the deeply personal crisis that he experienced at the end of the 1880s. The name drama had come to an end. The following decade would see its epilogue, and it is then that the name of Chekhov would be redeemed.

Michael C. Finke

"At Sea": A Psychoanalytic Approach to
Chekhov's First Signed Work

WITH THE publication of "The Requiem" (Panikhida) in February 1886, Anton Chekhov made his first appearance in *Novoe vremia*, a Petersburg daily published by Aleksei Suvorin. He had submitted the story under the pseudonym Antosha Chekhonte but was persuaded by the paper's editors to attach his real name.[1] That this moment receives special mention in biographies of Chekhov is natural, given the significance Suvorin was to have in the development of Chekhov's career and the meaning commonly attached to the signing of one's proper name. But it is in equal measure odd that so little attention has been afforded the first story published under the name of A. Chekhov at the author's own initiative. This was "At Sea," a very short tale published in *Mirskoi tolk* in 1883.[2] Two more stories signed by Chekhov, "He Understood" and "The Swedish Match," soon also appeared in different journals.

"At Sea" has an interesting publication history, as told by the editors of Chekhov's complete works. Soon after its submission, Chekhov apparently grew anxious enough about the provocative subject matter to write a letter to the editors asking that they return the story; he was told it was too late, although the editors would be happy in the future to receive "less spicy" tales. A short time later, in the letter of December 25, 1883, to Nikolai Leykin, Chekhov complained of the tactics of unscrupulous publishers regarding his name.[3] He explained: "I sign with my full family name only in *Priroda i okhota* [where "He Understood" appeared], and once I put it under a large story in *Strekoza* [this was "The Swedish Match"]." Less than two months after "At Sea" appeared in *Mirskoi tolk*, Chekhov neglected to mention it when listing the few stories he had published under his own name to date—a striking indication of his ambivalence regarding the story.

Almost two decades later Ivan Bunin asked Chekhov to contribute somthing to an almanac projected by the publishing house Skorpion.

Chekhov, who had been revising his early pieces for the Marks edition of his collected works, offered a slightly reworked "At Sea" under a new title, "At Night"; but he was then appalled by the decadent company in which he found himself printed. He was also irritated at the sloppy proofs Skorpion sent him to correct, and he was angry that the proofs arrived with postage due. What seems to have especially provoked Chekhov, however, was the overprominent use of his name to advertise the almanac in the newspaper *Russkie vedomosti*. As happens to the narrator of "A Boring Story" (1889), Chekhov saw his name detached from his self and circulated as a coin of exchange. His letter of complaint to Bunin (March 14, 1901) ended with a pun: "Having read this announcement in *Russkie vedomosti*, I swore never again to become involved with scorpions, crocodiles, or snakes."

If the first publication of a story under Chekhov's own name involved a great deal of anxiety, then republication of the same story many years later became an occasion for manifestly hostile feelings; in both instances the issue of Chekhov's name was central. When revising the story, Chekhov did not disturb its spicy plot, nor did he remove some astonishingly suggestive erotic imagery. Indeed, Skorpion's editor, Valery Bryusov, complained in his diary that Chekhov had intentionally sent a story that would be unlikely to pass the censors.[4] What Chekhov suppressed—what, perhaps, he wished he had suppressed before he sent the story in eighteen years before—were, first, overt signals of intertextual connections with Victor Hugo's *Toilers of the Sea* and Shakespeare's *Hamlet* and, second, details about the relationships between the story's sailor-narrator, his father, and his late mother.

Chekhov normally cut material when making revisions. But the anxiety and ill will that accompanied each publication of this tale, together with the singular fact of Chekhov's signature, lead one to suspect an excessive degree of emotional, even unconscious, involvement. Might not something in the story be at least partially responsible for both Chekhov's signature and his discomfort? The following assay at a psychoanalytic approach to "At Sea" reveals a deep nexus between the story's most remarkable features: its provocative erotic plot and imagery and the author's revisions, anxieties, and signature. But first we will briefly examine the story's plot and Chekhov's revisions.

THE PLOT

The plot tension of "At Sea" is explicitly based on the dynamics of erotic desire: the sailors aboard a steamer have drawn lots to determine which two of them will spy on a newly wed English pastor and his young wife in the bridal suite. The winners are father and son, and the son is also the tale's first-person narrator. Since both the debauched sailors and the story's reader anticipate as payoff or denouement the culmination of two others' sexual act, the reader's position here is no less voyeuristic than the narrator's.[5] The familial relationship between the two peeping Toms creates additional expectations: scenes of mastery and initiation will occur on both sides of the wall.

The two sailors take their places at the peepholes, but there is a hitch in the bridal suite: the bride appears to be reluctant. When she does finally assent, we peeping Toms, who were unable to hear the husband's words, assume that he was pleading for himself and that the marriage's consummation will follow. In the surprise denouement, a banker with whom the couple had been socializing earlier enters, gives the pastor some money, and is left alone with the bride. The stunned sailors leave the peephole without witnessing the sexual act, thereby also depriving the reader of the voyeuristic titillation promised earlier.

The denouement provokes a moral reevaluation of the sailors, earlier self-described by the narrator as "more disgusting than anything on earth." For had the peepers' desires been strictly pornographic, the exchange of privileges for money should have been no cause for them to give up their stations. At the same time, a man of the cloth is the last husband we would expect to be pimping his own bride. Finally, the roles of father and son are reversed: the son, whom his father addresses as "laddie" or "little boy" (*mal'chishka*), becomes father to his own father as he helps him up the stairs.

Every detail in this miniature relates to the denouement, either as anticipated by the sailors or as it actually takes place. The setting at sea and at night—both of which Chekhov underlined in various published versions by alternately using them as titles for the story—suggests a space, cut off from the normal world, where anything might happen; it is a space tailor-made for liminal states. Each of the first three short paragraphs culminates in images that, if interpreted with the story's anticipated denouement in mind, suggest erotic culmination: the heavy clouds wishing to let go of their rain in a burst; the joking sailor who, as lots are drawn to determine who will spy on the newlyweds, crows like a rooster; and this bold image—"A little shudder ran from the back of my head to my very heels, as if there were a hole in the back of my head from which little cold shot poured down my naked body. I was shivering not from the cold, but from other reasons."

Next follows a digression that sets up an opposition between the debauched seaman's world and the virginal world of the newly wed pastor, his bride, and idealized love. This opposition, which will be reversed in the denouement, is later made explicit in the passage juxtaposing the space where the peepers stand with the space of the bridal suite. At the moment, however, the narrator focuses on the sailor's world. His view of his own and his comrades' moral state is summed up by the special kind of space they inhabit. Both literally and figuratively, it is the vertical space necessary for a fall: "To me it seems that the sailor has more reasons to hate and curse himself than any other. A person who might every moment fall from a mast and be immersed forever under the waves, who knows God only when he is drowning or plunging headfirst, needs nothing and feels pity for nothing in existence." Here the sailor embodies man in his fallen state, man who falls all the time, compulsively. In the denouement the narrator jumps back from his peephole "as if stung" or bitten, as by a serpent (the Russian word here, *uzhalennyi*, would be used for a snake bite). The father's face is described as "similar to a baked apple"; this motif has special resonance in the context of a story about falls, carnal knowledge, and egregious sin. The inhabitants of this anti-Eden are compelled to repeat forever the moment of the Fall.

The digression ends: "We drink a lot of vodka, we are debauched, because we don't know who needs virtue at sea, and for what." Yet the anticipated coupling between pastor and bride is special precisely because of its aura of idealized love and virtue, while the sailors' reactions in the denouement demonstrate that virtue is necessary to them, even if they do not expect to take part in it. Here we might compare the way negotiations are carried out between the banker and the pastor with the sailors' method of deciding who among them will receive voyeuristic satisfaction of their erotic desires. The latter cast lots; they rely on luck, God's will, to decide the matter. For the pastor, God's representative, he who can pay gets what he wants. The woman whom the sailor idealizes as a love object becomes a commodity for the pastor and the banker.

"At Sea" begins as a story about the depravity of the sailor's world but ends as a tale depicting the depravity of the "aristocratic bedroom"—a reversal perhaps banally moralistic, but not untypical of the early Chekhov. The last image is one of the father and son moving upward in space.

SUBTEXTS

Now we return to the question of Chekhov's revisions. These can be divided into three chief areas: his handling of subtextual references to Hugo, his handling of references to Shakespeare, and his decision to drop certain details regarding the familial relations of the two peepers.

The characters and setting of "At Sea" are quite exotic for Chekhov, and one suspects from the start that they have been imported. The

Russian scholar R. G. Nazirov recently revealed the story to be a parody of Victor Hugo's *Toilers of the Sea* (Les travailleurs de la mer, 1866).[6] "At Sea" picks up where *Toilers* leaves off: the English pastor, Ebenezer, is departing on a steamer with his bride, Deruchette. Left behind in despair is the extraordinary seaman, Gilliatt, who once saved Ebenezer's life and to whom Deruchette was promised. Chekhov's story echoes the opposition between the coarse laborer of the sea and the refined representative of God, and it repeats certain central motifs, such as that of peeping: the lovesick Gilliatt spies on Deruchette for four years before he takes action to win her; he is spying on her when the pastor declares his love and kisses her for the first time; and even at the novel's melodramatic end, as Gilliatt commits suicide by allowing the rising tide to cover him where he sits, he is watching Deruchette and Ebenezer hold hands on the deck of a departing steamer. To the echoes Nazirov notes can be added Chekhov's handling of the plot device of reversal: men whose exemplary virtue is remarked on by Hugo's narrator repeatedly turn out to be utter scoundrels.

One effect of Chekhov's revisions was to distance "At Sea" from Hugo's novel. Here the customary strategy of improving the rhythm of his prose, shortening dialogues, and pruning some of the melodramatic imagery eliminated the excesses so characteristic of Hugo's style and thereby weakened the links between this parody and its target text. In particular, "Chekhov cut a direct 'bibliographic key'—an allusion to the original object of parody: 'the loud, drunken laughter of *toilers of the sea.*" It has been suggested that Chekhov's diminution of "stylistic mimicry" of Hugo was meant to place greater emphasis on the story's critique of romantic aestheticism.[7] Debunking romantic love, however, is a theme that has lent itself to lighthearted narrative treatment for ages (e.g., in the fabliau), and it is a staple of the early Chekhov. It is highly improbable that when Chekhov returned to this story while editing his early stories for the Marks edition of his works he revised it to further a project of setting the world straight on the issue of romantic love. Rather, he likely found the story unsatisfactory in form and no less unsettling in content than when it was first published.

The second subtext obscured in the revisions was *Hamlet*. Chekhov's career-long involvement with Shakespeare, especially with *Hamlet*, certainly deserves the epithet *obsessive*. As one Russian critic has put it, "Shakespeare is mentioned so often in the stories and plays of Chekhov that one could call him one of Chekhov's heroes."[8] In the 1883 version of "At Sea," the steamer's name, *Prince Hamlet*, is mentioned five times—this in a work of under five pages. Such an underlining of the *Hamlet* motif leads one to look for other allusions, and several can be found.

The cock's crow and the narrator's shudder, discussed above, recall the appearance of the ghost of Hamlet's father:

BARNARDO: It was about to speak when the cock crew.

HORATIO: And then it started like a guilty thing
Upon a fearful summons.[9]

For the sailor imitating the sound and those who are amused by it, the cock's crow is an erotic allusion; for the narrator, however, who has been contemplating his fallen state and is full of self-reproaches, it is also a "fearful summons" heard by a "guilty thing." In the Gospel tale of Peter's denial, retold in Chekhov's short masterpiece of 1894, "The Student," the rooster's call has a similar meaning.

In *Hamlet* this shudder at the recollection of one's guilt is repeated when Claudius sees his crime portrayed in Hamlet's mousetrap. The moment is paralleled in "At Sea" in the narrator's reaction during the dumb show of the wedding night: if the crime of treating the bride as an object to be bought and sold stuns him, this is perhaps because it echoes what he and his shipmates did when they created and raffled the use of the peepholes.

In the original version of the story, the narrator goes on deck and previews in fantasy the scene to be staged in the bridal suite:

I lit a pipe and began looking at the sea. It was dark, but there must have been blood boiling in my eyes. Against the night's black backdrop I made out the hazy image of that which had been the object of our drawing lots.

"I love you!" I gasped, stretching my hands toward the darkness.

This expression "I love" I knew from books lying around in the canteen on the upper shelf.

As he utters "I love you" and stretches his hands toward the phantasm he has conjured, the narrator imagines himself in the place of the one man who in reality has the right to utter these words and embrace the woman—the bridegroom. In a sense, this fantasy places the narrator on the other side of the wall at which he will soon be standing. The motifs of dreaming and reading also associate the narrator with Hamlet; in particular, they recall act II, scene ii, where Hamlet enters reading, in which he utters the line "Words, words, words," and which ends with a torrent of self-reproaches, including his calling himself "John-a-dreams." As we have seen, the narrator of "At Sea" is no less liberal with criticism of himself. It is also in act II, scene ii, that Hamlet calls Polonius "Jephthah, judge of Israel," thereby accusing the father of sacrificing Ophelia to gain favor with Claudius. There is a clear thematic connection with "At Sea," where the bridegroom sacrifices his wife for financial gain.

Chekhov's recourse to *Hamlet* in this story appears distinctive when compared with references in his other early narrative works. There allusions to Shakespeare are usually comically distorted citations that sharpen a character's speech characteristics, reveal a farcically pretentious character's lack of culture, or lampoon Russian pseudo Hamlets and latter-day superfluous men.[10] Something more substantial is taking place in "At Sea." And yet Chekhov chose to obscure the story's connection with *Hamlet* when revising it.

The third area of changes in Chekhov's revision of "At Sea" involves suppressing all mention of the narrator's late mother and toning down the hostility between the narrator and his father. In the 1883 version, the elder sailor addresses his son after they win the lottery:

> "Today, laddie, you and I have gotten lucky," he said, twisting his sinewy, toothless mouth with a smile.
> "You know what, son? It occurs to me that when we were drawing lots your mother—that is, my wife—was praying for us. Ha-ha!"
> "You can leave my mother in peace!" I said.

The "that is" (in Russian, the contrastive conjunction *a*) separating the two designations "your mother" and "my wife" underlines the different functions this one woman held for the two men. (The erotic connotations that can be associated with "getting lucky" work in Russian as well as in English translation.) In the 1901 version this exchange is replaced by the father's words: "Today, laddie, you and I have gotten lucky. . . . Do you hear, laddie? Happiness has befallen you and me at the same time. And that means something." What this odd coincidence means, perhaps, is what it has displaced from the story's earlier version: the mother.

In addition to leaving the mother in peace, Chekhov cut out explicit motifs of antagonism between father and son. In the original version, when the father asks the son to switch peepholes so that he, with his weaker eyes, might see better, the son strikes his father. "My father respected my fist," he says.

THE PRIMAL SCENE

"At Sea" is so laden and ready to burst with motifs of Oedipal strivings that, had the story not been written some sixteen years prior to Freud's first public discussion of Oedipus and Prince Hamlet in *The Interpretation of Dreams*, one would be sorely tempted to conjecture about Freud's influence on Chekhov.[11] To the extent that Chekhov departed from the situations and configurations of characters given him in Hugo's *Toilers* and, at a deeper level, *Hamlet*, his alterations of these subtexts in the original version of "At Sea" directly parallel Freud's interpretation of Shakespeare's play: they superimpose direct conflict with the father onto an impossible erotic desire.

The story's English characters and Shakespearean steamer led the censors to take its original version as a translation from English; "At Night," the version rewritten for Ivan Bunin in 1901, was received as an imitation of Maupassant.[12] Perhaps this helps explain why, in spite of Bryusov's concerns, the story was passed by the censors: giving works non-Russian settings and characters and presenting an original work as a translation or an imitation of a foreign author were long-standing techniques for evading prohibition. But if elements of foreignness acted as a screen from government censors, might this not be true of Chekhov's internal censor as well? Recourse to the exotic Hugo subtext and to *Hamlet* may have facilitated the emergence of very sensitive material. Years later, when Chekhov revised the story for Skorpion, he attenuated the agonistic relationship with the father and the Hugo and *Hamlet* connections in equal measures.

Behind the incident of voyeurism we can see many features of the "primal scene," that archetypal peeping situation, defined in psychoanalytic literature as a "scene of sexual intercourse between the parents which the child observes, or infers on the basis of certain indications, and phantasies. It is generally interpreted by the child as an act of violence on the part of the father."[13] In "At Sea" the scene is portrayed with idiosyncrasies and distortions characteristic of the work of the defense mechanism of repression. These include splitting the father into two figures, the old sailor at the peephole and the pastor (or the reverend father), whose conjugal place the narrator has already taken in his fantasies (when he is on deck with outstretched arms in the story's first version). They also make it possible for the father and the son to share the object of desire even as they contest for her; that is, there is a transformation in which the "either me or you" or "not me but you" as rightful agents of erotic desire for the mother figure into a "both me and you."[14] This helps explain the uncanny stroke of luck—"that means something"—by which both father and son have won the right to stand at the peepholes.

The narrator's positioning at his peephole actually begins as a dreamlike image of penetration into a low and dark place: "I felt out my aperture and extracted the rectangular piece of wood I had whittled for so long. And I saw a thin, transparent muslin, through which a soft, pink light penetrated to me. And together with the light there touched my burning face a suffocating, most pleasant odor; this had to be the odor of an aristocratic bedroom. In order to see the bedroom, it was necessary to spread the muslin apart with two fingers, which I hurried to do." The Russian here for orifice, *otverstie*, can refer to an orifice in the anatomical sense as well. The aristocratic bedroom, with its ambivalently perceived scent, is revealed only after a parting of the hymeneal "muslin"; the notion of hymen is, after all, what makes the anticipated coupling of newlyweds special.

The dialogue between father and son as they are waiting in anticipation at their stations vocalizes, after a process of displacement, thoughts belonging to the situation of the primal scene: "Let me take your place," and "Be quiet, they might hear us." In theory it is the child who can be traumatized by his lack of potency in the Oedipal stage; here the old man complains of his weak eyes. We can interpret the "stung" reaction of the narrator at the denouement—once again, on a different plane of meaning—as just such a castrating trauma, with potency redefined in pounds sterling and the idealized pastor-father exposed in his lack of it. The shock is all the more effective when juxtaposed with the images of excessive and impatient potency at the story's start. At the same time, the exchange represents the uncanny event of a wish fulfilled: the narrator's investment in this scene is predicated on a fantasy of taking the pastor-father's place, and now, before his eyes, just such a substitution is made. Once again, on the model of Hamlet's mousetrap, the sailor's conscience has been captured—with the difference that his most serious crime was no more than a transgressive wish. The narrator's sudden solicitous attitude toward his father—helping him up the stairs—may be interpreted as an attempt to undo this fantasy, a mechanism typical of obsessional neurosis.[15] Earlier, the sailor's reaction was interpreted as revealing an essential morality; now it appears to be a neurotic symptom. The two traits are deliberately entangled in Chekhov's 1889 story "An Attack of Nerves" (Pripadok).

A full-scale psychoanalytic interpretation of the story would only be beginning at this point. In tracing the vicissitudes of the peeping compulsion, Freud treats scopophilia and exhibitionism as inextricably linked opposites "which appear in ambivalent forms."[16] This is certainly the case in "At Sea," where Chekhov can be said to expose himself in a story depicting scopophilia. Indeed, Chekhov himself consciously associated publishing and exhibitionism when he told I. I. Yasinsky that he wrote under a pen name to avoid feelings of shame: "It was just like walking naked with a large mask on and showing oneself like that to the public."[17] The narrator's fantasies and voyeurism are fundamentally autoerotic acts, while the contradictory situation of father and son peeping together, which then culminates with the father's order to desist, could at once dramatize a wish for union with the father and the father's injunction against autoerotic activity, both features of ambivalent Oedipal dynamics.[18] The narrator portrays his father as laying down the moral law and so impinging on his natural process of maturation: "Let's get out of here! You shouldn't see this! You are still a boy." By now, however, this gesture of paternal authority appears ludicrous.

CHEKHOV

Chekhov wrote "At Sea" as a twenty-two-year-old medical student, who at the time, incidentally, was following a patient in a clinic for nervous disorders.[19] The past few years had seen a "tangling up of the family sequence" in which Chekhov had become in a sense the father of his own brothers, sister, and parents.[20] This was chiefly a result of his ability to bring money—that same signifier of authority that displaces the Bible in "At Sea"—into the clan after his father's disastrous bankruptcy. In Chekhov's own family, moreover, the Bible can be associated with Chekhov's pedantically religious father, who was fond of reading religious texts aloud. Just what Chekhov's new status meant to him is hinted at in Tatyana Shchepkina-Kupernik's retelling of a favorite story of Chekhov's mother: still a student, Chekhov came to her and announced, "Well, Mama, from this day on I myself will pay for Masha's schooling!"[21]

The definite antierotic strain in Chekhov's life and works may well bespeak an inadequate resolution of the issues glimpsed in "At Sea." Chekhov's coy, ironic, at times even sadistic bearing toward women with whom he skirted serious involvement, notably Lika Mizinova, recalls Hamlet's treatment of Ophelia and his mother, the women he claims to love. It happens that the measure by which Hamlet quantifies his love for the dead Ophelia—more than "forty thousand brothers" (V.i.269)—was a favorite citation of the early Chekhov; in humorous paraphrasings it became a synonym for "a lot."[22] More to the point, some of Chekhov's later, full-length stories that are notable for their representation of psychopathological states—in particular "Ward Six" (1892)—very carefully situate certain characters' psychological problems in respect to their relations with their fathers.

Psychoanalytic theory has it that the son's identification with the father, his accession to the father's name, closes the Oedipal stage.[23] This comes about after acquiescence to what is perceived as the father's threat of castration and the renunciation of erotic desire for the mother. Fully one-third of "At Sea" involves the narrator's self-reproaches, all of which are based on his sailor's calling, that is, the professional identity shared with and given him by his father. It is clearly an uneasy identity. For Chekhov, too, any identification with his real father would have been terribly problematic.

Chekhov's very first ambitious literary attempt, the play he wrote while still in Taganrog and subsequently destroyed, was titled *Fatherless* (Bezottsovshchina). The first story Chekhov signed with the name of his father, "At Sea," depicts a son overtaking the father; in subsequent years Chekhov was to sign his own name only when he had already become a prominent literary figure and when his ascendency over the family of his father was beyond dispute. Later in life, just after his father died—when he must have been meditating on his relationship with his father—Chekhov made an oblique association between his own family and that of Oedipus. On receiving a telegram of condolence from V. I. Nemirovich-Danchenko on behalf of Konstantin Stanislavsky and the others in the Moscow Art Theater, Chekhov replied in a letter of October 21, 1898: "I am waiting for *Antigone*. I'm waiting, for you promised to send it. I really need it. I'm waiting for my sister, who, as she has telegraphed, is coming to me in Yalta. Together we'll decide how to arrange things now. After the death of our father, our mother will hardly want to live alone in the country. We've got to think up something new." Chekhov sets up a parallelism ("I'm waiting for *Antigone*. . . . I'm waiting for my sister") that casts the shadow of Oedipus's family onto his own, and the upshot of his comment is: Now that my father is dead, my mother will want to live with me.

But there may be more at issue than the Chekhov family dynamics and their reflection in the author's psyche. The allusions in "At Sea" to Hugo and Shakespeare—and their elimination in the story's revision—invite consideration of Chekhov's relations with his literary fathers.[24] "At Sea" juxtaposes two subtexts of vastly different literary value. In parodying Hugo's melodramatic situations and stylistic excesses (as Chekhov had done in the 1880 spoof "One Thousand and One Horrors," dedicated to Victor Hugo), Chekhov treats this predecessor as does the sailor-narrator his own father. Hugo may be openly and easily displaced; Shakespeare, however, is another matter. Whether imitated by would-be authors, misquoted by pretentious buffoons, or performed by un-talented actors, Shakespeare in Chekhov's works is a benchmark against which pretension stands revealed, very often to comic effect. And this notion of pretension might apply equally to the ill-equipped youngster who boldly advances an erotic claim on his parent and to the young author who declares his identity as an author for the first time by signing his proper name.

When Chekhov wrote "At Sea," the figure of Prince Hamlet had served Russian literature as a paradigm for the inability to translate desires and talents into action for decades. The allusion to *Hamlet* in "At Sea" is a kind of a joke about that paradigm, but one that perhaps nevertheless indicates anxiety about failure and a wish to forestall it. By the time Chekhov revised the story in 1901, however, his place as an author was secure. There is even evidence that he had become a conscious theorist of Oedipal anxieties and their implication in the problems of authorship: in *The Sea Gull* (1896), the young writer Treplev, who laces his speech with citations from *Hamlet*, must contest an established author of the preceding generation for both the affection of his mother and recognition as an author.[25]

In any case, the early Chekhov repeatedly associated the fateful moment of asserting one's identity in spite of feelings of inadequacy and probable failure with *Hamlet*. In "Baron" (1882), the seedy prompter, a failed actor who had shown great talent but lacked courage, is carried away during a performance of *Hamlet* and begins declaiming the lines he should have been whispering to the red-haired youth playing the Prince. It is his end. He is kicked out of the theater altogether, but at least for once in his life he has shown boldness; he has declaimed. How appropriate that the story in which Chekhov decides to be Chekhov, to sign his own name, should be engaged with *Hamlet*.[26]

Breakdowns in Communication

Robert Louis Jackson

"The Enemies": A Story at War with Itself?

> Die Botschaft hor'ich wohl,
> allein mir fehlt der Glaube.
> —Goethe, *Faust*

THE PRINCIPLE of symmetry governs Chekhov's story "The Enemies." Oddly enough, it is symmetry itself that is disturbing to the reader. Are there no imbalances in the story?

The title, "Vragi" (Enemies), carries us into one of the oldest and most disturbing realms of human experience. There are two protagonists who become enemies: Kirilov and Abogin. Kirilov's name has its root in the Greek *kyrios* ("Lord," "master") and echoes, incidentally, the name of a missionary who brought Christianity to Russia, St. Cyril (Constantine). Kirilov is a doctor, we are told, who has "experienced need and ill fortune." Abogin is a wealthy gentleman, the root of whose name appears in *bog*, Russian for "god," or *bogatyi*, "wealthy," "rich"; and in *obozhat'*, "to worship," "to adore." Indeed, we learn, Abogin worships his wife like a slave. Chekhov also may have meant the name Abogin to be understood as a Greek-Russian hybrid in which the Greek alpha privitive *a* combines with the Russian word *bog*, thus suggesting the Greek *atheos* (*a*-, "without" + -*theos*, "god"), atheist. Both of these men suffer misfortunes at the same time: Kirilov endures the death of his only child; Abogin experiences what he first takes to be the serious illness of his wife, but then turns out to be the deception of a woman who feigns mortal illness in order to run off with another man.

The story divides neatly into two parts. In the first part we are in Kirilov's house and learn how he meets his misfortune. Abogin arrives barely five minutes after the death of Kirilov's child. Terribly upset, he pressures the reluctant Dr. Kirilov into visiting his presumably sick wife. "I understand perfectly your situation," Abogin tells Kirilov several times. "You are in sorrow, I understand." In fact, in the blindness of his distress, he does not understand Kirilov's suffering. Every word he uses seems to violate it.

A transitional episode occurs in which both characters are on the road together traveling to Abogin's house. For one moment they seem joined in their misery. Even the crows, awakened by the noise of the carriage wheels, nonjudgmentally give out "an anxious pitiful wail, as if they knew that the doctor's son was dead and Abogin's wife was ill." Does nature, too, have a premonition that what unites these two men in their misery is their inability to communicate? "In all of nature one felt something hopeless, sick." Yet paradoxically these two men are closest to each other in their silence. Not without reason does the narrator early in the story observe that "the highest expression of happiness or unhappiness most often is silence; lovers understand one another better when they are silent." The equilibrium established through silence, however, is not long lasting. The carriage crosses a river, a line that seems to divide not only the two territories the men inhabit but also their social and psychic habitations.

The second part of the story takes place in Abogin's house. We discover how he meets his real misfortune, his wife's flight from the house with her lover. Abogin rages over this deception. It is now Kirilov's turn not to understand the suffering or distress that afflicts Abogin. "I do not understand," Kirilov keeps repeating as Abogin recounts the banalities of his bedroom melodrama, one in which, it turns out, he is the cuckold. "I do not understand." In fact, Kirilov does understand something of the world of Abogin, though what he understands he cruelly caricatures.

There is a stormy clash between the two men: Kirilov is outraged at being called upon to participate in what he calls a "vulgar [family] comedy" or "melodrama," and Abogin, who is mortally offended at the violent insults of Kirilov, likewise rages. These differences explode in class hatred. With the contempt of a man who obviously has faced the harsh realities of lower-class existence in his own and other people's lives, Kirilov compares the suffering of the wealthy Abogin to that of a contented "capon." In turn, Abogin, reaching back into the dark class history of Russia, responds furiously: "For such words people are thrashed! Do you understand?"

The story ends with Abogin and Kirilov going their separate ways, as enemies. Abogin drives off "to protest, to do foolish things." Kirilov drives off, not thinking of his wife nor of (his son) Andrei, full of "unjust and inhumanly cruel thoughts" about Abogin, his wife, and her lover, Papchinsky. Kirilov, the narrator tells us, condemns all three of them and "all people who live in rosy subdued light and smell of scent. All the way home he hated and despised them to the point of pain in his heart. And a firm conviction concerning those people took shape in his mind. Time will pass, Kirilov's sorrow will pass, but this conviction, unjust, unworthy of the human heart, will not pass and will remain in the doctor's mind to the very grave." The final words of the story, then, speak of Kirilov's permanent failure to overcome his deep hostility toward Abogin, that is, to reach out to him. The scales, it would seem, have tipped in favor of Abogin. Have they been tipping in that direction in the second half of the story? Do the prestigiously located words at the end of the story signal that on the deeper ethical plane of the story's meaning a reversal of roles has taken place, one in which the "godless" Abogin has overtaken the "Christian" Kirilov in the sympathies of the reader? So much for the symmetries and neat pattern of reversals on which this story and its conventional interpretation thrive.

The narrator himself interprets in a very judicious way the events he narrates: the "egoism of suffering," he observes, drives people apart. "The unhappy are egoistic, spiteful, unjust, cruel, and less capable of understanding each other than fools. Unhappiness does not bring people together but draws them apart." Suffering divides Kirilov and Abogin. Both are bearers of a certain measure of truth, but only as it relates to their own unhappiness; with respect to the whole truth both are blind.

The protagonists, then, are victims of a fundamental misunderstanding, the kind that lies at the root of so many divisions between human beings. Only Chekhov and his narrator—the narrator in this interpretation *is* Chekhov—are aware of the full and complex truth involving Kirilov and Abogin. Thus Chekhov emerges as a kind of arbiter: he holds in his hands the scales of justice, and they are balanced. Suffering is suffering, Chekhov appears to be saying. There is no such thing as a hierarchy of suffering, no foundation for anybody to say, "My suffering is deeper than yours," any more than there is a basis for somebody to say that "what I call beauty is beauty, but what you call beauty is ugliness."

There is much to recommend this interpretation of the story. Yet I find something—not everything, but *something*—wanting in this interpretation. Or rather, I accept it with my head—I see the design very well—but I do not wholly feel it with my heart. Chekhov does not appear to me to approach his two protagonists in an evenhanded way. His sympathies seem to lie with Kirilov, and his antipathies with Abogin. Let me be absolutely clear: Chekhov, the narrator, and the reader, I think, are all agreed that both men as they exchange insults at the end of the story really are equally at fault. Yet in the course of the story Chekhov presents the misunderstanding between the two men in the context of radical differences between these men in their personalities, modes of suffering, and life-styles. Approaching the story from this direction, we are inclined to say that the men part as "enemies" not only because an extraordinary coincidence of circumstances has plunged them into the "egoism of suffering" but also because they are enemies in some deeper sense. The crisis only brings into broad relief certain underlying realities. It is on this deeper level of their misunderstanding—a misunderstanding, as it were, between two different realities—that I find Chekhov's sympathies and my own leaning toward Kirilov.

Whether or not we subscribe to the view that these two men are divided on a deeper level of enmity, Chekhov's near-caricature of Abogin's language and personality complicates an exclusively ecumenical understanding of the story, an understanding well formulated in Beverly Hahn's view that "the story is primarily concerned with the intersecting needs of different lives and consequently with the relativity of moral claims"; that the story is "a plea for understanding, against prejudice"; and that, finally, in this story Chekhov moves "beyond his instinctive sympathies and antipathies to defend the rights and dignity of a comparatively shallow man."[1] The apparent direction of Chekhov's effort is well stated here, and one might say that the design is brilliantly executed. Yet I would argue that Chekhov's instinct and intent are to some extent at cross-purposes with one another. Indeed, it is this fact that awakens the story, for me at least, from its ecumenical dream and makes it at once intriguing, enigmatic, and ambiguous, as so many of Chekhov's stories are.

I am not the first person seriously to raise some of these questions, though I may be the second. More than forty years ago the Soviet ideologist V. V. Yermilov, a heavy-handed but not unintelligent critic, suggested that Chekhov views were not expressed directly in the text: "They live as it were *under* the text, in the deep subterranean current of the story," in its "subtext." Chekhov's sympathy for the little man, Yermilov believed, was expressed in the poetic detail of the text. Yermilov, however, had no patience with what he called the "conciliatory" element in the story. Loudly blowing his class trumpet, he discovered only a repressed message of class antagonisms in the story, what he felt to be Chekhov's hatred of the "parasitical" and "banal" Abogin. "The 'conciliatory' element introduced by Chekhov in the story," Yermilov insisted, "is clearly alluvial, alien to the poetry of the work, and can be explained by the 'pacifist' influence of Tolstoy's teachings that Chekhov was experiencing just at this moment."[2]

The concept of class enemies, which was implemented in a grim way in the Soviet Union, seems to have unbalanced Yermilov's critical mind. But we must give the devil his due: Yermilov rightly calls attention to Chekhov's tendency, on the one hand, to elevate Kirilov and his suffering and, on the other hand, to undercut Abogin. We may object to reducing the conflict of Abogin and Kirilov to a Marxist class struggle, but we cannot avoid treating the question of Chekhov's uneven treatment of his two protagonists.[3]

What is the problem here? Perhaps it is only an aesthetic one. We need only imagine the problem a theatrical adaptation of "The Enemies" would present to a director who understood the story exclusively in its ecumenical dimension. How should one depict Abogin? How does one convey two realities: the fact that on the subjective plane of experience Abogin really does suffer the apparent illness of his wife and then her deceit (suffering is suffering), and the fact that on the objective plane of expression, where the spectacle of suffering and personality is concerned, Abogin comes across as slightly foppish, certainly shallow, and in some respects even comic? In his major plays, Chekhov resolved this kind of problem through characterizations that combine in miraculous ways the comic and the lyrical, the tragic and the ridiculous. There is no trace of such an approach here.

Let us now turn our attention to the question of imbalances in Chekhov's characterization of Kirilov and Abogin. "The most lofty beauty is not without but within," Dostoevsky once observed.[4] Unattractive and ungainly in looks and shape, harsh and embittered in manner, seemingly indifferent to life and people through prolonged contact with a bitter reality, Kirilov nonetheless emerges as a person of dark strength and integrity, one who has lived his values. "Looking at his desiccated figure," the narrator remarks, "one would not believe that this person had a wife, that he could weep over a child."

The opening two lines of the story introduce us to the Kirilovs' suffering. The first sentence is like a terse comuniqué: "At around ten o'clock on a dark September evening the district doctor Kirilov's only child, the six-year-old Andrei, died of diphtheria." Words here seek not to express an attitude toward the event, but simply to convey stark, terrible fact. Comment is superfluous. The second sentence is dominated by one image, that of the Pietà. "Just as the doctor's wife sank on her knees by the dead child's bed and was overwhelmed by the first wave of despair, there came a sharp ring at the bell in the entry." The bell that breaks the silence of the Kirilovs' suffering announces the arrival of Abogin and, as we shall see, the intrusion into the story of a radically different expression of suffering, one that announces itself at every turn and is full of superfluous commentary.

Abogin's first wave of words, his appeal to the doctor for assistance, is met by silence. "Kirilov listened and was silent, as though he did not understand Russian speech." Abogin's second attempt to break through the silence is met by a recapitulation of the story's terse opening line: "Excuse me, I can't go... Five minutes ago... my son died..." Abogin, stunned, momentarily seems to consider leaving; nevertheless, he continues to press the doctor to come. But "a silence ensued." In the moments that follow (a page and a half of the text) the reader is drawn into the bleak and tragic world of the death scene. Every detail speaks mutely of the catastrophe: Kirilov standing with his back to Abogin; his un-steady, mechanical walk; the unlighted lamp; Kirilov's glance into an unidentified "thick book" lying on the table (one may presume, perhaps, that the book is the Bible); the reference to a "stranger" in the entry. The stranger is not only Abogin; as in Chekhov's story "Kashtanka," the stranger is also death, as dark as the unlighted lamp that Kirilov abstractedly touches as he passes into the bedroom.

"Here in the bedroom reigned a dead silence," writes the narrator. "Everything to the smallest detail spoke eloquently of the storm that had just been experienced, about exhaustion, and everything was at rest." Again, the details are singular: the candle, the bottles, the large lamp illuminating the room, the mother kneeling down before the bed, and on the bed "a boy with open eyes and an expression of wonder on his face." Death is closure, but the open eyes of wonder erase the line that separates life from death. Only at the end of this silent scene does the narrator speak directly of the ensemble of death, suffering, and beauty we have witnessed.

> That repellent horror that people think of when they speak of death was absent from the bedroom. In the pervading numbness, in the mother's pose, in the indifference on the doctor's face, there was something that attracted and touched the heart, precisely that subtle, almost elusive beauty of human sorrow that it will take men a long time to learn to understand and describe, and that it seems only music can convey. Beauty was also felt in the somber stillness; Kirilov and his wife were silent and not weeping, as though besides the anguish of their loss they were conscious, too, of all the poetry of their condition.

The reader thinks the obvious: that Chekhov has learned to understand and paint such suffering, that "the elusive beauty of human sorrow" such as we find in this first scene of "The Enemies" is like music. The reader could think further that although there is absolutely no basis for anybody to say, "What I call beauty is beauty, and what you call beauty is ugliness," nonetheless Chekhov in "The Enemies" has presented to us in this tableau his own conception of the "beauty of human sorrow," his own "feeling of beauty," his own poetics of suffering. Whether or not Chekhov's own tableau of sorrow, anymore than Botticelli's or Michelangelo's, carries any objective weight is a matter for each reader to decide. What is certain, however, is that Chekhov stands in intimate relation to the Pietà he has created.

"I myself am profoundly unhappy," Abogin tells the increasingly disturbed and angry Kirilov after he, Abogin, has learned of his wife's betrayal. Kirilov responds scornfully, "Unhappy? Do not touch this word; it does not concern you." In any ordinary sense Kirilov's remark is absurd. Suffering is suffering. Abogin, our head tells us, suffers in his own way. Yet Chekhov depicts the suffering Abogin in a way that demeans his suffering. The spectacle of suffering of the Kirilovs is lyrical, tragic. The spectacle of suffering of Abogin is melodramatic and lowered by the details of his personality and surroundings.

Let us go back, for a moment, to the first scene in which the narrator introduces Abogin to us. "Is the doctor at home?" asks the person who enters the room. "I am at home," answers Kirilov. "What do you want?" "Oh, it's you? I'm very glad!" rejoiced the newcomer (*ochen' rad, obradovalsia voshedshii*), and he began feeling in the dark for the doctor's hand, found it, and squeezed it tightly in his own. "I'm very... very glad! [*Ochen', ochen' rad*] We are acquainted! I'm Abogin... and I had the pleasure of seeing you in the summer at Gnuchev's. I'm very glad [*ochen' rad*] that I found you in... For God's sake [*Boga radi*] don't refuse to come with me now... My wife is dangerously ill... And I've a carriage... . . . On the way to you I suffered terribly [*isstradalsia dushoi*]."

Abogin is distressed. The narrator notes in his shaking voice "an unaffected sincerity and childlike uncertainty." Frightened and overwhelmed, he spoke in brief, jerky sentences and "uttered a great many unnecessary, irrelevant words." His selection of words, indeed, contradicts the seriousness and urgency of his mission. The word *rad* (glad) is repeated often, by itself and within words: *obradovalsia, isstradalsia.* It produces a strangely incongruous effect, in view of Abogin's distress. Finally, his *Boga radi* and *radi Boga* almost pass into *radi Abogina* (for Abogin's sake). And indeed this is how Abogin incongruously comes across to us. It is a fact worth noting that the word *Bog* (God) in one form or another is repeatedly on Abogin's lips, in his name, A-bog-in, *Boga radi, radi Boga, Bozhe moi, vidit Bog, Ei-Bogu,* and *Dai-to Bog.* By contrast, the name of God only once passes the lips of Kirilov. Only the "thick book" hints at Kirilov's relationship to God. No words about love or sacrifice pass his lips. On the other hand, we learn that Abogin loved his wife "fervently like a slave" (*Ja liubil nabozhno* [the root of this word is *bog*, or god] *kak rab*), that "he sacrificed the civil service and music" (*brosil sluzhbu i muzyku*) for his wife. Indeed, there is no music in his life, or perhaps, religion—if we choose to remember the double meaning of *sluzhba* (both "service" as in civil service and "service" as in religious services).

The "irrelevant" words *rad* (glad, happy) and *udovol'stvie* (pleasure) that crop up in Abogin's speech are signal words: they are not merely expressions of a distressed man who has lost control of his language, but they point to a residual sense of self-satisfaction and egoism that characterizes the man. The narrator speaks of Abogin's "contentedness [*sytost'*], health, and assurance." Even before his quarrel with Abogin,

Kirilov early observes in Abogin's house "a stuffed wolf as substantial and content [*sytyi*] as Abogin himself." This expression of "contentedness" (*sytosti*), the narrator notes, only disappears when Abogin learns of his wife's deception. But as he waits for his carriage a short while later, we are told, "he regained his expression of contentedness [*sytosti*] and refined elegance."

There is, indeed, something childishly, naively, egotistically *radi Abogina* (for the sake of Abogin) about Abogin and his use of words. "Doctor, I'm not made of wood [*doktor, ja ne istukan*], I understand your situation perfectly. . . . I sympathize with you." But there is something oddly unfeeling about Abogin. We have translated the word *istukan* as "piece of wood"; it also means "idol" or "statue," figuratively, a person without feeling. Whether we ascribe it to his distress, to something basic in his personality, or to both, there is something out of place in Abogin's way of expressing himself: "My God," he says pleadingly to Kirilov, "You have suffering, I understand, but really I am inviting you not to do some dental work or to a consultation, but to save a human life! . . . . . A life is higher than any personal suffering! Really, I'm asking for courage, for heroism! in the name of humanity!"

Without any question, Abogin is terribly upset. He is out of touch with his words; it may even be said that Abogin's tone contradicts his words. Yet our words, even in crises, say something about ourselves. There is something banal and shallow about this man. "You never love those close to you as when you are in danger of losing them," Abogin says to Kirilov when, at last, the two men are on their way to Abogin's house. There is some truth in this observation. Yet it is a truth that is not usually uttered by one who directly faces the loss of a loved one. Authentic love does not comment on itself. "If something happens [to her]," Abogin exclaims in the carriage, "I won't survive it!" (*Esli chto sluchitsia, to… ia ne perezhivu*). The focus here is oddly upon himself. Later when he learns of his wife's deception, he more truthfully declares: "Oh, God, better that she should have died! I won't be able to bear it! I won't be able to bear it!" (*Ia ne vynesu! Ne vynesu ia!*). Again the focus is upon himself.

"Abogin was sincere," the narrator remarks early in the story about Abogin's way of expressing himself, "but it was remarkable that whatever words he uttered all sounded stilted, soulless, and inappropriately flowery and even seemed to do violence to the atmosphere of the doctor's home and to the woman who was somewhere dying. He felt this himself, and therefore, fearing to be misunderstood, did everything possible to give his voice a softness and tenderness, so that at least sincerity of tone, if not his words, would take effect." Abogin is by no means a

man without genuine feelings. He is arguably sympathetic in his tortured naïveté; he reaches out to Kirilov (he presses his hand on meeting
him, touches him several times as though to establish human contact
and to awaken Kirilov from the numbness of grief). Yet Chekhov makes
it difficult for us to respond sympathetically to him: "In general the
phrase, however lofty and profound it may be, acts only on the indifferent but cannot always satisfy those who are happy or unhappy;
therefore the highest expression of happiness or unhappiness is most
often silence; lovers understand each other better when they are silent,
while a feverish, passionate speech spoken at the grave moves only
bystanders, whereas to the widow or children of the deceased it seems
cold and insignificant."

The classical Greek view was that every character is at the root of
his own fate. In the case of Abogin, the style is the man. This slightly
foppish and contented man—this naive and shallow man who abandoned music and the service slavishly to attend to a capricious and fast-
living wife—is the kind of banal character to whom banal things happen. The more we learn about him and see him in his own environment,
the more we find some connection between his character and his bedroom melodrama. Just as his eyes "laugh with pain," so his suffering
has a touch of the burlesque. Here is how the narrator describes Abogin
at the time he discovers his wife's betrayal: The sound *a!* (is it only a
coincidence that the first letter of Abogin's name announces his grotesque
entry?) echoes from the room in which he first realizes that his wife
has absconded with Papchinsky. If, as suggested at the outset of our
discussion, Chekhov indeed intended the name Abogin to be understood
as a Greek-Russian hybrid (with the *a* in his name representing the
Greek alpha privitive meaning "without"), then the sound that he de-
spairingly utters when he discovers that his wife has deceived him may
conceal a Chekhovian joke: Abogin, who has worshiped his wife like
a slave, is suddenly "without" his deity, his god.

Abogin enters the living room.

His expression of satiety and refined elegance had disappeared; his face,
hands, his whole stance, were contorted by a repulsive expression combining horror and the torment of physical pain. His nose, his lips, his
moustache—all his features were moving and seemed to be trying to tear
themselves from his face; his eyes looked as though they were laughing
with pain. . . . Abogin took a heavy and wide step into the middle of
the drawing room, bent forward, moaned, and shook his fists. "She has
dece*iv*ed me!" he cried, strongly accenting the second syllable. She's gone
off! . . . with that clown Papchinsky! My God! Abogin stepped heavily
toward the doctor, thrust his white soft fists to his face, and shaking
them continued to wail: "She has gone off! Deceived me! But why this

lie?! My God! My God! . . . What did I do to her? She's gone off!"
Tears gushed from his eyes. . . . Now in his short coat and his fashionable narrow trousers in which his legs looked disproportionately slim,
and with his big head and mane, he extraordinarily resembled a
lion. . . . "A sick person! a sick person!" cried out Abogin, laughing,
weeping, all the while shaking his fists.

Echoes of the irrelevant *rad* appear, of course, in this last reference
to "laughing, weeping." Indeed, the melodramatic scene before us, like
Abogin's suffering, seems to border on tragicomedy or even farce. "If
you marry big-rich, rage around big-rich, and then act out a melodrama, what has this got to do with me?" exclaims Kirilov after listening
to Abogin pour out his family secrets. "Who gave you this right to mock
another man's sorrow?" Kirilov blindly observes. Yet what has Abogin's
suffering got to do with Kirilov's? And can we—how much are we supposed to—empathize with Abogin? We remember well Kirilov's gratu-
itous and cruel dismissal of Abogin as a clown, his characterization of
Abogin's bedroom drama as farce, his savage comparison of Abogin's
unhappiness or suffering to that of a capon who is unhappy because it
is overweight. "Worthless people!" Of course, Kirilov, like Abogin in
the first scene, has lost control of his words, his touch with reality; his
portrait of Abogin is a gross caricature. We forget, however, that Chekhov has provided us with an image of Abogin and his suffering that
lends a certain credibility to this cruel caricature. In this connection, it
is noteworthy that toward the end of the story the narrator suggests that
had the doctor been able to listen to Abogin instead of heaping abuse
on him, Abogin "might have reconciled himself to his sorrow without
protest." The suggestion here is that a more sympathetic response on
Kirilov's part might have helped assuage Abogin's grief. Yet it appears
that such a gesture was not necessary. We are informed a little later that
when Abogin leaves his house his usual "expression of satiety and refined
elegance" have returned to him.

Beverly Hahn maintains that "it is Abogin who progressively gains
the story's sympathy and Kirilov, in his arrogant rejection of Abogin's
suffering, who loses some of it."[5] I do agree that this is what should
happen. Unfortunately, I do not think Abogin rises very much in our
estimation at the end of the story or that Kirilov appreciably suffers.
In short, I do not think that Chekhov succeeds wholly in overcoming
a certain residual lack of sympathy for Abogin. More important, the
reader is ill prepared for the sermonic words with which the narrator
reproaches Kirilov at the end of the story. Chekhov's message is clear.
The point is that it is too clearly a message.[6]

Sisyphus in the eponymous myth is condemned to roll a stone to
the top of the mountain only to have it roll down again to the foot of

the mountain, and so on. I see Chekhov in "The Enemies" in the same position as Sisyphus. More than any other Russian writer in the nineteenth century Chekhov approaches humankind "with malice toward none, with charity for all" (to borrow our words from Lincoln). But Chekhov was also human. Had there not been a bit of the *vrag*, or "enemy," in him, there would have been no charity. I think Chekhov understood this when he wrote "The Enemies."

Vladimir Golstein

"Doma": At Home and Not at Home

The child is father of the man.
—William Wordsworth

He did not use his talent (the art of
depicting well) to hide his soul, as had been
done so often. He used it to turn his soul
inside out.
—Leo Tolstoy, on Ivan Turgenev

AT THE end of the sixth book of the *Iliad*, Homer
presents a touching moment in the life of the Trojan war hero Hector.
Wearing all his shining armor, the famous warrior returns from battle
to visit his wife and their infant son, Astyanax. When, however, Hector
leans over to embrace the boy, Astyanax begins to cry, for he is frightened by the bright reflection of the armor. Hector is forced to take off
his helmet in order to embrace and kiss his child. Thus Hector, who
is so often called "Hector of the gilded helmet," must shed his arms
and helmet, that is, his public persona, in order to fulfill his private
role of a father. Through this encounter Hector is forced to realize that
the conduct of familial relations is very different from the conduct of
military exploits. Amid his family Hector has to learn to function without his protective armor.

Remote as its events are from those of the *Iliad*, Chekhov's story
"At Home" (Doma, 1887) conveys a similar message. Evgeny Petrovich,
a successful lawyer and the widowed father of seven-year-old Seryozha,
is made to think and act differently from the way he does in public in
order to make genuine contact with his son.

One does not have to travel to ancient Greece to search for antecedents of Chekhov's story. "At Home," set up as a confrontation between
two value systems (that of a grown-up and that of a child), bears the
undeniable mark of Tolstoy. This is not surprising, since at the time
when "At Home" was written, Chekhov was under Tolstoy's influence
to such a degree that a number of his stories of that period are conventionally called Tolstoyan.[1] And Tolstoy, who often praised works

74

that echoed his own thought, considered "At Home" among the fifteen best Chekhov stories.[2] "At Home," I believe, is based on the twenty-sixth and twenty-seventh chapters of part 5 of *Anna Karenina*, that is, the chapters that describe the education of Anna Karenina's son, also named Seryozha. Similarities between the experiences of the two boys are striking. They both have to cope without their mothers: in Chekhov's story the mother is dead, and in *Anna Karenina* Seryozha has been told that his mother is no longer living. When dealing with grown-ups, both boys look for love but are faced with dry formality in their fathers. Their fathers' rationality and formalism are manifested even in their involvement in legal professions: Evgeny Petrovich is a public prosecutor, and Karenin participates in the government legislature. Similarities run even to minute details: both boys, for example, are preoccupied with the beards of the adult men they know.[3]

Let us consider how Chekhov elaborates on Tolstoy, confronting his character's rationality and bookishness with the immediacy and spontaneity of his son. Chekhov's protagonist, Evgeny Petrovich, liberal, skeptical, and tired from a day's work as a prosecuting attorney, comes home to relax in the world of comfort, only to be faced with a new unpleasant task. He learns that Seryozha has been smoking on a number of occasions. The governess who first discloses Seryozha's smoking to his father says that she tried to convince the boy to stop but to no avail: "When I began to appeal to his conscience [*stala ego usoveshchivat'*] he closed his ears, as he usually does, and began to sing loudly so as to drown out my voice."[4] The father's task is thus defined at the outset: he has "to catch the conscience" (*usovestit'*) of Seryozha; that is, he has to break through the child's rather active resistance toward boring moralizations and then convince him of the dangers of smoking. As the story unfolds, Evgeny Petrovich tries various strategies in order to achieve his goal.

In appealing to his son, Evgeny Petrovich resorts to the methods of three human activities that are supposedly able to awaken an individual's conscience. Evgeny Petrovich mentions these activities explicitly when he skeptically reviews his options: "How little rationally comprehended truth and reasonable confidence are to be found even in those activities that are fraught with so much responsibility and that are so terrifying in their consequences, such as education, law, literature." Regardless of Evgeny Petrovich's skepticism, the actions he takes and the words he uses to convince his son to stop smoking fall neatly into these three categories. The consecutive use of legal, pedagogical, and literary modes of persuasion turns out to be the organizing principle of the story. The first two approaches fail, however, and only a fairy tale, which Seryozha asks his father to narrate, actually succeeds.

Evgeny Petrovich starts his war on smoking by appealing to the legal sphere, that is, to the sphere with which he as a public prosecutor is most familiar. He investigates the charge and comes up with an indictment: "You've been caught doing three bad things: you smoke, you take tobacco that doesn't belong to you off my table, and you tell lies." The child fails, however, to grasp the significance of abstract notions of private property or of right and wrong. During the father's pronouncements he is preoccupied with an investigation considerably more important to him: he is wondering what glue is made of.

Having failed with the legal method, the father appeals to pedagogy. He addresses Seryozha like a teacher or preacher: "Second, you have been smoking. That is very bad. If I smoke, it doesn't mean that smoking is fine. When I smoke I know it is a foolish thing to do, and I reprimand and dislike myself for doing it ('Oh, what a crafty teacher I am!' thought the prosecutor)." Yet neither abstract lecturing on the moral or physical dangers of smoking nor the sophistry of self-accusation achieves Evgeny Petrovich's goal. Even the direct threat of the lethal effects of smoking does not scare the child. Seryozha's face darkens for a moment when his father mentions death, but then the boy becomes lost in meditations on the whereabouts of his dead mother.

Having failed with these two approaches, Evgeny Petrovich finds himself at a loss.[5] He contemplates his failure:

> If one of our teachers or jurists could look into my head at this moment, he would call me a pushover and would probably accuse me of excessive subtlety. But after all, these cursed questions are resolved much more easily *at school* or *in court* than *at home*. At home, one has to deal with people whom one madly loves, and love is demanding and complicates things. If this boy were my *pupil* or a *defendant* rather than my *son*, I would not be such a coward, and my thoughts would not wander as they now do. (my emphasis)

Evgeny Petrovich realizes that life at home is different from life in the public domain: at home he must deal with a unique individual whom he loves, not some unrelated person playing a predetermined role at school or in court. Evgeny Petrovich, for whom home is a place for "light, vague, relaxed, homelike musings," now reluctantly admits that home offers new demands and complexities instead.[6]

While Evgeny Petrovich contemplates his defeat, Seryozha begins to draw. He resorts to art, whose concrete images are an obvious indication of the kind of language to which he can respond. What is more, he draws "a little house," as though attempting to attract his father's attention to the specific nature of the world he inhabits. Evgeny Petrovich, tired after his unsuccessful attempts to convince Seryozha, begins to discuss Seryozha's drawings with him; the father begins to pay attention to his son's manner of experiencing the world. Still, Evgeny Petrovich does not know how to proceed, as repetition of his exasperated question "What shall I say to him?" betrays. As though in answer, Seryozha caresses his father and says: "Tell me something. Tell me a fairy tale" (*rasskazhi mne chto-nibud'! Rasskazhi skazku*). Instead of logical discourse, signaled by the verb "say" (*skazhi*), the child demands artistic discourse, narration (*rasskazhi*).

The fairy tale that Evgeny Petrovich tells Seryozha is the story of an old king and his son, the young prince, who is perfect in all respects except for his predilection to smoking. The two inhabit a beautiful palace located in the most beautiful garden.[7] The son's smoking leads to his premature death, however. The king subsequently finds himself defenseless against his enemies, who conquer the kingdom, destroy the palace, and kill the king. This rather didactic and unimaginative tale has a tremendous effect on the boy. The child falls silent for a minute and then pronounces: "I won't smoke anymore." Why has the tale had such a strong and successful impact upon Seryozha?

Evgeny Petrovich, who appears almost disappointed with the success of his tale, offers his own answer. He thinks that success has been brought by artistic embellishment of the unpleasant facts. That he deems "trickery." He observes:

> It will be said that beauty and artistic form were the influences in this case. . . . let it be so, but it is hardly consoling. This approach is not a real one, after all... Why is it that morals and truth must be presented not in their raw state but in a mixture, always sugar-coated and gilded, like pills? That state of affairs is not normal... It is falsification, deceit, trickery... Medicine must be sweet; truth must be beautiful. Man has been prone to such folly ever since Adam... Well, perhaps it is all natural and ought to be so. Nature is rife with useful deceptions and illusions.

Evgeny Petrovich's interpretation of the success of his tale is echoed by later critics.[8] In 1988 Wayne Booth, in the epilogue to his book *The Company We Keep*, cited Evgeny Petrovich's philosophizing and wholeheartedly accepted his views on the mysterious power of art. Booth sees the story as Chekhov's musings on "the corruptions of art" and on the power of stories in general.[9] Such a reading might support Booth's arguments concerning the power of stories and the need to choose between good and bad stories that constitute our lives, but it clearly oversimplifies the subtlety of Chekhov's message by limiting it to the prosecutor's idle thoughts.

I believe that both the prosecutor's hackneyed opposition between fact and fiction and Booth's opposition between useful and harmful fictions miss the key component of Chekhov's story. The fairy tale that Evgeny Petrovich narrates is special and effective not because it is a gilded pill, but because it discloses such elements of the prosecutor's psyche that he prefers to overlook. In fact, Evgeny Petrovich's opposition should be reversed: it is the story itself that conveys the real, bitter truths, while all the platitudes the prosecutor has poured upon the child so far are the sugar-coated deceit and trickery.

While listening, Seryozha manages to transcend the didactic message of the fairy tale and perceive aspects of the story that remain hidden from Evgeny Petrovich. The child grasps that it is Evgeny Petrovich himself who is unwittingly exposed in the weak and frightened figure of the king. Having been emotionally awakened by the loving intimacy with his son, Evgeny Petrovich inadvertently reveals his innermost fear in the tale he narrates. It is the fear of being left alone, weak and helpless, with no one to provide protection from enemies. He concludes the tale thus: "The old man, weak and ill, was left without any help. And there was no one to govern the kingdom or to protect the palace. Enemies came and killed the old man and destroyed the palace." It is to this self-exposure on the part of the father that Seryozha ultimately responds.

The verb "was left" (*ostalsia*), used by Evgeny Petrovich in his narration, alerts Seryozha to his own experiences. Seryozha uses the same verb when contemplating the deaths of his mother and uncle: "Death carries mothers and uncles to another world, and their children and violins are left behind [*ostaiutsia*] on earth." Seryozha clearly identifies his own trauma of separation, of being abandoned, with the experiences of the old king, who is also left alone after the death of his cigarette-smoking son. The fact is further stressed when at the end of the fairy tale the child's eyes express the same fear and sorrow they expressed at the thought of the death of his relatives.[10]

Another key word of the fairy tale to which Seryozha instinctively reacts is *protect*. After the prince dies from smoking, the king and the garden are left unprotected. Seryozha can easily respond to these images, because he is a child obsessed with protection: he draws a house and next to it a soldier with a bayonet; he speaks of doorkeepers and the need to protect the home from thieves. This obsession is a result of painful losses he has already experienced: by the age of seven he has already been deprived of his mother and uncle. To be sure, seven-year-old Seryozha hardly perceives death in the same tragic light as grown-ups do, but he knows very well the grief of separation. When his father mentions death, Seryozha begins to wonder how his mother handles it: "Dead people live in heaven, somewhere near the stars, and from there they look at earth. Can they bear the separation?" Clearly, it is very hard for Seryozha himself to handle the pain of separation from his mother.

The plight of the king who is left unprotected reflects the father's fears in terms that the son can comprehend and identify with. To the father the tale is simply naive, for he fails to recognize himself, that is, his own fears and emotions, in it. Seryozha, on the other hand, perceives in the king's predicament both his own grief and his father's. And that makes it possible for him to respond to his father's needs.

Evgeny Petrovich has captured his son's conscience, not by threatening to cancel his own love for the child (as he tried to do at the beginning of the story), but by evoking Seryozha's own love and empathy. It is not thus sweetened medicine, as Evgeny characterizes the fairy tale, but real human compassion that makes the boy say, "I won't smoke anymore." The miracle of the child's conversion has occurred not because of the abstract artistry of the father's narration but because the son's own love and pity for his father are invoked through the medium of art.

In order to become a successful narrator or artist, Evgeny Petrovich had to become a father first, to take off his protective helmet and expose his humanity and vulnerability. It should be emphasized that throughout the story the narrator, describing Evgeny Petrovich's actions, refers to him either by his profession, "prosecutor" (*prokuror*), or by his name, Evgeny Petrovich or Bykovsky. Only once is he called by the narrator "the father." And this appellation is employed after Evgeny Petrovich has told Seryozha the fairy tale and the son has surprisingly capitulated, agreeing not to smoke. The narrator then records that when Seryozha "had said good night and gone to bed, his father [*ego otets*] walked quietly from one corner to another and smiled."

The child would have remained totally blind to the tale, however, had nonverbal contact not been established between the father and the son. The father's narration is both improvisation and oral performance, and as such it is characterized by nonverbal aspects of communication: tone of voice, gestures, glances. It is this communication that attunes the son and the father to each other and creates the loving and sharing atmosphere necessary for the father's conception of the fairy tale and the son's proper reception of it.

Among the aspects of nonverbal communication, which enable Evgeny Petrovich to achieve a real rapport with his son, physical contact is crucial. In the course of the story Seryozha moves closer to his father not only emotionally but physically as well. First, while sitting at his desk, Evgeny Petrovich pushes Seryozha away to accuse and interrogate the child. A bit later, Seryozha sits by the desk while his father lectures to him. And finally, when Evgeny Petrovich begins to talk about Seryozha's drawings, the son moves closer still to his father, climbing into his father's lap. For the son the physical contact in general is imperative. Several times in the story he is described as touching various things around him, often during his father's abstract arguments. He rubs against his father and plays with his beard. Through touch the child expresses and experiences love; the thought of his dead mother, for example, makes him touch the shade of the lamp that stands next to him on the table.

But it is not only the son who is susceptible to physical contact. Embracing Seryozha, Evgeny Petrovich looks into his eyes and is made to experience love again: "The prosecutor felt the child's breath on his face, touched the child's hair with his cheek, and his soul was getting warm and tender, as if not only his hands but his whole soul were lying on the velvet of Seryozha's jacket. He looked into the boy's large, dark eyes, and it seemed to him that his mother and wife and everything he had ever loved gazed at him out of those wide pupils." Evgeny Petrovich is being figuratively disarmed by his son, just as Hector was literally disarmed by his. The son's intimate behavior brings Evgeny Petrovich closer to home, so to speak, to the realm of intimacy and personal involvement. At home, he learns, he has to be neither a lawyer nor a teacher, but a father.

The nonverbal communication, however, is not restricted to touch. When Seryozha asks to hear a fairy tale, he wants it to be told, not read. The child wants an oral word, one colored by the tone and feelings of the narrator, a word addressed directly to him. Words as such have hardly any meaning for Seryozha. This fact is rendered emblematically when Evgeny Petrovich, in a fit of exasperation, tells his son: "Give me your word of honor that you won't smoke anymore." The son's response is illuminating. He sings back: "Wo-ord of ho-nor! Wo-ord! Ord! Ord!" (*Che-stnoe slo-vo! Vo! Vo!*). By deconstructing, so to speak, the very word *word* (*slo-vo! vo! vo!*) into meaningless sounds, Seryozha reveals that he fails to perceive any meaning in those words—words that do not have immediate emotional resonance to him. Seryozha's singing in response to his governess's warnings confirms his utter indifference and even hostility to words that convey abstract promises, threats, and so on.

But if Seryozha's singing can strip words of their meaning, perhaps some other artistic and emotional employment of words can invest words with new meaning and bring this meaning to life. In fact, that is exactly what happens during the narration of the fairy tale. The tale succeeds not because Evgeny Petrovich embellishes the unpleasant words of truth, but because the intense emotional involvement of both father and son brings to life for Seryozha the abstract and distant meaning of words. It is revealing that once the fairy tale is over, the son returns to the words of the promise, which his father has requested before ("I won't smoke anymore"). This time the words have regained their meaning.

There is one word in the text of "At Home" that reveals better than others why the fairy tale was so effective. The narrator tells us that in Seryozha's imagination, sounds, form, and color are "interwoven" (*soprikasalis'*). This word is emblematic, for it defines the condition of emotional and physical closeness that is established between father and son. The tale is told at the moment of warm embrace, with all of Seryozha's senses attuned to his father: "Seryozha was listening intently, looking steadily into his father's eyes." Moreover, it is the interconnection of all of Seryozha's perceptions and sensations that enables Seryozha to transcend the didactic message of the fairy tale and to perceive those aspects of the tale that are hidden even from Evgeny Petrovich.

There is a revealing tension between the title of Chekhov's story "At Home" and its very first sentence, in which the governess reports to the prosecutor: "Somebody came from Grigorievs to pick up a book, but I said you were not at home [*vas net doma*]." This tension between being both at home and not at home discloses the paradox of Evgeny Petrovich's situation. On the level of action and organic expression, he has indeed behaved like a father and has succeeded in rousing his son's conscience. On the level of thought and reflection, however, Evgeny Petrovich misses the implications of both Seryozha's conversion and his own behavior. Once the child goes to bed, Evgeny Petrovich prefers to drown the intensity of the emotional involvement with his child in his idle philosophizing about the ability of sugar-coated truths to succeed where unvarnished facts have failed. Evgeny Petrovich refuses to face the true reason behind the success of his story and in so doing hides from his child and, ultimately, from himself. On this level Evgeny Petrovich is not yet "at home."

The Sacred and the Profane

Nils Åke Nilsson

"The Bishop": Its Theme

"THE BISHOP" is Chekhov's last story but one. It was written in 1901–2 and published in the April 1902 issue of *Zhurnal dlia vsekh*. According to one of Chekhov's letters, however, the subject was not a new one; it was something that "I have had in my head for about fifteen years already."[1] The story tells of the illness and death of "His Reverence Peter." It begins with the midnight mass on the eve of Palm Sunday, and by the time the bells call the people to the Easter Day service, the bishop is already dead. His mother and his niece have come to see him because of the holiday, and it is together with them that he spends his last days, recalling his childhood, his whole life. Finally, we are told that a new bishop has been appointed, and though Bishop Peter apparently discharged his duties better than many of his colleagues, people are quick to forget him. His mother returns to her small provincial town, and she is the only one who still remembers him. Sometimes she tells the other women that she had a son who was a bishop, but this she does cautiously, fearing that they will not believe her. And—so ends the story—not everybody in fact does so.

"The Bishop" has often been called one of Chekhov's best stories. It is not difficult to understand why. The subject is simple, human, and moving. It is told without any sentimentality, with Chekhov's usual sense of balance and economy, and yet with an emotional tone contributing very much to the powerful impression we get from it. Even so, the story has attracted little attention as an object of study.[2] The reason may very well be that it has been considered merely simple and clear, not involving any complicated problems. It might appear difficult to say more than what is usually said about it: that it is one of Chekhov's best stories. Nevertheless, it seems to me that "The Bishop" raises certain interesting questions about subject, style, and structure. My purpose here is to discuss some of them.

On a first reading, the most natural reaction is to connect the story with Chekhov's biography. It was, after all, one of the last efforts of a writer approaching death, of a man who knew only too well that his days were numbered. It is a story of breakup and departure, a frequent theme in the plays and stories of his last years. But here the theme is not departure "for Moscow" but a breaking up from life. There is a tone of restrained sadness in the story, corroborated, it seems, by the special twist at the end: the bishop dies, and soon he and all his good work will be forgotten. It sounds like a final pessimistic chord on the vanity of all human endeavor.

But should we actually read the story in this way? Is it really as pessimistic as this synopsis would have us believe? A closer look at the structure gives a different answer; the story is in point of fact more ambiguous. It is not difficult, in the first place, to see that Chekhov has been very careful not to let the tone of pessimism dominate. And this he did in spite of—or, with our knowledge of Chekhov's art, we might even prefer to say exactly because of—the subject. We recognize a technique used in other stories and in his plays: he works with change and contrast, with a rhythmical play of bright and subdued light, with a balance of trivial and serious scenes.[3]

This interplay of rhythms is emphasized by something that could be called an impressionistic or a bloc technique. Such a technique, a result of Chekhov's demand for economy and objectivity, consists in placing small, complete scenes next to each other without any comments. There is still a clear chronological scheme and logical development from one scene to another, but the reader should never feel that there is a narrator guiding him, anxious to explain everything. Most of the conclusions should be drawn by the reader himself. The content and significance of the scenes will be clear by their contrast with the preceding or following scenes or by their places in the story as a whole. "The Bishop" is, among other things, an interesting example of the application of such a technique.

The first scene strikes a powerful emotional note. It reaches a climax when the bishop bursts into tears during the midnight mass and the whole congregation begins to sob and cry with him: "And for some reason tears flowed down his face. . . . Tears glistened on his face, his beard. Nearby someone else began to cry, then further away someone else, then more and more people, and little by little the church was filled by soft weeping."

The bishop's tears seem to be explained by his fatigue and irritation. But the whole episode is connected to the preceding sentence by an *and*. In this preceding sentence the bishop believes that he sees the face of his old mother in the crowd. The conjunction seems to tell us that it is the image of his mother that provokes his tears. The vision of his mother takes his thoughts back to his childhood; by this he also understands that he is now an old man, his life is over and done with, and he is soon going to die. The inexplicable tears presage what is going to happen in the story: the bishop's death. But all this is only implied. It is there behind the lines, in the "subtext," and we shall not fully understand the meaning of this scene until we have read further in the story.

In fact, the author tries to assure us that it is difficult to find any reason for the bishop's tears. This is said by the phrase *for some reason*, which seems to belong to the bishop rather than to the narrator: it is the bishop who cannot explain his own tears, who is surprised by them.[4] This is further stressed in the next sentence: "His soul was at rest, everything was well, but he kept gazing fixedly at the choir on the left, where prayers were being read, where in the evening haze it was already impossible to recognize a single person, and—he wept."

It is interesting to note that the original plan, as described by S. N. Shchukin, explicitly stated that the bishop cried because, while reading the story of Christ's Passion, he applied it to the fate of every human being and to himself in particular, knowing that he was ill and that he was going to die. In the final version all these explanations were left out. The reason might have been that Chekhov did not want to reveal the action of the story from the very beginning. Further, this introductory scene has a powerful emotional tone, skillfully conveyed by various stylistic devices. There was always the danger that such a scene might become sentimental; even as it is now, we can see how Chekhov has tried to tone things down and balance the emotional pitch by using *for some reason*, the markedly neutral phrases ending the first two paragraphs, and so on.

Now follows a scene set in a different key, yet quite clearly connected with the first. The bishop returns to his monastery. It is midnight, and the moon is shining. It would have been very easy here to continue the sad tone of the introduction by simply allowing the night landscape and the moon to do their work. It is true that Nature is said to live her own incomprehensible, mysterious life, but at the same time a different atmosphere is evoked: gay light and colors clearly dominate, and the bells resound joyfully. In the air there is a hint of spring, and everything seems close and friendly: "Everything around was alluring, youthful, so intimate—everything, both the trees and the sky, and even the moon—and one wanted to believe that it would always be so." When the bishop reaches his monastery he is told that his mother has come to see him, and by now all sense of sadness is dispelled.

The arrival of his mother inevitably leads his thoughts back to his childhood. A new scene ensues. An emotional evocation of a kind we recognize from Chekhov's plays ("Dear, precious, unforgettable childhood!") is followed by memories of a mostly unsentimental and even joyous character: "And it seemed to His Reverence that joy quivered in the air (at that time he was called Pavlusha), and he followed the icon without a cap, barefoot, with naive faith, with a naive smile, immeasurably happy!"

The bishop's thoughts are then interrupted by a short description of the night outside: "The moon glanced in through the window, the floor was illuminated, and shadows lay on it. A cricket chirped." As we see, just a few simple details, familiar enough from many other descriptions of a moonlit night, here appear brief and stark, with the particular economy Chekhov so liked. In fact, the economy has an obvious explanation. The two simple sentences hark back to the description of the bishop's return journey from the midnight mass. The night atmosphere was already evoked there; a few sentences are now enough to bring it back to mind. This is a characteristic means whereby Chekhov recalls an underlying mood merely by hinting at images conjured up before.

The sentences also serve as a transition to the next scene, where a new key is introduced through Father Sisoi: Father Sisoi with his snoring, his yawns, and his "I don't like it" (*ne ndravitsia*). He brings the bishop back from the past with its many pleasant memories, back to the present, a trivial, petty present.

The first section thus consists of a series of small scenes, each set in a different key and introducing the persons and the themes that will appear in the sections to come. The changing mood is connected with what constitutes the main principle of structure of the story: the blending of time. The story lives on all three levels of time. The bishop looks back on his life; the verb *remember* is used frequently, and it is worth noting how Chekhov varies it all the time. These forms occur twice: *vspominat'*, *vspomnit'*, *vspominal*, *vspomnil*, *vspomnilos'* (to remember, to recollect, kept remembering, recollected, was remembered). The following are used only once: *vspomnilas'*, *vspomnilsia*, *vspominalas'*, *pomnil*, *pomnila*, *pripomnilsia* (was remembered, was reminded, kept being remembered, remembered, [she] remembered, was reminded). But he also looks ahead to the future, symbolized by approaching spring. His memories of the past and his dreams of the future are contrasted with the present. From this emerges a reevaluation of his life and of himself. In the first section all this is still not clear to him or to the reader, but it will become increasingly evident from section to section as the contrast is given ever-increasing stress.[5]

The second section takes up the same themes as the first; that is, there is a new combination of time levels. In the first section they were simply introduced, but now they begin to work together, unveiling the idea of the story. The second section opens with a bright note, the promise of spring, already encountered in the first section in the description of the night landscape: "All through the dinner the spring sun looked in the windows from the courtyard and gaily lit up the white tablecloth and Katya's reddish hair. Through the double windows one could hear the rooks bustling about in the garden and ʻie starlings singing."

This mood is soon toned down, however; the focus moves from the future to the present. The meeting and dinner with his mother do not bring the bishop the joy and pleasure he had been looking forward to. They have nothing to say to each other, her small talk irritates him, and it is characteristic that she finds a sympathetic haven in Father Sisoi. In the middle of the section the shift of humor is underlined: "Somehow his mood suddenly changed." He flies back again to his memories. In the first section he recalled childhood, and now we come to know of his life and career as a priest.

The second section also introduces a new theme. It begins: "The next day, on Palm Sunday, His Reverence celebrated mass in the cathedral in town. Then he called upon the archbishop, paid a visit to the widow of a general who was very ill, and then went home. Between one and two he had dinner with his dear guests: his old mother and his niece, Katya, a girl of eight." There are quite a few such passages in the story, written in a strikingly objective style, having almost the character of a report. They are, for that matter, easy enough to find in other stories by Chekhov, occuring particularly in descriptions or at the beginnings of sections, clearly being part of his program of objectivity and economy. But here in "The Bishop" they serve a further function. They record briefly and swiftly what the bishop is doing during the last days of his life: he goes to the church, he visits various people, he receives others: "After dinner two rich ladies arrived, landowners, who sat for an hour and a half in silence, with long faces; the archimandrite, taciturn and hard of hearing, came on business. Then the bell for vespers rang, the sun disappeared behind the woods, and the day was over. On returning from the church, His Reverence said his prayers hurriedly, got into bed, and covered himself as warmly as possible. . . . On Tuesday after the service His Reverence went to the archbishop's house, listened to petitioners, got upset, angry, and then went home."

This is his duty, part of the routine he has performed day after day all through his life and that has to be done even now, in spite of his illness. Compare the use of an expression like *nado bylo: nado bylo itti v tserkov', nado bylo priniat' ego* (had to: he had to go to church, he had to see him). Such passages stand as stylistic contrasts to the more emotional, lyrical passages, but they also have another function. They mark the rhythmic interplay of rest and movement in the story: they themselves give us the movement, the point of rest being the bishop's recollections. They tell us that time passes, that the bishop's fate is sealed, that death is approaching inexorably. They also consitute a present tense from the point of view of the story, a present tense as against the bishop's looking back to the past or ahead to the future.

The bishop's illness strengthens his sense of the negative side of life around him. As often happens with the sick, he becomes irritated and nervous. He sees people around him in a new way, naked, petty, egoistic, uneducated. But this is more than a sick man's irritation. Step by step, from section to section, we come to understand that this is a deep, suppressed dissatisfaction with life, coming to the surface for the first time now that approaching death has given him a new perspective on what is essential in life.

This direction is already intimated in the first section with Father Sisoi's snoring and his "I don't like it" (*ne ndravitsia*). In the second section it is the main theme. Here again we have Father Sisoi with his silly remarks about the Japanese: "The Japanese, Mother, they're the same as the Montenegrins, from the same tribe. They were together under the Turkish yoke." But not only is Father Sisoi involved. The bishop's own mother also belongs to this short-sighted, petty world, his own mother with her constantly repeated "And then we had a cup of tea": "And it was always 'we had a cup of tea,' or 'after having a cup of tea,' and it was as though all her life she had been only aware that she was drinking tea."

It is worth noting how Chekhov uses Father Sisoi's and the mother's conversation as inserts in the bishop's recollections. The bishop has retired to bed, and while he is lying there, his thoughts once again focus on memories of the past. In the other room Father Sisoi and his mother sit chatting; their trivial exchanges intermingle with the pictures of the past. What Chekhov is applying here is a technique designed for the stage: as we know, his plays often contain two kinds of dialogue going on in different parts of the stage (see the first scene of *The Three Sisters*). Here, in the story, there are no comments from the narrator, but it is easy to understand the function of the contrast between the pair of unwitting chatterboxes and the lonely bishop trying to discover some meaning in his life.

In the third section the notes of triviality and pettiness appear in a more intense form. The bishop is struck by this when he has to receive visitors and listen to their little requests and complaints: "And now when he was ailing, he was struck by the emptiness, the triviality of everything people were asking, weeping over; ignorance and timidity irritated him; and all this that was petty and unessential oppressed him by its mass, and it seemed to him that he now understood the diocesan bishop who in his younger years had written "Teachings of Free Will," but now, it seems, was lost in trivia, had forgotten everything, and no longer thought about God."

People are backward and uncultured. The bishop is able to make comparisons on this point because he has lived outside Russia for several years; Chekhov apparently added this detail as a further explanation of the bishop's critical view: "While abroad His Reverence, apparently, had lost touch with Russian life; things were not easy for him; people seemed coarse to him, the women petitioners—dreary and stupid—the seminarians and their teachers—uncultured, at times savage."

His nervous irritation eventually reaches its peak in the fourth section and manifests itself as hatred of the whole environment that is threatening to suffocate him, of a way of life that is unendurable: "When he covered himself with his blanket, he suddenly craved to be abroad, craved unbearably! It seemed he would give his life if only he did not have to see these miserable, cheap shutters, these low ceilings, did not have to put up with that heavy monastery smell. Would that there was one person to whom he could speak, unburden his soul!"

But along with the levels of past and present there is also the level of the future. Initially it appears only indirectly, in the first and second sections, in the bright scenery and the feeling of spring in the air. In the third section it appears in the bishop's thoughts, mingling with his recollections of the past. This is an emotional scene again, reminding us of the introduction. Tears flow down his cheeks now as then, but this time he is already aware of the reason: he understands that he is going to die, and he thinks he is not yet ready for it. There is still something missing in his life, and he is sure that there must be an answer to all his questions in the future: "He thought about how he had really achieved everything that was possible for a man in his situation. He had faith, but still not everything was clear to him. Something was still lacking, he did not want to die, and it still seemed to him that he was lacking something that was most important, about which he had at one time vaguely dreamed, and that at the present time he was stirred by the same hope for the future that he had had in childhood, in the academy, and abroad."

At the end of the story this theme is brought to a climax in the joy of Easter Day. The mood and even the details from the second scene of the introduction return, now fortified and stressed. Again the bells ring out merrily: "The joyous sound of the bells rang out over the town from morning until night without ceasing, stirring the spring air." There is spring in the air, and instead of a bright moon there is bright sunshine: "The birds were singing, the sun was shining brightly." In the marketplace people are enjoying themselves: "It was noisy on the big marketplace: swings were swinging, barrel organs were playing, an accordion was squeaking, drunken voices echoed."

What we have here is a characteristic application of Chekhov's bloc technique: scene is added to scene—the bishop's death, the boisterous market scene, and, at the very end, the mother in her provincial town— but there are no clear transitions, no comments. The scenes are connected, and yet at the same time they contrast with each other in an effective way. The contrasting of life and death, of death and the indifference of nature, in the way done here is a device rather frequently used by various prose writers and even poets, but not just for the sake of effect. Behind them is a personal view on these questions, a view that has much in common with the concluding scene of "The Bishop" and with the whole idea of that story.

To understand the meaning of the climactic scene, let us first see what happens to the bishop during the last days of his illness. While sitting in the church listening to the choir (in the third section), he does not want to die. There is, he thinks, something missing; there are certain things still not clear to him, a truth he has been looking for all his life. But before he dies, the realization that the past is gone forever and will never come back is thrust home to him. His recollections, the review of his whole life, are finally brought to an end. His only comment is "How wonderful." When the past is put aside he becomes a changed man, a different man, a man of truly humble dimensions: "It already seemed to him that he was thinner and weaker, more insignificant than anyone."

Now we understand the function that the arrival of his mother performs in the story. He becomes like a child again, a long-lost child returning to his mother; the immediate contact, lost during the years of service to the Church, is renewed. To his mother he is no longer an imposing and venerable bishop but simply her son of old: "And for some reason it seemed to her too that he was thinner, weaker, and more insignificant than anyone, and she no longer remembered that he was a bishop and kissed him as if he were a child, someone very close, dear."

What happens to the bishop before he dies is that responsibility and duty are lifted from him; the pressure that prevented him from being simple and human, prevented him from achieving personal contact with his congregation, is released. In his way, he too was one of those "men in a case" whom Chekhov depicted in several stories from the late 1880s. Contrary to those, however, the bishop realizes what has been wrong, even if it is too late.

Easter day and its mystery of resurrection has a special significance in this context. It is connected with the bishop's new attitude to his surroundings, with the feeling of freedom that comes to him just before he dies. This, too, seems to be a form of resurrection. But what kind of resurrection is it, and how are we then to understand the end, which could promise the bishop nothing but oblivion? It would, I think, be rather interesting at this stage to compare Chekhov's story with another very well-known story on a similar theme, Tolstoy's "The Death of Ivan Ilych." This Ivan, as Tolstoy emphasizes, is a very ordinary man living a very ordinary and, as he himself thinks, normal, honest, and true life. When he is told by his doctor that his time is up, he realizes that this was all wrong. He starts reviewing his life and arrives at a new understanding of what is essential to man. When he finally dies, death is no longer any threat to him; he has accepted and overcome it, and he looks forward to a new life, to a resurrection: "'It is finished!' someone said above him. He heard these words and repeated them in his heart. 'Death is finished,' he said to himself. 'It no longer exists.' He drew a breath into himself, stopped in the middle of his breathing, stretched out, and died."

It seems that Tolstoy's and Chekhov's stories are different. Ivan Ilych is an ordinary man, while the bishop is definitely not. The bishop, as he himself realizes when looking back on his life, has come far and attained all that was possible for a man with his background and qualifications. Ivan Ilych has lived a dull, commonplace existence, unconscious of the essentials of life. The bishop, on the other hand, has lived a life of righteousness and truth, at least in the eyes of the Church and the general public. Still, at the end, what awaits him is not resurrection, as for Ivan Ilych, but oblivion.

The difference between the stories is a difference between the authors: Chekhov the agnostic and Tolstoy the believer. Yet the stories have a great deal in common. Facing death, the bishop also comes to the conclusion that there has been something amiss with his life. His journey into the past does not have the same character of self-criticism, of showdown, as we find with Tolstoy's hero. The bishop feels that something has been missing from his life, but he is unable to put a finger on it with the ease of Ivan Ilych. His irritation first turns against his immediate environment, the people around him, the poor, dull, ugly life of the world at hand as symbolized by the fence, the low ceilings, the peculiar smell of the monastery. But before dying he understands that the fault was also in part his own, that he never allowed himself to be a simple, straightforward human being. He does not face resurrection as Ivan Ilych does, but still a promise of freedom and rest suddenly opens itself to him.

Let us now turn to the theme of oblivion. Tolstoy's story also stresses people's indifference to death. This is the main idea underlying the introductory chapter. Ivan Petrovich visits the widow to pay his respects to the deceased, but it does not prevent him from going directly from the scene of mourning to the card table. We also learn that the widow's thoughts gravitate toward very practical things, above all how to get as much money as possible from her husband's employers. All these details are part of Tolstoy's purpose to unmask people, to show them naked in all their egotism, to present the other side, the true face of such an official function as a funeral, to stress the contrast between appearance and reality. The whole episode is given with the clear, hard, and merciless strokes of a moralist with a purpose and a plan, so different from Chekhov's lyrical tone, his comprehension of human weakness and his unwillingness to comment.

In "The Bishop" the theme of human indifference only appears in clear-cut form at the end. It is true that the story has already hinted at people's pettiness, egotism, and ignorance. In a way, then, the conclusion has been prepared for, but it comes as a surprise nevertheless. It has the character of a moral. The whole story has endeavored to evoke our sympathy for the aged bishop, but death is brought to him. Instead of words of consolation, all we are told is that he was quickly forgotten.

We might call this an unsentimental agnostic's calm and simple view of death. It was needed for the purpose of precluding any direct religious interpretation of the bishop's death, but also as a counterbalance to the nostalgic atmosphere brought to its peak in the death scene. But further, hidden in this special twist at the end, there is an idea of apparently great importance to Chekhov, one that we can find in many other of his stories. If we scrutinize it, the meaning of the final scene will stand out more clearly, and we shall find that it is not so pessimistic after all.

A main theme of the story is, of course, the contrast between time and eternity. It is easy to understand that the bishop as a young man thinks that he will live forever: "Life was then so easy, pleasant; it seemed to go on and on, with no end in sight." Now, as an old man, he knows that there is an end. But he also knows that, in contrast to his temporal life, there is something eternal, something that will go on living after he is dead and forgotten. When he returns from the midnight mass he looks at the landscape and feels that "everything around was alluring, youthful, so intimate—everything, both the trees and the sky, and even the moon—and one wanted to believe that it would always be so."

It is not only nature that can prove the existence of eternity. While officiating at the service in the cathedral, the bishop sees before him the congregation like a sea of lights, "and it seemed that these same people would be here every year, and for how long—only God knows." There will always be a congregation, and the cathedral will always be filled by the same people or people who appear to be the same. And outside the church, too, the holiday will be celebrated in the same way, with barrel organs and accordions and drunkenness: "In a word, it was gay. All was well, just as it was last year and, in all probability, as it will be next year."

From the point of view of the congregation, the bishop himself is a link in a chain, a tradition, that seems to be without end. When looking back on the past, he recalls that there had always been a priest in the family: "His father had been a deacon, his grandfather a priest, his great-grandfather a deacon, and his whole family, perhaps, from the days Russia accepted Christianity, had belonged to the clergy." We are not told if the bishop had a son to carry on the tradition, but this is not important. There will always be a successor. The chain will not be broken: "A month later a new suffragan bishop was appointed, and no one remembered His Reverence Peter any longer."

Individual man is mortal, but life is eternal as mankind is eternal. Every individual is a mortal link in an immortal chain, a member of an unbroken tradition. Placing the last part of the story in such a context, we are better able to understand that the seemingly pessimistic note at the end is not so pessimistic after all. And this is not an isolated example in Chekhov's works. If we go through them we shall find many other examples proving that this was, in fact, a favorite twist.

Willa Chamberlain Axelrod

Passage from Great Saturday to Easter Day

in "Holy Night"

HOLY NIGHT takes place at a unique moment in the Russian Orthodox Church: at the moment of transition from Lent to Easter. As the midnight service of Great Saturday, beginning at about 11:30 P.M., flows into Easter matins, beginning at midnight, the Church "passes over" from the sorrow of death and burial to the joy of new life.

Chekhov's story "Holy Night" (Sviatoiu noch'iu, 1886) falls clearly into four episodes: waiting for the ferry, crossing the Goltva River to the monastery, attending services at the monastery, and leaving the monastery by ferry.[1] Liturgical allusions suggest that "Holy Night" opens shortly before the midnight service. The first-person narrator, who should not be confused with Chekhov, waits for the delayed ferry to bring him across the Goltva to the monastery. The quiet and darkness of the night and the anxious waiting evoke the liturgical tone of Great Saturday.[2] As the ferry crosses the Goltva, the midnight service implicitly is celebrated at the monastery, and as the ferry arrives, Easter matins implicitly are about to begin.[3] Thus, the crossing of the Goltva represents the Church's liturgical passage from Lent to Easter. Although the Goltva River actually exists, the biblical "Golgota" (Church Slavonic) is echoed in the name Goltva. As Golgotha represents Christ's passage from death to life, so the Goltva crossing is a metaphor for spiritual transition.[4] By the end of the story, the Church has completed the Easter liturgy and broken the Lenten fast.

It is against this background of liturgical transition that the spiritual passage of the first-person narrator unfolds. His spiritual odyssey follows the course of the Church, but it lags behind. On the ferry, he is exposed to the grief of death and burial, characterizing matins of Great Saturday, and to the Resurrection, anticipated in Great Saturday's liturgy. The stop at the monastery or "enchanted kingdom" is a detour into the underworld, which signifies the harrowing of hell, commemorated on Great Saturday. At the monastery the narrator imbibes the excitement and anticipation of Great Saturday, not the joy of Easter Day, and he experiences the sacrament of baptism, traditionally performed on Great Saturday. In the final scene, embarking from the monastery's shore, the narrator perceives the world as sorrowful and listless and does not detect the signs of resurrection present in nature. He does show, however, a budding spiritual sensitivity. As the Easter canon proclaims and the novice monk Ieronim illustrates in "Holy Night," it is through "purified senses" that one realizes the paschal passage. During Easter matins, the Church sings, "Let us purify our senses so that we may see the unapproachable light of the Resurrection."[5]

CROSSING THE GOLTVA RIVER

During the Goltva crossing, Ieronim, a novice from the monastery who mans the ferry, narrates a figurative story-within-the-story. He laments the death of his dear friend the monk-priest Nikolai, who died during the Old Testament readings of Great Saturday's liturgy, and he sings glory to Nikolai's talent of writing *akathistoi*, specialized hymns of praise. It is through Ieronim's account of Nikolai's "sweet" nature and language that the narrator is introduced to the services of Great Saturday and Easter Day. Through Nikolai, who is a Christ figure, he is exposed to death and resurrection. During the crossing, however, the narrator is not sensitive to the spirituality of Ieronim's story. In his anxiousness to arrive at the monastery, he is more interested in the material, in the career of Nikolai as writer of akathistoi. "Are akathistoi hard to write?" "Did he publish his akathistoi?" "Why did he write?" are some of the questions the narrator asks.

In his great grief, Ieronim does not understand why such a wonderful person as Nikolai had to die. His confusion is expressed by the question mark his body forms as he bends over the ferry's cable, and his misery is vocalized by his show of exertion: "Ieronim grasped the cable with both hands; he bent over in the form of a question mark and gasped." Ieronim's grief, tinged with bewilderment, mirrors the sorrow of Great Saturday. In particular, he evokes Mary, the Mother of Christ, lamenting at the foot of the Cross, a central image carried over from Great Friday and vivid in "The Praises" (Pokhvaly), a funeral hymn sung at matins on Great Saturday: "In her bitter grief, Mary laments, 'Woe is me, Light of the World! Woe is me, my Light!'" She too is bewildered by the burial of her son: "With a mother's grief she cried, 'How shall I bury you, my Son?'"[6] Similarly, Ieronim wants to "bitterly cry." His grief, which he cannot forget "even at a moment of such great happiness . . . does not listen to reason. . . . But Nikolai

97

actually died!" Ieronim explains. "No one else but Nikolai. It's even hard to believe that he is no longer on earth!"

Ieronim grieves at the foot of a figurative Cross. The cable of the ferry, mentioned ten times in the eleven-page story, suggests the Cross, a sign of Christ. As the narrator sees the ferry in the distance, he notes its resemblance to a gallows. No doubt this is due to the cable, which apparently runs above the ferry. Thus, as the Cross is an emblem of death, so is the cable. In addition, in standard Christian symbolism, the Church is a boat guided by Christ, "the rudder of those sailing."[7] As the rudder guides the Church, so the cable guides the ferry.

Another parallel to the services of Great Saturday occurs in Ieronim's praise to Nikolai. As the Resurrection is announced in the Gospel reading of Great Saturday's liturgy (Matthew 28:1–20), so in the eulogy to Nikolai, resurrection is anticipated. Ieronim suggests that Nikolai lives eternally in the word of the akathistoi or, more generally, in the liturgical word. Nikolai and his creative word are a metaphor for Christ the Word, the theme of Easter Day's Gospel (John 1:1–3, 14). As the Word made flesh lives eternally, Nikolai lives after death in the words of the akathistoi. Ieronim's description of the beauty of akathistoi is very similar to his description of Nikolai's personality. Nikolai's word, however, never published, is not found in "either conversation or in books." His word is so overwhelming that Ieronim exclaims: "I cannot express to you how he used to write!" This is true. Ieronim does not quote from Nikolai's religious poetry. He speaks of the beauty of his language in the context of published akathistoi, quoting from three of the best-known akathistoi in Russian worship. Thus, the word of Nikolai, neither written nor spoken, and indescribable, associates Nikolai with the spiritual Word.

AT THE MONASTERY

When the narrator eagerly jumps off the ferry onto the grounds of the monastery, a Dantesque atmosphere calls to mind Christ's descent into the underworld on Great Saturday to bring the faithful to heaven. "We floated straight out of the darkness and stillness of the river into the enchanted kingdom," writes the narrator. The darkness and stillness represent the burial and the disappearance of Christ before the Resurrection. The "enchanted kingdom" (*zakoldovannoe tsarstvo*), which evokes sorcery or magic (*koldovstvo*), is opposed to the heavenly kingdom (*tsarstvo nebesnoe*).

The shore of this enchanted kingdom is ablaze with crimson light and thick with smoke rising from ignited barrels of pitch. Such fire and smoke represent the flames of Gehenna. The "impenetrable, black darkness" beyond the crimson blaze represents the depths of Hades, void of divine light and life. The dark monastery gates look like a "hollow" or "cavity" (*vpadina*). Thus, as the narrator approaches the monastery, it is as if he steps further down into the underworld or enters a tomb. Inside the gates, again smoke and crimson light fill the air. Restless crowds on both sides of the gates, wandering among the gravestones or selling bread, suggest the souls of Hades awaiting liberation. "Pure chaos! . . . . What an uneasy night! How nice!" exclaims the narrator to himself, enjoying the commotion. The liveliness and uneasiness of the crowds is even more intense inside the church, where Easter matins and the liturgy are being celebrated. The congregation, cuaght up in the anticipation of Great Saturday, pays little attention to the Easter services. It does not desire prayer and contemplation but rather perpetual motion, as if "looking for something." It wants to "escape outside and stream into some sort of movement." The "holy doors" (*tsarskie vrata*) on the altar, representing the gates of heaven, are ajar, as if beckoning the restless congregation to "pass over" the threshold into heaven.[8]

The congregation moves like a big wave. The narrator uses this image five times in describing the activity inside the church. Such waves evoke the burial canon of Great Saturday, sung at matins and the midnight service. This canon is usually referred to by its opening words, "By the waves of the sea," or *Volnoiu morskoiu*. Considered second in poetic beauty to the Easter canon, and equally well known, it begins with the *irmos*, "By the waves of the sea, he who in ancient times hid the pursuing tyrant is hidden beneath the earth by the children of those whom he once saved."[9] As with all initial verses of canons, this *irmos* refers to the miracle of the Red Sea (Exodus 15:19). The account of the parting of the sea is recited during the liturgy of Great Saturday and is considered a prefiguration of Christian baptism.[10]

The allusion to the Red Sea, the ebb and flow of the congregation, and the spring torrents of the Goltva, mentioned earlier in the story, suggest the waters of baptism. As a ritual of transition, marking the passage from the death of sin to a life of grace, the sacrament of baptism is traditionally administered to catechumens and renewed by the faithful on Great Saturday. The sea of people in the monastery church suggests a congregation of catechumens being baptized. More precisely, however, it is implied that the narrator is the one at the baptismal font. Three times he is thrown back and forth by the wave of the congregation: "The wave gushed forth and threw me backwards. . . . the crowd pushed me back to my former place. . . . ten minutes had not passed before a new wave burst on me." This image of the narrator, thrice carried by the wave of the crowd, evokes the threefold immersion of the catechumen at the baptismal font. Furthermore, it is after this threefold immersion that the narrator for the first time cites the Resurrection canon and experiences an awakening sensitivity. For the first time he feels strong sympathy for Ieronim and responds to the liturgical word. Now he understands what Ieronim means by "grasping the beauty of the holy phrase," in that he realizes that no one in the congregation, including himself, is capable of this. Only Ieronim, in ecstasy over the beauty of akathistoi and of the liturgical word in general, is capable of such sensitivity.

REBOARDING THE FERRY

At the end of "Holy Night," the Church has celebrated the Easter liturgy and is breaking the fast. The liturgical "passover" is complete. Despite his figurative baptism, the narrator has not yet realized the passage from sorrow to joy. As he leaves the monastery church, he still lingers behind in the mood of Great Saturday.

Shortly before dawn on Easter morning, he sees gloom and exhaustion in the world around him. The sky is "gloomy," and the weather is no longer "magnificent," as it was during the night, when he was filled with anticipation. Now the air is cold and damp. The chiming bells do not ring as happily as they did during the night. The horses and people seem exhausted and sleepy, and they hardly move. "It seemed to me that the trees and the young grass were sleeping." Ieronim still mans the ferry, and his expression is "unusually sad and exhausted." Sleep and stillness evoke the Sabbath rest of Christ and all creation, rather than the awakening joy of Resurrection. A white fog, mentioned four times in the last scene, drapes the ferry. In the context of the narrator's dreary tone, this fog conjures up the shroud or *plashchanitsa* venerated on Great Saturday and on which the burial of Christ is depicted.

The narrator does not yet have the "purified senses" of which the Easter canon sings, which are required to detect and experience resurrection. He notices the dew on Ieronim's face, but he is not sensitive to the beauty and significance of this detail, which reveals that the monk has passed over from a Lenten to a paschal disposition. The narrator writes: "'No one has taken your place?' I asked [Ieronim] in surprise. 'My place?' he asked, turning toward me with his face, cold and covered with dew, and he smiled."

In the Old Testament, dew is a blessing of God, a sign of God's grace and of new spiritual life. In a messianic promise, Isaiah proclaims, "Thy dead men shall live, together with my dead body shall they arise. Awake and sing, ye that dwell in dust: for thy dew is as the dew of herbs, and the earth shall cast out the dead" (Isaiah 26:19, KJV). In the prophet Daniel's "Song of the Three Children," dew from heaven saves the children in the fiery furnace. This event, a prefiguration of the Resurrection, is the subject of the fifteenth and last Old Testament reading of Great Saturday's liturgy (Daniel 3:1–30). Earlier, when the narrator leaves the monastery church, he remarks on the dew covering "the iron slabs, the tombstones, and the buds on the trees." The tombstones and the cold iron slabs of the pathway, resembling the slabs of the tombstones, suggest death. Dew, a symbol of renewal, is superimposed on these emblems of death. Dew also covers the ferry's cable, thus transforming this representation of the Cross from a sign of death to a sign of resurrection. The buds themselves are obvious signs of renewal, as are the egg and hemp seed mentioned at the beginning of the story. Unconscious of the religious implications of his similes, the narrator remarks that some stars are big "like goose eggs" and others are small "like a seed of hemp." The egg and seed are traditional symbols of resurrection. In matins of Great Saturday, for example, God is likened to a "life-giving seed" planted in the earth, which "brings forth joy to the world."[11]

At the end of the story, a peasant helps Ieronim man the ferry. Together they lean over the cable and groan as they set the ferry in motion. This groan does not suggest grief as before but rather friendship: "They leaned on the cable, gasped together, and the ferry started." The word for "together" in this sentence is *druzhno*, derived from *drug*, or "friend." The peasant's fur hat, curiously enough, is likened to a tub in which honey is sold. Reference to honey brings to mind the adjective "sweet" or *sladkii*, which Ieronim earlier used several times to describe Nikolai as well as Christ.[12] Thus it is suggested that the peasant who helps Ieronim is a new friend, a surrogate Nikolai or perhaps the risen Nikolai.

In the final scene, Ieronim directs his stare at a young merchant woman. The narrator remarks: "It seemed to me that in the face of the woman Ieronim was searching for the soft and tender features of his deceased friend." This searching gaze calls to mind the narrator's search for Nikolai at the monastery. He steps out of the church to seek the "dead Nikolai," but to no avail. This search for Nikolai parallels the Gospel reading of Great Saturday, in which the "myrrh-bearing women" look for Christ in his tomb, but without success (Matthew 28:1–20). An angel tells them that he is risen. In a hymn from Easter matins, quoting Luke 24:5, an angel asks the myrrh-bearing women, "Why seek ye the living among the dead?"[13] Likewise, Nikolai, a Christ figure, is not to be found among the gravestones of the enchanted kingdom but rather among the living. Ieronim, renewed by the symbolic dew, knows to look for Nikolai among the living, in the young woman with the rosy cheeks, the only passenger who specifically is wrapped in the white robe of fog. In the context of the dew and resurrection, the fog represents the white garments of Easter, not the shroud of burial. Thus, the resurrected Nikolai is not on the monastery grounds but on the ferry. And it is on the ferry, the living Church, that Christ's death is mourned and his eternity as Word is praised. The ferry coheres well with abundant Christian symbolism of the Church as ship.

Given this imagery, "Holy Night" ends on a hopeful note. That is, as the ferry departs from the "enchanted kingdom," the narrator still has the chance to leave burial Saturday behind and to "pass over" to new beginnings. Ieronim is the first to see the risen Nikolai or Christ, just as Mary in Russian tradition is the first to know of the Resurrection. But perhaps the narrator will soon experience renewal also. The final sentence, in which he perceives Ieronim looking for Nikolai, illustrates increasing sensitivity. On the other hand, Chekhovian ambiguity pervades the end of the story. In the final two words, the narrator refers to Nikolai as Ieronim's "deceased friend" (*usopshii drug*), as earlier when he refers to "dead Nikolai" (*mërtvyi Nikolai*). Thus, in the final two words of the story, the narrator emphasizes death and still shows inadequate awareness of resurrection.

Alexandar Mihailovic

Eschatology and Entombment in "Ionych"

> To be buried alive is, beyond question, the
> most terrific of these extremes which has ever
> fallen to the lot of mere mortality. That it
> has frequently, very frequently, so fallen will
> scarcely be denied by those who think. The
> boundaries which divide Life from Death are
> at best shadowy and vague. Who shall say
> where the one ends, and where the other
> begins?
> —Edgar Allan Poe, "The Premature Burial"

> A month later Belikov died. All of us went to
> the funeral—that is, everyone from the two
> schools and the theological college. Then, as
> he lay in his coffin, his face looked gentle
> and pleasant—even cheerful—just as if he
> were rejoicing that at last he had found a
> container from which he would never
> emerge. Yes, he had achieved his ideal!
> —Chekhov, "Man in a Case"

CHEKHOV'S "IONYCH" begins abruptly, in me-
dias res, with a defense of the provincial town of S———.[1] The narrator
states that in spite of certain complainers in the community, the op-
portunities there for the life of the mind and spirit are available for
those who want it. He then adds, almost as an evasive afterthought,
that these opportunites can be found in only one place in town, the
house of the Turkins. It soon becomes clear that the three members of
this family preside muselike over the cultural life of the town: on a
typical evening Ivan Petrovich Turkin arranges amateur shows and
regales his dinner guests with a vaudevillian repertory of mugging and
painful mimicry. Vera Iosifovna reads aloud short stories that she herself has scribbled, and their daughter, Ekaterina, nicknamed Kotik,

103

performs on the piano. The narrator concludes by saying, "In short, each member of the family had some talent or other."

A newcomer to the town, the doctor Dmitry Ionych Startsev, begins to frequent the Turkins' home; he falls in love with Ekaterina and is ultimately spurned by her, while her parents seemingly remain oblivious to the goings-on between them. Over the fevered objections and migraines of her mother, Ekaterina finally goes to Moscow to study piano seriously. Startsev soon forgets about her and becomes overwhelmed by greed in both his medical practice and his property holdings. Four years later Ekaterina returns from Moscow, disillusioned, with wistful and regretful recollections of Ionych; she now responds warmly to him, while his reaction to her is indifferent and cold. The story ends with the physical decline of the characters: Ionych is now overcome with obesity, as Vera Iosifovna and Ekaterina depart to the Crimea for a rest cure.

Many scholars in both the former Soviet Union and the West have asserted that Chekhov's goal in "Ionych" (written in 1898) was to portray in the character of Startsev the effects of moral degradation upon an almost Everyman-like figure.[2] The corruption of Startsev's conscience in the form of his slide into avarice and his corresponding physical deterioration are, however, *post factum* and do not wholly explain the disquieting effect of this muted tragic process. The step-by-step and painstaking characterization of Startsev's decline over the five sections or parts of the story indicates not merely an ethical crisis but a spiritual one as well. A network of Christological associations and references throughout the text throw into sharper relief Startsev's self-mortification, describing it in the metaphorical terms of the ossification and entombment of the self. The disturbing pathos of his fate is brought home by the reiterated suggestion in the imagery of the story that he rejects the possibility of salvation.

Both the time of year and the specific day of Startsev's first visit to the Turkins' home are crucial hints to what follows in the story. In the third paragraph the narrator informs the reader that the season is spring and the church holiday is Ascension (*Voznesenie*). The holiday, celebrating the bodily ascent of Christ described in Acts 1:1–11 that occurred forty days after his Resurrection naturally occurs at that time of the year.[3] This strikingly redundant and therefore highly marked information is followed by another odd statement. In an otherwise sober and highly detached narrative, the mythic burden of spring as a time of renewal and reawakening is brought to the fore in an abrupt and explicit, even jarring manner with the entrance of Ekaterina: "Her expression was still childish, her waist slender and delicate, and her already fully developed virginal bosom, healthy and beautiful, held promise of spring, of real spring [*o nastoiashchei vesne*]." In an otherwise straightforward description of events and people, this statement emerges as a complement to the preceding tautological reference to the calendar. The ambiguity of *nastoiashchaia*—the key adjective in the Russian text—is patent, signifying not only the "real" but also the "present" or "ongoing" spring.[4] The entrance of Ekaterina signals the intrusion of nascency, youth, and renewal onto a barren field; her affiliation with the natural phenomenon of the season and, associatively, with the holiday at hand impels her beyond the confining pale of her family's domain.

As Vera reads one of her stories to the dinner party and Ekaterina stridently performs a piece on the piano, however, this idyll is abruptly shattered. Vera's sentimental tale serves as a dissonant counterpoint to the multileveled intimations of "real spring," its wintertime setting sharply contrastive of the actual setting of her narrative act:

> Then they all sat in the drawing-room, looking very serious, and Mrs. Turkin read them her novel. It began: "The frost was getting harder..." The windows were wide open, the knives made a terrific clatter in the kitchen, and there was an overpowering smell of fried onions. It was very restful [*bylo ochen' pokoino*] sitting in the deep, soft armchairs [*v miagkikh, glubokikh kreslakh*]; the candles blinked so enchantingly in the twilight of the drawing-room, and now, on a summer evening, when the sound of voices and of laughter was coming from the street and the smell of lilac was blowing in from the garden, it was difficult [*trudno bylo*] to imagine how the frost was getting harder or how the setting sun's cold rays could be lighting up the snow-covered plain and the lonely wayfarer on the road. Mrs. Turkin read about how a beautiful young countess opened up schools, hospitals and libraries on her vast estates, and how she fell in love with a wandering artist—read of things that never happen life, and yet it was quite pleasant and comforting [*bylo priyatno, udobno*] to listen to her, and such calm, delightful [*khoroshie, pokoinye*] thoughts passed through one's mind—one simply did not want to get up [*ne khotelos' vstavat'*]...

The Soviet scholar V. V. Golubkov has noted the occasional and obtrusive lyricism of Chekhov's story, certain passages of which practically lend themselves to scansion.[5] Thus, like the guests at the dinner party and against his better judgment, the narrator of "Ionych" falls under the rhythmic and balmlike spell of Vera's story, his description of the scene momentarily dissolving into fragmentary, vaguely sympathetic apperceptions suggestively evoked by the use of past-tense impersonal constructions (*bylo pokoino . . . trudno bylo . . . ne khotelos'*). The dividing line between the real and the spurious, the present and the past, becomes temporarily blurred. The reader, however, never truly loses sight of this distinction, which is accentuated by the opposition between indoors and outdoors that prevails throughout the story but especially in this passage. The scents and sounds from without represent both the genuine and concurrent awakenings of nature that, like Ekaterina, are intrusive and potentially disruptive of the contrived order of things in the Turkin household.

Not surprisingly, a closer look at this passage reveals that the absence of the life principle in Vera's story, so flatly asserted by the narrator (she "read of things that never happen in life"), inevitably approximates a state verging on death. The repeated use of various derivatives of *pokoi* (peace, [eternal] rest), such as *pokoino*, plays upon the motifs of peace and death, virtually merging them. Furthermore, the secondary and archaic meaning of *pokoi* as a chamber or room is also hinted at here. The entire parlor in which Vera tells her story becomes a macrocosm of each armchair with its entranced, virtually paralyzed occupant; its depth and padded softness (*v miagkikh glubokikh kreslakh bylo pokoino*) suggest a coffin. The burning candles and the entire hushed scene of the drawing room in fact suggest an almost funereal atmosphere. In this light, the final, laconic utterance "did not want to get up" (*ne khotelos' vstavat'*), evocatively followed by suspension points in the Russian, gains additional significance. Translated into the scheme of life (*zhizn'*) versus immobility and stasis, the disruption of Vera's siren song would signal a rousing and rising to a more genuine existence implied by the Russian verb prefix *voz/vz* (*vos/vs*) that denotes upward movement; the sharply focused time frame of spring and Ascension Day in this part of the story suggests the possibilities of reawakening and resurrection, the lifesaving movement from *vs-tavat'* (to get up) to *voznesenie* (ascent, Ascension).

As Vera finishes reading her story and closes her notebook, a choir outside sings the folk song "Luchinushka," and the narrator makes another jarringly blunt comment: "[The song] told them more of life than the novel they had just heard."[6] Although nothing more is said of this interruption, the detail is significant in several respects. The folk song itself tells of a woman waiting through the night for her husband, whose absence is ominously associated with a vicious mother-in-law (*svekrov' liutaia*).[7] The subliminal violence of the song offsets the banality of Vera's tale of the star-crossed affair between the countess and the itinerant artist. Vera's reading and the song are followed by another musical performance, her daughter's on the piano. The stridency and barely concealed anger of Ekaterina's playing, presented in all its appalling, naturalistic detail, echoes the pain of the folk song, whose portrayal of generational strife correlates to the tense mother-daughter relationship in the Turkin family: "Then she struck them [the keys] with all her might, again and again; her shoulders and her bosom shuddered . . . and one could not help feeling that she would go on hitting the keys till she had driven them into the piano." The song also anticipates the relationship between Startsev and Ekaterina, although the genders of the song are reversed in Chekhov's story, where Startsev becomes the one maintaining an apprehensive vigil. In "Ionych" music suggests the possibility of judgment, both in the sense of a critical self-awareness and of a decisive reckoning. The enervating dinner party of the first section of Chekhov's story is even framed by melody as Startsev hums melancholic romances to himself both on his way to the Turkins' house and during his walk back home, as if dimly cognizant of an elusive malaise.

By the beginning of section 2, more than a year has passed since Startsev's last encounter with the Turkins. His acquaintance with them is resumed when Vera asks him to treat her for a migraine, which is exacerbated by Ekaterina's stubborn insistence on leaving the town to study music seriously. The professional reasons for Startsev's visits become increasingly pretextual as he becomes infatuated with Ekaterina. Startsev's abortive rendezvous with her in the graveyard is the crux not just of the second section but also, as Chekhov's contemporary Ovsyaniko-Kulikovsky notes, of the entire story.[8]

The pivotal nature of the section is signaled by an arresting, if brief, textual interpolation. As he is about to enter the graveyard, Startsev notices a truncated biblical quotation in Slavonic inscribed at the top of the gate: "In the moonlight the inscription over the gate could be read: 'Behold, the hour is at hand.'" The source of this quotation is John 5:28. The immediate context is Jesus' prophecy of the resurrection of the dead on Judgment Day, an event also alluded to in Revelation 20:4–5. The verse quoted in the story and the subsequent one in the same Gospel, however, contain the fullest expression of this prophecy:

> 28. Marvel not at this: for the hour is coming, in the which all that are in the graves shall hear his voice,
>
> 29. And shall come forth; they that have done good, unto the resurrection of life; and they that have done evil, unto the resurrection of damnation.

The appropriateness of the citation and the resonance it has with the entire story are unmistakable. Here, as in the earlier episode of Vera's storytelling, transcendence becomes ascendancy (resurrection, *voskresh-enie*); a rising is needed to escape the insidious lulling effect and physical confines of a deathlike state (Chekhov's *pokoi*). The Christological intimations of the time frame of section 1 are thus made more explicit in section 2.

The time frame of section 2, while never stated, can be gleaned both from references made by the characters and the descriptive iconography of the graveyard scene. This section, like the preceding one, also takes place on a holiday, although here it is not explicitly named. En route to Startsev's first meeting with Ekaterina in this section, the narrator makes various remarks on the natural setting: "Autumn was approaching, and . . . dark leaves lay thick on the path." The vegetative and diurnal changes described in this passage strongly suggest the month of September in Russia, during which the Orthodox calendar recognizes only two holidays: the Nativity of the Mother of God (*Rozhdestvo bogoroditsy*) on September 8 and the Exaltation of the Honorable and Life-Giving Cross (*Vozdvizhenie chestnogo i zhivotvoriashchego Kresta Gospodnia*) six days later, on September 14. When Startsev pleads with Ekaterina at the beginning of the section, he reminds her that he has not seen her for an entire week. Given the Turkins' relish of holiday dinner parties (one of which occurs on the night of Startsev's abortive meeting with Ekaterina) and the six-day interval between the September church celebrations, the events of section 2 most likely occur on the night of the Exaltation of the Cross (*Vozdvizhenie Kresta*). Once again, Chekhov reiterates the thematics of ascent in the story.

The reverberations of diction between the graveyard scene and section 1 are especially revealing in this regard. Startsev's initial impression of the cemetery is remarkably resonant of the ambience surrounding Vera's storytelling, although here the overarching presence of the narrator's censorious voice is seemingly absent:

> At first Startsev was struck by the fact that he was seeing something he had never seen before and would probably never see again: a world that was unlike any other world, a world in which the moonlight was as soft and beautiful [*khorosh i miagok*] as though this were its cradle, a world where there was no life [*zhizni*], none at all, but where in every dark poplar and in every grave one felt the presence of a mystery which held out the promise of a quiet, beautiful and everlasting life. From the tombstones and the faded flowers there came a breath of forgiveness, sorrow and peace [*pokoem*].

A subtle parallel is drawn between the graves and the armchairs of the Turkins' parlor: both types of enclosure are described in benign terms, each imbued with softness and *pokoi* in its various connotations. Moreover, in each instance the context suggests that this situation is dangerously deceptive, one in which enchantment loosens the listener's grip on the life force and ultimately prettifies the image of death.

The opposition between the inertia of provincial life and the hypothetical true life of the spirit, however, is still at this point in the story highly provisional and sketchy. So far, the nature of those things

108

that actually "happen in life" has only been hinted at in the form of family conflict with its potential ugliness. The passage above introduces a new element into this polarity with the word *cradle*. The appearance of this term provides an ironic contrast to the elegiac decay of the autumnal scene and Startsev's mounting unease. On his way to their meeting place, Startsev is suddenly beset by a vision of his own mortality as the church bells ring in observance of the holiday: "It was only when the church clock was striking the hour and he imagined himself dead and buried forever, that he had the odd feeling that someone was looking at him, and for a moment it occurred to him that this was not peace and stillness but the dull anguish of non-existence, suppressed despair." Suddenly Startsev realizes the horror of being buried alive and its corollary, described by Poe: namely, the illusion of life belied by a static or deathlike existence. The rising from a state of inertia is either a procreative or a regenerative act. The offering up of death and birth, womb and tomb, as analogues to or coefficients of one another heightens the level of spiritual unease experienced by Startsev and Ekaterina and pervading the entire story.

These conflicting categories of existence are raised to their peak volume and greatest dissonance in the tableau of Startsev's vigil by the gravestone. Earlier in the evening Ekaterina relents to Startsev's pleading and tells him to wait by the tombstone marked "Demetti." Her nonarrival makes clear that the site was chosen for reasons that were probably not so much romantic as they were whimsically alliterative of Startsev's name, Dmitry. And yet this phonetic association somehow does not exhaustively explain her choice of this particular gravestone from among so many others; the subconscious workings of Ekaterina's decision making are patent even if their specific drift appears obscure. Demetti was a singer in an Italian opera company who had died during a stopover in the town of S——. The headstone is certainly suggestive in light of Ekaterina's own musical aspirations; a highly plausible scene outside the strict confines of the text would be her lingering by it and reflecting on her artistic aspirations. The image of the grave implies a certain equivalence between life in the provincial town and death itself. The prospect for a restored and reactivated life is external to both the town and the Turkins' parlor.

The physical aspects of the gravestone are particularly significant. While waiting, Startsev notices the distinctive appearance of the marker ("in the form of a chapel with an angel on top"), and the lamp by the tomb seems to flicker in the moonlight: "The lamp over the entrance to her tomb reflected the moonlight and seemed to be burning [*gorela*]." These details are significant as echoes of the holiday of the Exaltation of the Cross. According to the legend behind the holiday, St. Helen, the mother of Constantine the Great, sent an expedition to Jerusalem in search of Christ's Cross. All three crosses from the day of the Crucifixion were found buried under a pagan Roman temple; as Christ's was taken from the excavation site, it brushed against and revived a corpse being carried in a funeral procession. On September 14, 335, a church was built over Christ's tomb, and the original Cross was raised over an enormous multitude of praying Christians so that all could see it.[9] The lamp over Demetti's tomb comes to life in virtual commemoration of the reestablishment of Christ's own monument; in turn, the chapel emerges as a diminutive analogue to the church built on Christ's tomb, and the angel on top evocatively parallels the elevated pinnacle of the Cross. The double significance of the symbolism of ascent—as a rising either to salvation or to damnation described in the citation from the Gospel According to St. John—is increasingly accentuated over the course of the second section. It appears that Startsev experiences a crisis in his growing awareness of the crucial choice to be made between submitting to the soothing blandishments of the town or escaping from the spiritual entropy that it inevitably represents.

The unbearable tension of this duality reaches its height in the next paragraph, when Startsev emits a *cri du coeur* as he begins to hallucinate that the women buried in the cemetery are on the verge of fulfilling the prophecy inscribed over the gate. The moonlight seems to ignite Startsev as well as the lamp of Demetti's tomb, and the flame in his soul provides the illumination for his visual imagination:

> There was no one there. And who would be coming to the cemetery at midnight? But Startsev watied, and waited ardently [*strastno*], as though the moonlight was merely inflaming his passion [*strast'*], and in his imagination he saw kisses, embraces. He sat there beside the monument for half an hour, then took a walk through the side paths, his hat in his hand, waiting and wondering how many of the women and girls buried in those graves had been beautiful and fascinating, had loved, burning with passion at night [*sgorali po nocham strast'iu*] as they yielded to the caresses of their lovers. What a silly joke mother nature really played on man, and how humiliating to be conscious of it! Startsev was thinking thus, but at the same time he felt like shouting aloud that he wanted love, that he waited for love, that he must have it at all costs; he no longer saw before him slabs of white marble but beautiful bodies, he saw shapes that hid bashfully in the shadows of trees, he felt their warmth, and this agony of unfulfilled desire was becoming unbearable.

Agonizingly, Startsev becomes even more aware of the deathlike quality of so many lives, for whom existence is no different from a protracted illness or sleep. But the iconography of this passage suggests much more than simply a rumination on wasted lives. Here the religious imagery evident earlier is developed to a further extent. In the Orthodox tradition, the story of Christ's Transfiguration through light (Matthew 17: 1–8) occupies a place of special importance; according to Byzantine patristic literature, the Transfiguration prefigured the Second Coming. St. Gregory Palamas asserted that the true Christian is capable of witnessing the light of the Transfiguration within himself and, as the theologian John Meyendorff puts it, is thus "sacramentally united to the Redeemer after his death and Resurrection."[10] The presence of light also plays a significant role in Orthodox hagiographies, where the bodies of saints are sometimes transfigured by light.[11]

Both types of light, internal and external, are amply displayed in this passage, especially in the instance of the emotional conflagration that Startsev experiences as the slabs of marble appear, Pygmalion-like, to come to life. Love provides the opportunity for transcendence and a rising from a sepulchral state. In the context of the connotations of light just described, repetition of *strast'* (passion) and *strastno* (passionately, ardently) in this passage takes on new meaning. Sexual passion becomes merged with Christ's Passion, the apparent revivification of the women offering a further playing out of the biblical legend to its denouement of ascent and resurrection. Within this paradoxical context of a curious, almost pagan animism and a feminization of Christology, Startsev's bitter and vaguely misogynist cry against "mother nature" emerges as a profoundly ambiguous gesture. In section 2 of the story Startsev half-defames and blasphemes against the life force while admitting to his tragic alienation from it; he moves toward a rejection of what in section 1 is prosaically referred to as "life" (*zhizn'*) but is later identified with the eschatalogical salvation of John 5:28–29.

In the fourth section of the story Startsev's repulsion from possible salvation hardens into an almost principled renunciation, a shift reflected in the imagery invested in his last conversation with Ekaterina. She, by this time disappointed in her musical ambitions, asks him to remember (*A, pomnite*). A few years have already passed since their last encounter, and at first he responds to her indifferently, almost as if nothing had happened between them. As he recalls his near-visionary vigil in the cemetery, however, he soon finds that he remembers everything (*vspomnil vsë*), and the spark of memory turns into a flame: "He suddenly felt a sadness and pity for his past. And a little flame was kindled in his soul." In section 2 the motifs of memory and light are conflated in the description of Demetti's tomb, a *momentum mori* illuminated by an *ignis fatuus* of a lamp. As the narrator states then, "One of the singers had died and had been buried there, and this monument [*pamiatnik*] had been erected in her memory. Nobody in the town remembered [*pomnil*] her any more." In all of these instances memory and salvation emerge as an inextricable pair; the former is certainly evident not only in the verbs *pomnit'* and *vspomnit'* but also in the derivative *pamiatnik*, while the latter is represented by the motifs of light and heat. The tomb becomes the representational focus of the variant desires of Startsev and Ekaterina; for him it is a place of worship for his ardor, and for her it is a temple of the art to which she aspires. As reflected in their idolatrous lingering by the tomb, however, Ekaterina's and Startsev's muted yet obsessive narcissism ultimately prevents them from breaking out of their own emotional prisons as well as the prison of provincial life. The emotional developments of both characters, at first so different, converge in section 4. By this point an overwhelming elegiac sense has taken over the story, as if both characters have lived and died before the reader's eyes.

The last section of the story depicts the final stages of Startsev's and Ekaterina's self-mortification and ossification of personality. At Ekaterina's last appearance in the story, she is being packed off with her mother to the Crimea for the rest cure as the train car seals them off, casketlike, from the views of both the reader and Ivan Petrovich Turkin as he waves good-bye on the platform. The last memorable image of Startsev is of him, too, being conveyed. By this point in the story Startsev becomes physically indistinguishable from his obese and ill-mannered coachman, Panteleimon, as he profiteers from his property and practice. When the two ride through town in their carriage, the sight proves to be a formidable one: "When he drove about, red-faced and corpulent, in his carriage drawn by three horses, harness bells jingling, and Panteleimon, also red-faced and corpulent sitting on the box, holding his arms straight in front of him as if they were made of wood and shouting 'Keep to the r-r-right!' the overall picture was quite an impressive one and it seemed that it was not a human being but a pagan god [*iazycheskii bog*] driving past."[12] Startsev loses his identity to his coachman, and in fact here it is not clear to whom "pagan god" refers. The background of the name Panteleimon is particularly revealing in this regard: St. Panteleimon was a late third-century saint who worked as a physician and came to be known as a patron saint of doctors.[13] The application of this name to Startsev's coachman heightens the sense of interchangeability between the two characters.

Ivan Shcheglov rightly stresses the special and triumphantly iconic significance of this final, strangely frozen portrait of Startsev. As he notes, the merging of the doctor's being into the image of a primitive idol reinforces the chthonian and pagan connotations of the graveyard scene.[14] Not noted by Shcheglov but fully in keeping with his observations are certain aspects of the story's onomastics. The etymology of Startsev's first name, Dmitry, can be traced to Demeter (in Russian,

Demetra), the Greek goddess of agriculture.[15] According to legend, as Demeter mourned the abduction of her daughter Persephone into Hades, the once-rich soil was blighted, and the subsequent compromise of Persephone's periodic sojourn in the underworld resulted in the seasonal barrenness of the earth. The separation of Demeter from her daughter is echoed in Vera Iosifovna's hysterical response to her daughter's departure for Moscow. Startsev's troubled thoughts at the cemetery over all the stifled female consciousness trapped there, his resentful evocation of mother nature, and the autumnal setting of the scene even more clearly resonate with the myth.[16] Both the Christian and the pagan imagery of the graveyard scene are powerfully elegiac yet posit the loophole of a restoration to life.

The confluence of these two sets of imagery ends, however; the final comparison of Startsev to a pagan god clearly demonstrates this. Moreover, this shift from the potentially transcendent to the vulgar and profane is at least anticipated in the graveyard scene: Startsev's idolatry of Demetti's marker represents the turning point in his consciousness, the foreign name also serving as the mediating element or link in the phonological triad of Dmitry-Demetra-Demetti. The operation of Startsev's free will, the revelation that salvation and life are a matter of choice and not the passive and cyclical inevitability of nature, is ultimately expressed in the eschatalogical terms of the biblical text from John 5:28–29. The unconcealed paganism in section 5 stands in stark contrast to the earlier Christological imagery of transcendence and points up Startsev's spiritual demise. By the end of the story, the people in the town begin to call him simply by his patronymic, Ionych. Startsev's life tapers off to a single name, as mute and unrevealing as a solitary inscription on a headstone, such as "Demetti." The movement of onomastics to the forefront represents the triumph of the external and secondary, the final ossification of the shell surrounding the person. The name becomes the epitaph.

> This is the dead land
> This is cactus land
> Here the stone images
> Are raised, here they receive
> The supplication of a dead man's hand
> Under the twinkle of a fading star.
>
> Is it like this
> In death's other kingdom
> Waking alone
> At the hour when we are
> Trembling with tenderness

Lips that would kiss
Form prayers to broken stone.
—T. S. Eliot, "The Hollow Men"

The portrait of Startsev that finally emerges from "Ionych" completes and confirms the protagonist's movement toward self-mortification. In a series of masterly, economical brush strokes, Chekhov gives the reader a cumulative depiction of Startsev's physical person, vaguely indicated in sections 1 and 2 but later gaining in detail as the protagonist does in weight. Only by the end of the story is the reader treated to a thoroughgoing physical characterization of him. As Startsev becomes a Chichikov-like figure, all that seems to remain of him is his body, the opaque receptacle of his soul.[17] Vladimir Nabokov perceived Chichikov's obesity as a sort of metaphoric envelope or protective container for the putrefying essence of his character; he evocatively likened Gogol's protagonist to a punctured can of lobster carelessly left forgotten.[18] The worm in Startsev's soul eviscerates him. His body becomes a tomb and his soul a corpse, submitting to the powers of decay. As his body burgeons and the quantum of his soul dwindles, he becomes a desiccated and empty figure. Finally, the emergence of the eponymous patronymic decisively reaccentuates the topoi of ascent and renewal that the story's protagonist fails to realize. The name Iona (Jonah or Jonas) stands in ironic contrast to Startsev's actual fate: with its origin in the old Hebrew word meaning "dove" (*ione*) it possibly alludes to the Holy Spirit.[19] Perhaps more significant in this regard, however, is the biblical legend of Jonah and the whale. In Matthew 12:40 this event is represented as a prefiguration of both the entombment and the subsequent Resurrection of Christ: "For as Jonas was three days and three nights in the whale's belly; so shall the Son of man be three days and three nights in the heart of the earth." Ionych, like T. S. Eliot's hollow men, is for a crucial moment acutely aware of the prospect of liberation in the form of Judgment Day: "Not that final meeting / In the twilight kingdom."[20] He, however, is incapable of attaining the love that would release him from his sepulchral state.

114

Julie W. de Sherbinin

Life beyond Text: The Nature of Illusion
in "The Teacher of Literature"

> I played this morning with titles [for a book
> on Chekhov]. . . . À vrai dire, j'aimerais
> mieux 'Le Message Implicite': mais qui
> comprendrait?
> —Charles Du Bos, *Journal, 1924–1925*

A YOUNG woman named Aurelia Groman wrote to
Chekhov in 1899: "You say that each must bear his cross. But who will
show us how to bear that cross? In your works we see ourselves as in a
mirror. They show us our faults with the precision of a photograph, but
we don't know how to improve ourselves."[1] A Yalta resident responded to
Chekhov's "The Teacher of Literature" in a similar vein: "Give us at least
a few major chords—encourage us, give us some hope!"[2] The nineteenth-
century Russian *intelligentsia* was actively engaged in the quest for answers to a broad range of social, cultural, and spiritual questions. Writers served as sages, proffering answers that often propounded Christian
ethics as an ideal. Chekhov, a professed non-Christian, was broadly re-
proached for failing to show Russia "how to bear its cross." Yet a close
reading of certain Chekhovian texts suggests that he tenders answers that
are at once subtle and complex.

Chekhov's "The Teacher of Literature" (1894) has been widely regarded as a story that condemns the vacuous morass of provincial Russian life ("a mirror of our faults") but presents only a tenuous idea of
possible alternatives. In fact, the story offers a highly insightful message,
but one concealed from immediate view. "The Teacher of Literature"
follows a year in the life of the provincial gymnasium teacher Nikitin,
who falls in love with Maria Shelestova (Manya), the daughter of a
wealthy local family. Nikitin's courtship takes place during outings on
horseback and at social gatherings at the Shelestov home, where he is
in the company of Manya, her older sister, Varya, and a menagerie of
domestic animals. Nikitin proposes to Manya and is accepted. After

the wedding, he settles happily into provincial life, absorbed by teaching duties and adoration of his new wife. After a year of bliss, however, cracks begin to appear in the existence Nikitin had considered so ideal. He begins to recognize that his wife and her family value nothing beyond the satisfaction of physical comfort. Gradually he understands that "happiness is no longer possible for him in the two-storied house" and that the "illusion had dried up." He conceives a hatred for Manya, writing in his diary: "My God, where am I? I am surrounded by banality, banality [*poshlost'*]! . . . I must escape, escape from here this very day or I'll go out of my mind!"[3]

Scholarship has focused on Chekhov's negative assessment of *poshlost'* (banal and vulgar commonality, philistinism) and has variously assessed what is broadly viewed as an indeterminate end to the story. *Poshlost'* is a major theme in Russian social thought and one that Chekhov himself clearly identifies in the story itself and also in an epistolary reference to an early version of the story as "a frivolous trifle from the life of provincial guinea pigs."[4] Assumptions that the author's central aim is the condemnation of *poshlost'*, however, eclipse more important questions: Why does the banality of life in the provincial town elude, and delude, Nikitin for so long? What is the immanent nature of the illusion that "dries up"?

A second, symbolic plane of the story offers insights into the nature of Nikitin's illusion. The Russian title reads "Uchitel' slovesnosti," or "Teacher of *slovesnost'*," drawing attention to the role in the story of literary texts (the formal meaning of *slovesnost'*). An auxiliary meaning of *slovesnost'* also resonates here, for the term embraces oral tradition and folklore. Chekhov cites an array of literary and cultural texts in the course of the story. Moreover, the central figure is a man who calls literature his profession. It would seem worthwhile, then, to investigate the role of textuality in the protagonist's life.

Allusions to an important set of texts that derives from Russian religious culture are subtly woven into the story. A dual archetype of central importance in Orthodox thinking is the paradigm of the virgin and the harlot. Christian doctrine and legend firmly associate the virgin-whore dichotomy with the name Mary. The Virgin Mary (in Russian Orthodoxy, *Bogomater'*, *Bogoroditsa*, or the Mother of God) represents the female ideal of purity, tenderness, and obedience. Mary Magdalene and Mary of Egypt, on the other hand, were widely regarded as sinful women, although revered as saints in Christian dogma and practice. These Marias were known to Russia through a broad body of texts: iconography, acathists (liturgical hymns), hagiography, Scripture, and Apocrypha. Chekhov concerns himself with the psychology of images generated by this Marian paradigm in a number of stories.[5] In "The Teacher of Literature" the heroine's name initially signals the presence of the paradigm. Chekhov accentuates his choice of the name Maria with a series of derivative nicknames: Manya, Maniusia, Masha, and Marie Godefroy.

Nikitin unconsciously views both female characters, Manya and Varya, through the prism of this Marian paradigm. The artistic function of references to the virgin-whore cultural complex in Chekhov, however, is unique in the annals of Russian literature. The surprisingly consistent convention observed by his literary forebears was to establish a direct relationship between archetypal Marian qualities and characters named Maria.[6] In contrast, Chekhov dissociates a given character from the projections of the paradigm imposed upon her. Dissimilarities, inversions, and reversals of the cultural associations emerge as a key to understanding the thoughts and behavior of the protagonists.

Epithets characterizing the Mother of God mark Nikitin's attentive courting of Manya, whom he regards "with joy and tenderness [*s umileniem*]" as they ride together on horseback. These terms frequently characterize the Mother of God. The word *tenderness* evokes icons of the Virgin of Tender Mercy (*Bogomater' Umilenie*). Iconic overtones also appear in Nikitin's continual attention to Manya's immobile eyes: "[her] large, motionless eyes were shining"; "she gazed at him motionlessly, without blinking." In the story "Grief" Chekhov explicitly highlights this striking iconographic feature when he writes, "She gazed sternly and motionlessly, just as saints on icons gaze." Nikitin's marriage proposal to Manya is interlaced with some details that recall liturgical and apocryphal accounts of the Annunciation, the Angel Gabriel's announcement to the Virgin Mary that she would bear the Son of God.

The presence of a staircase, *lestnitsa*, in the small entryway where the proposal takes place is noted thrice. In Byzantine exegesis, Jacob's dream of the ladder (Church Slavic, *lestvitsa*) in the Old Testament (Genesis 28:12) prefigures the advent of the Virgin Mary in the New Testament, for she was to bridge heaven and earth with the birth of her son. On icons known as the Burning Bush, she is depicted holding a ladder in her hands, and in the major Marian acathist she is addressed as "the Heavenly Ladder."[7] In Nikitin's mind, his plea for Manya's hand is to be just such a moment of attaining "heaven." The episode develops in a symbolic manner. Nikitin never actually ascends the staircase. On his way "up" he is interrupted from mounting the "narrow wooden staircase" by the sudden entrance of Manya. She slams the door to the nursery so hard that the staircase shakes.

During the proposal itself we encounter a detail that, like the staircase, is mentioned three times—a flag of significance in Chekhov's economical prose. This is a piece of blue fabric that first appears in

Manya's hands, is then grasped by Nikitin, and finally falls to the floor when Nikitin moves to embrace Manya.[8] Apocryphal versions of the Annunciation portray the Virgin Mary spinning a thread for the temple veil when Gabriel appears to her. In iconographic depictions of the Annunciation, the thread and spindle are shown falling away from Mary's hand when she turns from her work to accept her "spiritual assignment."[9] Dark blue, the color of the material that falls from Manya's hand, is a sacred color in Eastern iconography and the consistent color of the Mother of God's robe on icons. Textile and thread are metonymically associated by contiguity. We recall that Nikitin hears the sound of a seamstress's scissors coming from the nursery when he enters the hall to make the marriage proposal. Manya, like Mary, emerges from her girlhood occupation (the temple, the nursery) to participate in a "coming of age" event.

The parallels in Chekhov's text, of course, serve to contrast rather than compare the biblical Annunciation and Nikitin's proposal of marriage. The marriage proposal takes place in a rather profane mode: the sacred value of the Annunciation is inverted at every step. This scene reveals the deep discrepancy between Nikitin's striving for an ideal that conforms to his cultural milieu and the reality of the Shelestov home, utterly devoid as it is of true intellectual, emotional, or spiritual values. The miracle of the moment at which the Virgin Mary drops the thread concerns immaculate conception; the moment at which Manya drops the blue fabric heralds erotic contact between Nikitin and his fiancée. The meaning of the proposal has to do with the physical initiation of Nikitin into a world of sensuality, at odds with Christian notions of the ideal woman.

The scene of the marriage proposal suggests a distinct discrepancy between Manya and the prototype in whose shadow she is being cast, and such a lack of correlation also exists between Varya and Marian images of womanhood.[10] Chekhov holds Varya up to the light of motherhood but subverts the correspondence. We are told that she has taken the place of her deceased mother in the family. Furthermore, "she called herself an old maid [*deva*], which meant that she was sure that she would get married." *Deva* means not only "maiden" but also "virgin" and figures as one of the appellations of the Mother of God (*Prechistaia deva, Prisnodeva Mariia*). From the outset, this is a portrait of unrealized motherhood, for the emphasis is on substitution for the real mother and on barrenness.

That Varya fails to conform to Nikitin's vision of exalted womanhood is clear from the literary debate in which they argue about Pushkin's status as a psychologist. (Interpretation of text on the level of plot thus parallels the question of the meaning of text developed on deeper

planes.) Nikitin's singularly unperceptive view of Pushkin is matched
by Varya's insistence that Pushkin is "a great poet and nothing more."
To escape the deadlock that the argument reaches, Nikitin yells, "I
won't argue anymore!... Of his kingdom there shall be no end! Basta!"
Chekhov, who commanded a thorough knowledge of Scripture, could
have only chosen this citation intentionally, for it is a line from an
account of the Annunciation (Luke 1:33). These are the words of the
Angel Gabriel, who proclaims to the Virgin Mary that the reign of the
Son of God shall be eternal. The impetuous exclamation "Basta!" in-
trudes on this citation as an index of its inversion. The Christian prophecy issues from Nikitin's mouth as a profanity, a curse, as it were, on
his own inability to articulate a convincing argument in his supposed
field of expertise—literature. In disgust at his intellectual impotence,
Nikitin harnesses a quotidian expression bearing reflexes of Christian
rhetoric to reject Varya's claim to a voice in the domain of the intellect.
The reversal of the sacred text is meaningful, for it is precisely Varya's
lack of feminity in the Christian sense, which extols a yielding, submissive nature, that dooms her hope for marriage and motherhood.
The image which Nikitin projects on Varya, in accordance with his
(mis)understandings, is the complementary component of the Marian
paradigm, the sinful woman.

Chekhov's design in regard to the theme of the fallen woman is
evidenced by the presence of a literary citation from Aleksei Konstan-
tinovich Tolstoy's 1857 poem "The Sinful Woman" (Greshnitsa). The
reference appears to be an incidental detail in Chekhov's story. It is
used to characterize the hackneyed acting of the amateur theater en-
thusiast Shebaldin: "He himself took part in performances, always playing, for some reason, comic servants or reciting 'Greshnitsa' in a singsong
voice." The actual significance of this "minor" detail underscores the
necessity of regarding every word in a Chekhov story as a critical
component of its semantic structure.

The poem is about a beautiful young prostitute who boasts to a
crowd that she will seduce Christ. Upon seeing him, however, she
immediately repents. In short, this is a reworked version of popular
tales about Mary Magdalene. At the moment of spiritual awakening
and repentance, A. K. Tolstoy's sinful woman drops her wineglass on
the floor and collapses at Christ's feet:

The ring of a goblet falling from hands
sounded out in the silence...
A moan is heard from her constricted
breast, the young harlot pales,
Her open lips tremble,

She falls down, sobbing,
Before the sacred figure of Christ.

Chekhov invokes this scene in Nikitin's diary account of Varya's hysterical collapse at the wedding reception: "Varya, Manya's sister, ran into the study with a *wineglass in her hand*. . . . she apparently wanted to run further, but suddenly she burst out laughing, then *sobbing*, and her wineglass began to *roll across the floor with a ring*" (my emphasis). In both texts, the same action occurs at a moment of crisis. Nikitin's adulation of Manya reaches its apotheosis in the wedding scene, and suddenly Varya feels acutely her own unwed status. Varya is no more a "sexually compromised" woman, of course, than is Manya the embodiment of Marian virtues. Rather, Varya as "sinner" reflects Nikitin's dualistic view of womanhood. She fails to correspond to the Virgin ideal, so Nikitin projects onto her the role (and "text") of the fallen woman.

This citation from A. K. Tolstoy's poem, which appears in Nikitin's diary at the opening of part 2, signals a change in contextual orientation for the story overall. We recall that fabric falling from Manya's hand situated the marriage proposal in reference to a sacred text about the Virgin. Here a glass falling from Varya's hand alludes to a secular text about a sinful woman. Indeed, at the wedding itself Nikitin is disconcerted by the old general's description of Manya as "a rose" for what it implies about her sexual attractiveness. (The rose as a symbol of the Virgin, a Catholic convention, was replaced by the white lily in Orthodox theology, for the rose's thorns, it was felt, suggested the taint of sin.[11]) This comparison initially embarrasses Nikitin, for it clashes with his own lofty image of Manya's virtues, but it eventually leads to new understandings.

Nikitin comes to view Manya as a sinful woman as his eyes open to the visceral quality of her life, confined as it is to the satisfaction of physical urges and desires. An incident early in the story hints at this connection. During the parlor game called "Fate" played at a Shelestov soiree, Nikitin is instructed to play the role of a priest at confession. Entranced by the sight of Manya's large, motionless eyes as she comes to "confess," he poses the question "How have you sinned?" Her response is to screw up her eyes and show him the tip of her tongue. These actions defiantly undermine the iconographic associations discussed above.

An image suggesting the duality of the Marian context in the story is the pair of Egyptian doves that dwells on the porch at the Shelestov home. Chekhov, who features Saint Mary of Egypt as a cultural referent for the prostitute in "The Requiem" and "An Attack of Nerves," was well aware of the possible connotations of the word *Egyptian* for the Russian mind. Nikitin's initial emphatic hostility toward the Egyptian doves reflects the same impulse that causes him to balk at the appellation *rose*. At the same time, doves may be associated with icons of the Annunciation, on which a dove represents the Holy Spirit descending to the Virgin. Nikitin's hostility gives way to a conviction that the doves moan because they have no other way to express their joy. The Egyptian doves point to Nikitin's polarized conceptualization of womanhood.[12]

Another indication of Manya's dissociation from qualities of the Virgin can be traced through the imagery of milk. The Virgin Mary's status as a nurturing spiritual mother was sometimes portrayed through the suckling breast.[13] Manya founds a dairy enterprise that could not be more remote from the essence of maternal benevolence: "With three cows, Manya set up a genuine dairy business. She kept a lot of pitchers of milk and pots of sour cream in the cellar and the pantry, which she saved to make butter. Now and then, as a joke, Nikitin asked her for a glass of milk. This gave her a scare, since it violated her sense of order, but he would embrace her with a laugh and say: 'Never mind, I was just joking, my golden one, just joking!'" Instead of exemplifying motherly nurturing, Manya hoards her milk and turns it into solids, a petrified parody of the milk that flows from the Virgin's breast. An acathist line reads, "Rejoice, for honey and milk flow from her!"[14] Manya's refusal to give Nikitin milk becomes a symbolic gesture, a sign of her utter lack of identification with Nikitin's ideal woman.

Emblematic of the onset of change in Nikitin's understandings of Manya is the scene in which he pontificates to her on the nature of his happiness. As he tells her that he regards his happiness as something that he himself has created, Nikitin plays with Manya's hair, unbraiding and then rebraiding it. In figurative terms, the sexual overtones of Nikitin's action reverberate with the symbolism of the Virgin—one braid is the Orthodox prescription for the modest female—and the harlot, who is depicted with loose hair, both in works of art and in Chekhov's oeuvre. Nikitin's action, the movement between braiding Manya's hair and letting it fall loose, indicates the direction in which his own thoughts are moving and belies his own confident assertions about his happiness.

The Marian holiday of the Dormition (*Uspen'e*) marks the resumption of Nikitin's teaching duties. The holiday, signifying the death of the Mother of God, coincides with the onset of the period in which Nikitin's illusions concerning Manya disintegrate. When Nikitin first imagines a different and meaningful life, it is imaged as a world beyond the icon lamp: "He mused that besides the soft light of the icon lamp, which smiled at this quiet domestic happiness, besides this little world, in which he and that cat lived so peacefully and sweetly, a wholly different world existed." He then regards Manya, lying on the bed beside the white cat, with her neck and her full shoulders and breast, and for the first time he understands the appellation *rose*. Nikitin comprehends that she whom he imagined as virgin really belongs to the world of spiritless sensuality associated in Christian doctrine with the whore. Nikitin has moved irrevocably beyond the stage of idealization of Manya.

The story's final paragraph is saturated with Marian signs that no longer exercise authority in Nikitin's life. The date of March 20 and the sun rays suggest the Annunciation (celebrated on March 25 and represented as a ray of light descending on the Virgin from heaven). The words *garden, miraculous,* and *joys,* which describe his surroundings, all resonate in the mode of Marian praise. But Nikitin sees no value in the scene that evoked euphoria in him a year before. In the last lines, he recognizes Manya's obsession with milk as a perversion of real value. Nikitin has shed his projections and moved beyond the "texts" of his culture that propagate a polarized vision of life.

The question of cultural texts and context in "The Teacher of Literature" is paralleled by Chekhov's attention to literary texts. Inversions of meaning also distinguish an important literary subtext in the story, Pushkin's narrative poem "Count Nulin."[15] In the first line of Chekhov's story, three horses are introduced: Nikitin mounts the black Count Nulin, Manya mounts the white Velikan, and Varya mounts Maika. Pushkin's poem portrays the dandified Count Nulin, who stops at a squire's estate for the night on his return from Europe to "Petropol'" and attempts to seduce the squire's lovely wife. Chekhov encourages an assocation between Nikitin and Nulin by the phonetic resemblance of their names. This turns out to be a false lead, however, for Nikitin corresponds poorly to the Pushkin prototype.

"Count Nulin" is a spoof on the effect that literature has on ways of imagining life. Pushkin originally planned to call his narrative poem "A New Tarquin," a reference to Tarquinius's ravaging of Collatinus's wife in Shakespeare's "The Rape of Lucrece." Pushkin parodies Shakespeare's plot by turning a tragedy into a comedy: he refashions Tarquin's sexual conquest of the chaste and faithful Lucrece as Nulin's blundering effort to seduce Natalya Petrovna, who rebuffs him with a slap in the face.[16] Chekhov, clearly conscious of the literary legacy, takes a further step in this textual series by sketching Nikitin in the shadow of Nulin but subverting the meaning once again.

Count Nulin, after an evening spent with Natalya Petrovna, is annoyed with himself when he returns to his quarters for failing to make a sexual advance on his hostess. In an analogous situation, Nikitin, returning from an evening at the Shelestov home, reproaches himself once back in his quarters for another reason: he regrets having missed the opportunity to make a marriage proposal. In the wake of this initial failure to propose, Nikitin lies on his sofa and indulges in a fantasy, imagining a letter he will wrote to his future wife: "'That's how I'll start my letter: My dear little rat... That's it! My dear little rat,' he said, and began to laugh." This odd detail acquires meaning by its reference to Pushkin's poem, for Nikitin's imagined epistle is a reverse echo of Nulin's seduction plan. The Pushkin text reads:

> Thus at times a wily cat,
> The maid's mannered favorite,
> Steals after a mouse from his perch:
>
> . . . .
>
> Sharpens the claws of his cunning paws
> And—bam!—snatches up the poor thing.

This image of mouse as sexual victim parodically echoes lines from "The Rape of Lucrece": "Yet, foul night-waking cat, he doth but dally, / While in his hold-fast foot the weak mouse panteth." Chekhov fashions Nikitin's fantasy in this Nulin/Tarquin mode. Nikitin's imagination conjures up a trip to Petersburg (Nulin, we recall, was also headed thence), although Moscow is the city familiar to him. He pictures a nocturnal "assault" on the bedroom. Even Chekhov's linguistic fabric imitates Pushkin's: "Or, even better, he'd be cunning: He'd return noiselessly at night, the cook would let him in, then he'd sneak to the bedroom on tiptoe, quietly undress and—plunk!—into bed." The many lexical rhymes with "Count Nulin" ("cunning paws"/"he'd by cunning"; "maid"/"cook"; "steals"/"sneak . . . on tiptoe"; "bam"/"plunk") leave little doubt about the intentionality of the semantic link. The point here, again, is that Chekhov transforms Nulin's crude erotic metaphor into a fantasy of consummated love in Nikitin's conscious mind. But in Nikitin's subconscious, Manya assumes the features of a rat rather than a mouse. His fantasized escapade involves returning to the bed of a pernicious rodent, not a victimized female.

Chekhov's reversal of text foregrounds the question of sexuality. Nikitin is dissociated from the aggressive sexual role allotted the "cat" by both Shakespeare and Pushkin. Chekhov's protagonist repeatedly expresses his hostility toward the Shelestov cats, considering them at one point the sole obstacle to his happiness. The implied presence of cats on the staircase during the marriage proposal may thus be considered an ominous sign. Instead, Manya becomes associated with the white cat, which, as we have seen, coincides with Nikitin's reevaluation of his wife's virtues.

The question of sexuality also resonates in Nikitin's preoccupation with his age. On several occasions he is mistaken for a very young man, barely old enough for marriage. Early in the story Nikitin fumes at such as implication: "'How swinish!,' thought Nikitin. 'This fellow also takes me for a suckling [*molokosos*]!'" *Molokosos*, literally "milk-sucker," suggests a psychologically puerile, dysfunctional state, which aptly describes Nikitin's romantic interest in Manya. The milk theme, of course, also relates to the Marian imagery. Not coincidentally, Chekhov borrows the word from Pushkin. At the end of "Count Nulin," Natalya Petrovna's husband has his say:

> He said that the count was a fool,
> A *suckling* [*molokosos*]; that being such,
> He'd make the count yelp,
> He'd hunt him down *with dogs*.
> (my emphasis)

The husband's comic and empty threat is reversed in Chekhov's story. Nikitin is figuratively "hounded by the dogs" of the Shelestov household. The reversal is brought full circle when Manya orders that a scrap of cheese be sent to the servants' quarters despite remonstrations on Nikitin's part that it is only fit for a mousetrap. The theme from the letter fantasy ("my little rat") converges here with the milk imagery (the cheese is "hard as a rock") to indicate the complete bankruptcy of his ideal. Nikitin turns out to be analogous to the victimized rodents of the Shakespeare and Pushkin verses. He is caught in the trap of his misapprehension of Manya.

In addition to the A. K. Tolstoy and Pushkin subtexts, Chekhov relies on a series of other literary allusions in his portrayal of Nikitin. Nikitin's erudition in the field of literature is repeatedly subjected to doubt. His rejoinder to Varya's claim that Shchedrin and Dostoevsky outstrip Pushkin as psychologists is the lame remark "Shchedrin is one thing, and Pushkin is another." When it is Varya's turn to "confess" during the parlor game, Nikitin avers that he "knows her sins" and teases her about her suitor by misquoting a Lermontov epigram. Nikitin is haunted by feelings of inadequacy in the wake of Shebaldin's shocked reaction to the information that he had not read G. E. Lessing. While his students read Gogol and Pushkin aloud in class, Nikitin engages in daydreams of Manya.

Nikitin consistently views his life by comparison with literary genres. He compares his married life first to "poetry, novels, and stories," then to a "fairy tale," and yet again to "pastoral idylls." Each of these descriptions represents a trite cliché and bespeaks a poverty of imagination. The vehicle of his ruminations is, appropriately, his diary, a supreme example of life focused in text. But as Nikitin starts to openly

124

admit his deep dissatisfaction with life, he comes to the startling recognition that he has no talent for, or interest in, the vocation of pedagogy and, moreover, that he has never understood what he taught, that he knows nothing about the meaning of literature. Nikitin fails as both a scholar and a teacher. His identity as a teacher of literature turns out to be an illusion.

Nikitin's critical realizations about his misconceived life are ushered in by Epiphany (*Kreshchen'e*), the Orthodox celebration of Christ's baptism. On Epiphany Nikitin's intense dislike of the Shelestov animals comes to light. But the actual holiday is marked by a failed celebration: "The police wouldn't allow anyone out on the river for the Blessing of the Water since, they said, the ice had swollen and darkened." This detail serves as a signal that the notion of baptism is inverted, denoting a crisis in Nikitin's life.

Nikitin's awakening of understanding comes as he stands in the rain after an evening of card playing at the club. The card motif appears in the first part of the story, when two decks of cards are used to play the game called "Fate" at the Shelestov soiree. This telling semantic juxtaposition, *cards* and *fate*, bears on the scene outside the club. Card playing may be regarded as a metaphor for abnegation of will and capitulation to fate.[17] Nikitin's card partner's comment on his unearned wealth jolts Nikitin into the realization that forces over which he wields no control direct his life. He recognizes that his perceptions have been molded by a system of belief that he never consciously embraced. His "baptism" in the rain, then, is an ironic antibaptism. Rather than signaling the espousal of faith or a spiritual epiphany, it is an omen of his move away from the projections of artificial, even fraudulent, Christian images on the life around him. Nikitin's ultimate plan to leave the provincial town represents the act of surmounting the notion of a preordained existence.

When Leo Tolstoy's Ivan Ilych discovers that life has been "not right" (*ne to*), a revelation of the need for spiritual value ensues, but Nikitin's *ne to* is not capped by a prescribed solution. Chekhov wrote of his admiration for the individual feat, or *podvig* (the connotation of spiritual victory inheres in the Russian). Nikitin's feat is not awaiting him in the future but has already been achieved by the story's end. His act of self-liberation moves him beyond the "scripts" offered by the Russian literary and religiocultural traditions. Overcoming the past, freeing oneself from the fetters of perception dictated by cultural images and literary texts, is, in Chekhovian terms, a critical juncture of self-discovery, a crucial moment of triumph for the individual.

The perceptive reader of literature, like Chekhov himself, maintains a distance between "life" and "text," regarding with appreciation the literariness of literature and with irony the human inclination to textualize life. These distinctions elude Chekhov's teacher of literature until he musters the honesty to challenge the a priori cultural attitudes that determine his thoughts and behavior. The illusion that "dries up" in "The Teacher of Literature," then, is the illusion that the intelligent individual can base a satisfying existence on culturally determined ideas, images, and archetypes or on dogmas, doctrines, or texts of any kind. In place of the illusion comes the much more difficult bidding to discover and structure one's own meaning.

Rather than encouraging his reader with a prescriptive path to happiness, for which Aurelia Groman and the Yalta correspondent plead, Chekhov advocates accepting the uncertainty and responsibility for self that come with a mature apprehension of life. In so doing, he turns the quest for answers back on the individual.

Robert Louis Jackson

Chekhov's "The Student"

Man lives for those who have passed and for those who are coming, for ancestors and descendants alike. His personality is bounded by this double connection with continuity. Every moment changes everything that has preceded him in time. Hence the obligation *to live* is the only obligation. Because "obligation" is "connection." Teaching *how* to live is false ethic. The individual is free in the limits of a single *yes* to life. Every *no* must be an affirmation of a single *yes*.

—Vyacheslav I. Ivanov,
"About Law and Connection"

THE DRAMA of Easter, the paschal drama, is the center of Chekhov's "The Student." On the symbolic plane of the story one moves from Good Friday, the day on which Christ is crucified, to the "feast of faith" of Easter Day. As the Eastern Orthodox theologian A. A. Bogolepov has put it, "The joy of Easter can be fully realized only through [experiencing] the tragedy of the Passion. Only one whom his sufferings have penetrated can truly and joyfully feel in his soul the Resurrection with Christ."[1] And indeed, Ivan Velikopolsky, "a student of a theological academy and the son of a sacristan," passes through suffering; that is, he painfully experiences not only the tragedy of the Russian people, Russian history and life, but also the drama of Christ and the moral-spiritual sufferings of Peter.[2] Ivan's drama, like that of Jesus' disciple Peter, is one involving the idea of renunciation, separation, and negation. Ivan moves from a moment of despair in Russia and in life—well symbolized in the phrase "it did not feel as though Easter would be the day after tomorrow"—to a moment when he regains his faith in the essential truth and beauty of human life. Using some of the images in the opening part of the story, one may say that at the beginning Ivan Velikopolsky, like Dante's confused traveler, finds himself in a dark and threatening woods. He moves steadily along a path

127

that leads toward the widows' gardens; at the end he ascends a hill, where, spiritually renewed, he experiences a sense of the connectedness, of the "lofty meaning," of all life. The passage from forest to mount, from momentary despair through communion with the widow and her daughter to a moment of spiritual transfiguration, defines the journey of both student and story. The student, one can suppose, will descend again, like Peter, into the dark world of suffering. This time, however, he will be spiritually fortified: that much is suggested by the whole design of the story.

The opening line of Chekhov's story hints at a change for the worse: "At first the weather was fine and still." The line that follows, however, suggests more than a change of weather. Chekhov anthropomorphizes nature. "The thrushes were crying out, and in the swamps close by something alive droned pitifully with a sound like blowing into an empty bottle." Not all is well and tranquil in this world. The opening paragraph concludes with the lines: "Needles of ice stretched across the pools, and it felt cheerless, remote, and lonely in the forest. There was a whiff of winter."

Ivan begins to think about the world, and his thoughts about it seem to relate to his response to the changes in nature. "It seemed to him that the cold that had suddenly come on had destroyed the order and harmony of things. . . . All around it was deserted and peculiarly gloomy." Except for a shimmering fire in the distance from the widows' gardens—this important image of light takes on symbolic significance in the story—everything was sunk in the cold evening darkness. Such is the setting for Ivan's somber thoughts about his poor and ailing parents and of Russian history: "And now, shrinking from the cold, he thought that just the same wind had blown in the days of Rurik and in the time of Ivan the Terrible and Peter [the Great], and in their time there had been just the same desperate poverty and hunger, the very same thatched roofs with holes in them, ignorance, misery, the very same desolation around, darkness, a feeling of oppression—all these had existed, did exist, and would exist, and the lapse of a thousand years would make life no better." As there is no harmony and order in nature, so there is none in the life of the people and of Russia. The bleak sounds of nature in the second line—"in the swamps close by something alive droned pitifully with a sound like blowing into an empty bottle"—become the blowing wind of Rurik's time. The thought that torments Ivan on Good Friday is that nothing has changed: everything is the same, the same, the same, the same. "All these had existed, did exist, and would exist, and the lapse of a thousand years would make life no better." These are bitter words. But there follow the most terrible words of the story: "And he did not want to go home." These words will find their parallel in Peter's denial of Christ in the story-within-the-story: "I do not know him."

Why is Ivan's wish not to go home so terrible? Because not to return home is to abandon the family, to forget wife, husband, daughter and son, mother and father; not to go home is to leave everything to chance; not to go home is to renounce all personal responsibility, duty, honor; not to go home is to deny the reality of human bonds, those moral, social, and spiritual connections that give meaning to the words *family* and *society*. Not to go home is the most basic and therefore the most terrible form of apostasy. Ivan Velikopolsky, however, unlike another Ivan in *The Brothers Karamazov*, overcomes his momentary impulse not to go home.

Precisely at this moment of despair Ivan approaches the gardens, the widow Vasilisa and her daughter, Lukerya, and the campfire "throwing out light far around on the ploughed earth." Ivan's words of greeting reflect his gloomy thoughts: "Here you have winter back again. . . . Good evening." For a moment Vasilisa does not recognize Ivan. Her response, however, is a warm one: "I did not recognize you; God bless you. . . . You'll be rich." Ivan, however, is relentless in his gloom. Not only the somber character of Good Friday but also personal thoughts about suffering and renunciation lead Ivan naturally into his recollection of the story of Peter's momentary renunciation of Jesus. "At just such a fire the Apostle Peter warmed himself. . . . So it must have been cold then, too. Ah, what a terrible night it must have been, Granny! An utterly dismal long night!"

What follows is the story of how Peter "from a distance" watched the beating of his beloved Jesus in the courtyard of the high priest. Ivan relates how deeply Peter loved Jesus—"passionately, intensely." The Russian words here translated as "intensely" are *bez pamjati*, literally "without memory." And ironically, Peter relates to Jesus as though without memory. Three times he denies Jesus: "I do not know him." Where there is no memory there is no recognition. Peter denies any *connection* with Jesus. Looking at him from a distance Peter remembers Jesus' prophetic words: "I tell thee, Peter, the cock shall not crow this day, before that thou shalt thrice deny that thou knowest me" (Luke 22:34, KJV).

Ivan directly identifies himself with the man, Peter, who denies Jesus. "Peter, too, stood with them [the laborers] near the fire and warmed himself, as I am doing." After recalling how Peter, after his denial, "wept bitterly," Ivan dwells especially on Peter's moment of grief and remorse: "I imagine it: the still, still, dark, dark garden, and in the stillness, faintly audible, smothered sobbing." At this recollection of intense suffering, Ivan himself undergoes a spiritual transformation. "The student sighed and sank in thought," the narrator writes. Not

129

accidentally is the Russian word *vzdokhnul* (sighed) connected with *dukh* (spirit) and *dyshat'* (to breathe)—a linkage that Chekhov will remember a few lines later. Ivan is overcome by the pathos of his own story. Vasilisa and Lukerya, moved to tears, give expression to their grief, to "a great pain." "Now the student was thinking about Vasilisa: since she had shed tears, all that had happened to Peter the night before the Crucifixion must have had some relation to her." Chekhov places trailing suspension points after the word *otnoshenie* (relation), the final word in Chekhov's Russian sentence, as though stressing the importance of the word. For to recognize a relation to something or to somebody or to some event is to affirm the reality of connections: it is the first step toward a consciousness of the unity of all human existence, toward establishing ethical bonds among people, holding people together, caring for people, loving them. The women instantly make these connections. Ivan's paschal revelation—and that is what is involved at this moment—is signaled by words that follow immediately after the word *otnoshenie*. The narrator writes, "He looked around. The solitary light was still gleaming in the darkness." The line evokes John 1:5: "And the light shineth in darkness; and the darkness comprehended it not." The light, of course, is always lonely—as Jesus was in the courtyard of the high priest and in the garden of Gethsemane—but it shines tranquilly, and its message is clear.

At this point Ivan develops his thoughts about connections: "The student thought again that if Vasilisa had shed tears, and her daughter had been troubled, it was evident that what he had just been telling them about, which had happened nineteen centuries ago, had a relation to the present—to both women, to the desolate village, to himself, to all people. The old woman wept, not because he could tell the story touchingly, but because Peter was near to her, because her whole being was interested in what was passing in Peter's soul." It is noteworthy that the old woman not only feels a connection with Peter but that she feels it with "her whole being." These words echo Mark 12:30–33: "And thou shalt love the Lord thy God with all thy heart, and with all thy soul, and with all thy mind, and with all thy strength. . . . And to love him with all the heart, and with all the understanding, and with all the soul, and with all the strength, and to love his neighbor as himself, is more than all whole burnt offerings and sacrifices."

What is important is that these women experience the suffering of Peter and the Passion of Christ with their entire being. Chekhov's thought is clear: One's commitment to one's fellow man, to the good, to God, cannot be abstract, "from a distance." It cannot be conditional or based on the expectation of returns, results, payment. It must be unconditional, total, above all deeply felt, that is, experienced with one's entire being, with all the heart.

At this point it is appropriate to ask: Who are the real heroes of Chekhov's story? The answer is clear: not the student, not Peter, but the women. Vasilisa and her daughter are the real heroes of the story, in the same way that Russian women have always been the real heroes of Russian life and literature, be they simple peasants or aristocratic wives of Decembrists. Vasilisa and her daughter are the heroes because in the most essential terms of human experience they have kept the faith: theirs is the light of the biblical "burning bush," and they have kept the fires burning. The women have nursed and nourished the children, served family and life; they have tended the garden, worked, endured the hardest labor; they have done the work of men as well as of women; and through it all they have maintained their humanity and image. Chekhov describes Vasilisa this way: "A tall, fat old woman in a man's coat was standing by and looking thoughtfully into the fire. . . . [She] expressed herself with refinement, and a soft, sedate smile never left her face." One may recall at this point some remarks by Dostoevsky in a little essay in *Diary of a Writer* entitled "On Love for the People: A Necessary Contract with the People." Dostoevsky writes: "One has to be able to separate out the beauty in the Russian belonging to the common people from the alluvial barbarism. Owing to circumstances, almost throughout the whole history of Russia, our people has been to such an extent subjected to debauchery and to such an extent corrupted, seduced, and constantly tortured that it is still amazing how it has survived, preserved its human image, not to speak of its beauty. Yet it preserved the beauty of its image as well."[3]

Vasilisa experiences the story of the suffering of Peter and of Jesus with "her whole being." These words prelude a qualitative change in Ivan's whole being: "And joy suddenly stirred in his soul, and he even stopped for a minute to take a breath." No detail is without meaning in Chekhov's great masterpieces. The Russian phrase for "to take a breath" is *perevesti dukh*. *Perevesti* means "to transfer," "move," "shift"; *dukh* is here, idiomatically, "breath," but in its main meaning it is also "spirit," that same *dukh* that is hidden away in *vzdokhnul*, as was noted earlier. One may say, then, that in both a literal and a figurative sense a transfer of the spirit takes place in Ivan; in other words, he experiences the paschal tranfiguration. Indeed, according to the Gospels, Jesus "yielded up the ghost" (in Russian, *ispustil dukh*) (Matthew 27:50) but was "quickened by the Spirit" (*ozhil dukhom*) (I Peter 3:18) and was resurrected by the Divine Spirit.[4] Such is the character of the paschal change that takes place in Ivan.

Ivan's grief and self-pity have been overcome through a deeply felt ethics of connection—through relating to people and life. Ivan's deep breath, his spiritual crossing over, leads immediately to often-quoted lines from Chekhov's "The Student," lines that articulate the central theme of connections in the story: "The past, he thought, is linked with the present by an unbroken chain of events flowing one out of another. And it seemed to him that he had just seen both ends of that chain; that when he touched one end the other quivered."

Ivan is filled with a sense of renewal. He now crosses the river in a boat—the moment is full of rich symbolism—and mounts the hill from which he looks out on "his village and towards the west where the cold crimson sunset lay in a narrow streak of light." There Ivan "thought that truth and beauty which had guided human life there in the garden and in the yard of the high priest had continued without interruption to this day, and had evidently always been the chief thing in human life and in all earthly life, indeed; and the feeling of youth, health, vigor—he was only twenty-two—and the inexpressible sweet expectation of happiness, of unknown mysterious happiness, took possession of him little by little, and life seemed to him enchanting, marvellous, and full of lofty meaning."

Ivan experiences the paschal transfiguration in a moment that seems to allude to Jesus' ascent to the mount. The life that had seemed senseless and unchanging to Ivan but a short while ago as he made his way homeward is now full of "lofty meaning." Ivan looks to the west, upon his village, and upon the crimson sunset with an expectation of happiness. There is an allusion in this final scene not only to Jesus' ascent to the mount but also to that moment when Moses on Mount Nebo looked west to the promised land and the Lord declared: "I have caused thee to see it with thine eyes, but thou shalt not go over thither" (Deuteronomy 34:4). Like Moses, Ivan will not see the promised land on earth; like Peter, he, too, will surely experience new trials and tribulations. What is important, though, is his sustaining vision, a profoundly ethical one, of "truth and beauty."

Relevant here are some words of A. A. Bogolepov on the significance of Easter: "Easter is the triumph of trampled truth and beauty. Granted—not in all fullness; granted—only in part; nonetheless, truth is attainable also on this earth. Granted—not always; granted—only at times, but it can be victorious even here. This faith has moved people."[5]

"What kind of a whiner am I? What kind of a 'gloomy' person? . . . What kind of a 'pessimist'?" Chekhov once exclaimed to the writer Ivan Bunin. "Really of all my pieces my favorite story is 'The Student.'

And 'pessimist'—that's a repellent word."[6] When Chekhov cited "The Student" as proof that he was not a pessimist, could he have had in mind only the ending of the story, that transitory moment when Ivan Velikopolsky breathes deeply of the joy of Easter? Hardly. "The Student" testifies abundantly to suffering and tragedy in human history, a tragedy of which the Crucifixion and Peter's denial, not to speak of his own martyrdom, are emblematic. Ivan may not end his life in martyrdom like Peter, but he will surely be tested again in the future. If one is to understand Chekhov's comment on "The Student," one must move from the banal, popular, and, above all, unproductive categories of pessimism and optimism, unhappy ending and happy ending, to the more vital and productive categories of affirmation or negation of life. Chekhov's "The Student," like almost all of Russian nineteenth-century literature, is profoundly affirmative in its eternal yes to life, its unflagging ethical and spiritual yes in the face of what Dostoevsky once called "contrary evidence."[7] Here is one possible reason for Chekhov's decision to change the title of his story from "In the Evening" (Vecherom) to "The Student."[8] Chekhov, one may surmise, changed the title not simply because the story moves from darkness to light—albeit to the crimson and pensive light of sunset—but because with respect to the essential lessons of life he believed that the human being is an eternal student, forever failing, forever drawing a deep spiritual breath, and forever restarting the journey.[9] Herein lies the affirmative character of "The Student" and Chekhov's work in general.

Fate and Responsibility

Richard Peace

"In Exile" and Russian Fatalism

IN APRIL 1890 Chekhov set out on a great adventure, his great "exploit" (*podvig*): the journey across Siberia to study penal settlements on the island of Sakhalin. This exploit, it should be noted, had two distinct elements. For if the aim was to live among convicts and to undertake serious work on their behalf, it did not necessarily entail a long and arduous journey across inhospitable terrain: he could have gone, as he returned, by sea. Chekhov's biographers have speculated on the reasons for his Sakhalin adventure, suggesting such motives as disappointment in love, a sense of stagnation in his life, and an attempt to rebut criticism that as a writer he lacked social commitment. The author himself, as usual, provided no clear answers of his own.

Nevertheless, Chekhov realized that now great things were expected of him as an artist, and yet the achievement of his stories must have seemed slight when set beside the novels of his illustrious predecessors. Dostoevsky had lived among convicts and then written his major works; Goncharov had made the arduous journey back from Japan across Siberia and then produced his masterpiece *Oblomov*. Chekhov had been reading both these writers the previous year, but his attitude toward them is far from ambiguous. His references to Dostoevsky are reserved, and Goncharov, whose name once stood alongside that of Tolstoy in Chekhov's table of literary ranks, was now diminished in Chekhov's eyes after a disillusioning rereading of *Oblomov*.[1] Yet both authors could claim to have analyzed Russian soul, and both were associated with a doctrine of acceptance and passivity before fate, be it Dostoevsky's well-known concept of humility (*smirenie*) or Goncharov's attempt to project Oblomov as the "Plato of the Vyborg side."[2]

In a letter to Suvorin of March 9, 1890, Chekhov advances two reasons for his journey. The first, a personal one, is the need to overcome a national (in this case Ukrainian) predisposition to laziness. If this suggests a struggle with incipient Oblomovism, then his second, more public-spirited reason, that red-nosed warders are not to blame for the convicts' plight, "but all of us," is strangely reminiscent of Dmitry

Karamazov's hopes for his own efforts among the Siberian convicts: "But there are a lot of them, hundreds of them, and we are to blame for them."[3]

Dostoevsky and Goncharov were clearly before Chekhov as he undertook, and later reassessed, his trip to Sakhalin. There are references, direct and indirect, to both authors in the fragmentary record of his outward journey, "In Siberia" (V Sibiri), as well as in the fruits of his labors in *The Island of Sakhalin* (Ostrov Sakhalin). Indeed, Goncharov's *Fregat Pallada* is listed by Chekhov as one of the works he consulted in writing *The Island of Sakhalin*, and in "In Siberia" he comments on Goncharov's own experience of Siberian travel. Moreover, *Oblomov* appears to have been in his mind while he prepared for his journey, to judge from a letter he sent his brother Aleksandr requesting newspaper information on Sakhalin, in which he draws a very disparaging comparison between Aleksandr and Oblomov's servant Zakhar, who were, apparently, both at one in their fatalistic acceptance of lice and bugs.[4]

After Siberia, Chekhov did not produce a major novel to compete directly with Dostoevsky and Goncharov, but the two stories "In Exile" and "Ward Six" not only reworked material from his Siberian and penal settlement experiences but did so in a way that attacked the doctrine of a philosophical acceptance of one's lot.[5] "In Exile" is set on the banks of one of those great Siberian rivers that present such an obstacle to west-east communication. It is spring, but it is bleak and cold. Snow is still falling. The forbidding scenery and the burning of last year's grass are details recorded by Chekhov in his letters. It is an experience that had left an indelible impression on Chekhov himself: "But what is most terrible of all, and what I won't forget all my life, is the crossing of the rivers."[6]

The basic form of the story is a conversation between two men exiled for criminal activity: the Russian ferryman Semyon, nicknamed Tolkovy (commonsensical), and a young Tartar boy, whose name nobody knows. The life of a third character, the "nobleman" Vasily Sergeich, provides Tolkovy with an illustration for his argument and the story itself with its main plot line.

Tolkovy and the Tartar boy are sitting beside a fire at night on the banks of a great Siberian river. Tolkovy is drinking vodka; the Tartar is frightened and depressed by Siberia and exile, but Tolkovy is totally unsympathetic: "You will get used to it [*privyknesh'*], he says." He expresses himself content with his lot. He argues that the secret for survival is not to want anything, not to expect anything, but to accept exile as it is. Desires, he says, only make one unhappy.

By way of illustration he tells the story of a man of gentry origin, Vasily Sergeich, who had been exiled for fraud, yet because he had money, he had been able to buy a house. Tolkovy would take him over on the ferry so that he could go to the post office in the local town to collect money sent to him from home. Tolkovy regards this as a bad sign: one should not want anything from outside. When Vasily Sergeich's wife, along with his young daughter, agrees to join him in Siberia, he is delighted and spends a lot of money on his wife to make life bearable for her. He now tells Tolkovy triumphantly that life is possible even in Siberia: "People live even in Siberia." Tolkovy is skeptical.

Unfortunately, Vasily's wife runs off with a lover. Vasily Sergeich tries to follow them but has to return empty-handed, and as he is being ferried back across the river in despair, Tolkovy mockingly reminds him of the reality behind his earlier words: "People live even in Siberia." In desperation, Vasily Sergeich does all he can to get himself a pardon to be allowed to go back to Russia. He writes constant petitions and crosses the river to go to the local post office, all to no avail.

Nevertheless he still has his daughter, and she is now growing up. He devotes all his attention and his love to her, and once more he is happy. Again he can tell Tolkovy that "people live even in Siberia. There is happiness even in Siberia." Tolkovy remains unconvinced. It is no life here for a young girl, he argues. Moreover, she soon falls ill from tuberculosis, and Vasily Sergeich is once more in despair. He now spends his time trying to get reasonable medical help for her in this Siberian backwater.

The Tartar does not like the moral that Tolkovy is trying to draw from this story. In his eyes Vasily Sergeich is right. It is better to have one day of happiness than nothing at all: "One day of happiness is better than nothing." He thinks of his own wife and mother and feels that he would be happy if they could join him here. He considers himself to have been wrongly convicted, that he is paying for the crime of his brothers and his uncle. Tolkovy's only comment is, "You will get used to it."

Having finished his story and his vodka, Tolkovy goes off to sleep with the other ferrymen in the hut, leaving the Tartar to dream by the fire. They are awakened by a demand for the ferry from the other side of the river. It is Vasily Sergeich. His daughter is worse, and he wishes to travel to another Siberian town, where, so he has heard, there is a new doctor. On the way across Tolkovy taunts him with his own words, "People live even in Siberia," and seems to derive real pleasure from Vasily Sergeich's predicament.

The Tartar is angry with Tolkovy and in his broken Russian tells him what he thinks of him: "You don't want anything; therefore you are not alive. You're a rock. You're clay. A rock doesn't want anything... You're a rock, and God does not love you, but he loves the nobleman."

The ferrymen laugh at this outburst and go back into the hut to sleep, leaving the Tartar outside by the fire. They hear a sound like a dog howling. It is the Tartar boy crying. Tolkovy's comment is his usual reaction: "He'll get used to it" (*privy-yknet*).

On the face of it, Tolkovy's philosophy of life might seem to be the only possible way to cope with the rigors of Siberia. Indeed, it has much in common with the commonsensical stoicism that will later characterize Solzhenitsyn's hero Ivan Denisovich and his view that one should be content with mere survival and live from day to day without trying to overreach oneself. Tolkovy is indeed a survivor. He is sixty and is strong and in good health. He was not born to the rough life of a peasant, however; as he boasts, he is the son of a church sexton and was used to wearing good clothing. Now, he claims, he has trained himself to sleep naked on the ground and to live off grass: "God grant everyone such a life. I don't want anything, and I am afraid of no one, and as I see myself, there's no man richer or freer than me." Such self-sufficiency should meet with approval. Here is a man who seems genuinely contented with what most would regard as less than the barest essentials of life. As he goes to sleep at the end of the story, he again proclaims his happiness: "'I am fine!' said Semyon as he dozed off. 'God grant everyone such a life.'"

Nevertheless, the moral validity of such an outlook, which in the harsh conditions of Siberian exile should be a positive philosophy for life and survival, is undermined by the evidence of the story itself. Tolkovy's vaunted self-sufficiency is entirely self-centered. The very circumstances in which he expounds his philosophy make this clear: he has some vodka left, and he prefers to remain outside with the non-drinking Tartar rather than to seek the shelter of the hut, where he would be expected to share his vodka with others. Tolkovy's egocentric self-sufficiency has turned him into "a stone," as the Tartar boy puts it. He shows no flicker of sympathy or compassion for the plight of the Tartar and positive delight at the recurrent problems of Vasily Sergeich, when they seem to vindicate his own philosophy of nondesire and nonaction.

It would, of course, be an exaggeration to call Semyon a philosopher. He is rather a man of common sense, as his nickname, Tolkovy, implies, and it is instructive to look at the way he himself uses the word *tolk* (sense). The fatalistic implications of Semyon's interpretation of *tolk* are clear from his reaction to Vasily Sergeich's desire to get urgent medical attention for his daughter: "'All right, you'll get there in time!' Tolkovy said in the tone of a man convinced that there is no need to hurry in this world. 'It's all the same, like, no sense will come of it [*vsë ravno, mol, tolku ne vyidet*].'" Not content with this gibe at

140

the distraught Vasily Sergeich, he seeks to develop this "commonsensical" point into a broader philosophical generality: "As if any sense [*tolk*] came out of traveling. But you yourself know that people are eternally traveling around both day and night, and there's just no sense [*tolk*]. That's a fact!" Tolkovy's commonsensical philosophizing is undermined by the reality of his own position, since a ferryman's material well-being depends on the constant traveling of others. It is through such understated ironies that Chekhov suggests the insubstantiality of Tolkovy's position. In this particular instance the irony is further compounded by the fact that the story itself came out of Chekhov's own traveling.

A paradox lies at the very heart of Tolkovy's philosophy. Thus he criticizes Vasily Sergeich's attempts to improve his lot: "'Yes,' I say to him, 'if fate has bitterly insulted you and me, then there's no point in begging its mercy and groveling before it. You must despise it and laugh at it. Otherwise fate itself will have a good laugh.'" But Tolkovy's way of laughing at fate is not to rebel against it: it is to accept it, and not even as something inevitable, but rather as something desirable. A welcoming passivity before fate is presented as a challenge to it; contempt is expressed through acceptance.

The elevation of the supine into an ideal may well have been one of the factors that so disconcerted Chekhov in his rereading of *Oblomov* the year before he undertook his Siberian journey. Oblomov's passivity and fatalism are clearly associated with an Asiatic element in Russian life. Thus his homeland, Oblomovka, is "almost in Asia," and the prime symbol of his outlook and way of life, his *khalat* (dressing gown), is characterized by its Asiatic features "without the slightest hint of Europe."[7] The ultimate irony of Chekhov's own treatment of this theme is that in this story it is the true Asiatic (who, significantly, comes from Goncharov's native province, Simbirsk) who denounces the fatalistic attitude to life, whereas its champion is the Russian with a nickname that proclaims him as the embodiment of "sense."

One cannot, of course, identify the nobleman Oblomov with the convict Tolkovy. Nevertheless, Goncharov had attempted to project through his hero a type he saw as quintessentially Russian in opposition to the Western values embodies in Shtolz, and Oblomovism, in its many forms, haunts the characters of Chekhov's own stories and plays. We see a similar supine fatalism in Dr. Ragin of "Ward Six" and in Dr. Chebutykin of the play *The Three Sisters*, for whom Tolkovy's (and Ragin's) phrase *vsë ravno* has become a set expression. In both these cases, as with Tolkovy himself, abnegation of responsibility is linked to drink; in spite of his apparently self-denying stoicism, Tolkovy does not forgo the pleasure of vodka. Indeed, he thinks that money, which Vasily Sergeich has spent on medical help for his daughter, would have been better spent on drink: "A terrible amount of money has gone on doctors, but what I think is it would have been better to spend this money on drink. She'll die all the same [*vsë ravno pomret*]."

The philosophical implications of the story are summed up in its concluding symbolism: "Everyone lay down. The door opened because of the wind, and snow blew into the hut. Nobody wanted to get up and shut the door: it was cold and too much bother. 'I am fine!' said Semyon as he dozed off. 'God grant everyone such a life.'" As they go to sleep, they hear the noise of the Tartar boy crying, to which Tolkovy adds his drawling comment: "He'll get used to it!" (*privy-yknet*). But the final words of the story are: "Soon even the others fell asleep, but the door remained, as it was, unshut." The moral is plain: no one is prepared to undertake the simplest of acts to ameliorate conditions either for himself or for others.

If Tolkovy embodies a form of fatalistic Oblomovism, then the overtones surrounding the Tartar boy are distinctly Dostoevskian. It is not merely that his words on "one day of happiness" would have been understood and approved by almost all the inmates of the House of the Dead, but he himself appears to have a Dostoevskian prototype; for in spite of Dostoevsky's veneration of the Russian common people, the most positive character in *The House of the Dead* is the Tartar boy Aley, who like Chekhov's own Tartar has been sent to Siberia because of the activities of his elder brothers.[8]

Moreover, the repeated phrase of Vasily Sergeich, "People live even in Siberia," seems to echo the positive attitudes of Dmitry Karamazov when he is faced with Siberia.[9] For him the human content of Siberian exile is epitomized by the men with little hammers, and in Chekhov's story "Gooseberries," which is a further attack on another variant of self-sufficient Oblomovism (and also, like "In Exile," ends on a symbolic note), the image of the man with the little hammer is projected as a universal image of human suffering and a necessary reminder to the self-obsessed of the "unfortunate ones" (the Dostoevskian word *neschastnye'* is used).[10]

The strongest attack on Oblomov-like values occurs in "Ward Six," a story that, like "In Exile," is the direct result of Chekhov's Siberian journey. Again there is a Dostoevskian echo, for the minor character of the Jew Moseika has obvious antecedents in *Notes from the House of the Dead*.[11] Critics who persist in seeing the story as an attack on Tolstoy's doctrine of nonresistance to evil are doing Tolstoy a great disservice. Tolstoy himself was a great resister of evil. He states his doctrine clearly: it is "nonresistance to evil by violence." Indeed, Tolstoy liked Chekhov's story and printed it in *Posrednik*. Chekhov's target is much wider than this. Gromov, the figure of the protester in the story, characterizes Ragin's ideas in a way that links them to Oblomov: "All this philosophy is most suited to the Russian lie-abed." The story also shows that religious fatalism can provide a similar pretext for nonaction. Ragin's helper, the medical assistant Sergey Sergeich, exhibits a comparable complacency before human suffering, though on a different philosophical basis: "We are ill, and suffer need because . . . we pray badly to the merciful Lord."[12]

Perhaps the most significant statement in the story is that of Gromov, repeated by Ragin at the end: "In Russia there is no philosophy, but everyone philosophizes, even the least significant of people." Tolkovy is certainly not one of the most significant of people, but he has pretensions to philosophy, and Gromov's statement links him with many characters in Chekhov who prefer philosophizing to taking action, notably Tuzenbakh and Vershinin in *The Three Sisters*.

If the outward journey across Siberia provided Chekhov with material for a negative evaluation of Russian fatalism, then the experience of his return trip by sea through the tropics seems to have softened his approach to the theme. The story "Gusev" is clearly related to this voyage, and it reveals an opposition of central characters similar to what we have seen in "In Exile" and "Ward Six." Gusev is a "submitter" (*smirennik*), and Pavel Ivanych is a "protester" (*protestant*) who, like Tolkovy, is of clerical stock. The submissive peasant soldier Gusev is portrayed in a positive light. He faces inevitable death with quiet, fatalistic resignation, and although he uses Tolkovy's phrase, "God grant everybody such a life" (*Dai Bog vsiakomu takoi zhizni*), nevertheless his last thoughts are that, if called on, he would be prepared to save a fellow Christian from drowning.[13]

Yet the story that appears to rework essential details of "In Exile" in the most positive light is "The Student." In "In Exile" Holy Week has already passed, but the riverside scene is wintry and bleak, and a sense of ancient timelessness is communicated through the image of the boat likened to an antediluvian creature with long paws. The setting in "The Student" is in European Russia near a river with a ferry, and although it is Good Friday, cold wintry weather has suddenly come to a landscape that, the student feels, has not changed since the time of Rurik. The story that Tolkovy told at the bonfire was of hope constantly betrayed, but the story told at the fire, in the growing dark, by a son of a deacon (the student) is of betrayal that unexpectedly turns into hope. It is the story of Peter's thrice denying Christ before the crowing of the cock. Cocks also crow in the earlier tale, but the weeping of the Tartar strikes no sympathetic chord in those around him, whereas the tears of Peter in the student's story evoke those of Vasilisa, a widow, who is listening to it.

The influence his story has on Vasilisa and her daughter, two simple women, makes the student realize the link between past and present in a way that seems to refute his earlier feelings about the bleak Russian landscape with its suggestion of eternal gloom and oppression. Like Dostoevsky's Zosima, he perceives that everything is interconnected, that events are a chain, and that when one touches one end the other end trembles, that beauty, truth, and justice are, and always have been, at work guiding human life.[14] If "In Exile" suggests a psychological correspondence between an eternally remorseless landscape and the attitude of those condemned to live in it, then "The Student" points to the way in which faith and art can give inner meaning to the bleakness of the external world. The narrow, fatalistic acceptance of one's own lot can only make sense in the context of the chain linking all human fates, both past and present.

The examples of Goncharov and Dostoevsky may well have been in Chekhov's mind as he undertook the great Siberian exploit, and their artistic influence can certainly be detected in the stories resulting from it. Yet, as we have also seen, in treating the theme of Russian fatalism, Chekhov portrays supine Oblomovism in all its forms as negative, whereas Dostoevsky's more metaphysical concept of humility appears to meet with some authorial approval.

Liza Knapp

Fear and Pity in "Ward Six":

Chekhovian Catharsis

IN THE middle of "Ward Six" (Palata No. 6, 1892), Chekhov notes in passing that "people who are fond of visiting insane asylums are few in this world."[1] And yet Chekov has conspired to make the reader of his story feel like an actual visitor in the mental ward of a provincial hospital. After an initial paragraph describing the exterior of the hospital, he invites the reader to enter the hospital premises with him as a guide: "If you are not afraid of being stung by the nettles, let us go along the narrow path." As soon becomes apparent, these nettles are not all the visitor to ward 6 or the reader of "Ward Six" need fear. Warnings of the perils and hardships of a journey to this godforsaken place recall the beginning of Dante's *Divine Comedy*, for to enter ward 6 is indeed to "abandon all hope."

Chekhov found himself writing this story, one he considered uncharacteristic and in some ways unappealing, since it "stinks of the hospital and mortuary," in 1892, less than two years after his journey to the penal colony of Sakhalin.[2] As he worked on "Ward Six," a fictional "visit" to an insane asylum, Chekhov had for various reasons interrupted work on the factual, scholarly account of his visit to the penal colony. Still, in many ways, "Ward Six" was a response to the trip, a response more indirect, in form, than *The Island of Sakhalin*, but, in essence, perhaps just as immediate.[3]

That mental wards and penal institutions were associated in Chekhov's mind is demonstrated by a series of comparisons made in the story. In the first paragraph he mentions "that particular desolate, godforsaken look which is exclusive to our hospital and prison buildings." When Dr. Ragin first puts on his hospital *khalat*, he feels "like a convict." At one point, ward 6 is called a "little Bastille." Repeated references to the bars over the windows of ward 6 emphasize its likeness to a prison: lack of physical freedom and of human dignity is suffered in both places.

Chekhov directly formulates the link between these two locales in a letter he wrote to Suvorin, explaining his motivation for visiting Sakhalin. "The much-glorified sixties," writes Chekhov, "did *nothing* for the sick and for prisoners and thereby violated the chief commandment of Christian civilization."[4] Chekhov believed that he and others shared a collective responsibility for eliminating, alleviating, or at the very least acknowledging the suffering that takes place, with an exceptionally high concentration, in these two locales, penal institutions and hospitals, places that nobody wants to visit, much less, of course, to inhabit.[5]

In this spirit, Chekhov visited the island of Sakhalin, this "place of unbearable suffering of the sort only man, whether free or subjugated, is capable of."[6] Chekhov visited Sakhalin partly because he felt that it was time that Russia stopped ignoring the suffering that went on there.[7] He wrote: "It is evident that we have let *millions* of people rot in jails, we have let them rot to no purpose, unthinkingly and barbarously. We have driven people through the cold, in chains, across tens of thousands of versts, we have infected them with syphylis, debauched them, bred criminals and blamed it all on red-nosed prison wardens. Now all educated Europe knows that all of us, not the wardens, are to blame."[8] Furthermore, he tells Suvorin that were he a "sentimental man, [he'd] say that we ought to make pilgrimages to places like Sakhalin the way the Turks go to Mecca."

"Ward Six" stands as the literary equivalent of a pilgrimage, not to a penal colony, but to an analogous place, a mental ward, with its own "red-nosed warden," whose guilt, Chekhov would have us believe, we all share. The point of a pilgrimage, be it that of a Muslim to Mecca, a Christian to Golgotha, a Russian subject to Sakhalin, or Chekhov's reader to ward 6, is to gain greater understanding of another's experience and suffering (Muhammad's, Christ's, an inmate's) by imitating the experience and suffering of another, by following physically in another's footsteps. Pilgrims do whatever they can to make the other's experience their own. They may not be able to duplicate what the other has lived through, but they can try to find out what it is like. The experience of a pilgrimage becomes the empirical equivalent of a simile.

The premise of Chekhov's story, like that of a pilgrimage, is that suffering cannot be understood in the abstract. One needs to have it made as immediate as possible. That reading Chekhov's story has the effect of making one feel as if one were in ward 6 has been attested by many of its readers, prominent among them being Vladimir Lenin, who commented: "When I finished reading the story last night, I started to feel literally sick; I couldn't stay in my room. I got up and went out. I felt as if I, too, had been incarcerated in Ward 6."[9] Such a statement suggests more than the notion that, as Leskov put it, "Ward 6 is everywhere. It's Russia," for it also reveals what seems to have been Chekhov's intent in the story: to play on the reader's emotions so that he or she feels what it is like to be locked up in ward 6.[10]

In evoking in the reader a response to the suffering that is witnessed in ward 6, Chekhov aims at evoking pity and fear, the same emotions that, according to Aristotle, a good tragedy will evoke in its audience. In his *Poetics*, Aristotle defines *pity* as the emotion we feel for undeserved suffering and *fear* as the emotion we feel when we witness the suffering of someone like ourselves.[11] Aristotelian pity and fear at times cease to be two discrete emotions, since, as one scholar puts it, "we pity others where under like circumstances we should fear for ourselves. Those who are incapable of fear are incapable also of pity."[12] Both emotions are related to the concept of *philanthropia*, or love for one's fellow man, which for the Greeks meant that one should have sympathy for one's fellow man, this sympathy stemming from a recognition of solidarity with others. One should take another's "misfortunes as a warning of one's own insecurity." Tragic events reveal "the precariousness of the human condition" and thus "make men fear for themselves." At the root of the fear is a recognition that one is much like the tragic protagonist, that one is "endowed with similar capacities and exposed to similar dangers."[13]

Fear, as understood by Aristotle, is predicated upon the recognition, however subliminal, of a similarity between the self and the other whose suffering is witnessed. The basic mental operation involved is the same as that described by Aristotle elsewhere in the *Poetics* when he discusses similes and metaphors, which are based on the intuition of similarites between different phenomena. In recognizing similarities between disparate phenomena, we should not go so far as to equate them. At the same time that we recognize similarities, we must bear the differences in mind. We need not have lived through what tragic heroes live through; rather, we, as audience, put ourselves in their place and fall into a mood in which, according to Butcher, "we feel that we too are liable to suffering."[14] Tragedy thus has the effect of making the public less complacent and of reminding them that their own good fortune may be precarious.

A strategy to be learned from Greek tragedy and epic is that if you want another to take pity on you and do something for you—for example, to give your father asylum (Antigone in *Oedipus at Colonus*) or to surrender your son's body for burial (Priam in *The Iliad*)—the best way is to make that person fearful. You make that person realize that what you are suffering could happen to him or her. Hence, Antigone tells the people of Colonus who were shunning her and her father to look on her "as if [she] were a child of [theirs]" and to "take pity on [her] unhappiness."[15] By bringing her plight home to them in this manner, Antigone gains their sympathy. Similarly, Priam, trying to get Achilles to give him Hector's body, tells him: "Take pity upon me remembering your father." He creates fear in Achilles by reminding him that his own father will be in an analogous situation, since Achilles is fated to die soon. The strategy works, for, as "he spoke, [Priam] stirred in [Achilles] a passion of grieving for his own father," and this, in turn, moved Achilles to relinquish Hector's body.[16] These Greek heroes implicitly realize that fear for oneself serves as a catalyst for bringing about pity for another, insofar as people use themselves as a point of reference.

Chekhov demonstrates his understanding of the dynamics of Aristotelian fear and pity in "The Duel," written in 1891, a year before "Ward Six." We are told that earlier when Laevsky loved Nadezhda Fedorovna, her suffering (in the form of her illness) "evoked pity and fear in him" (*vozbuzhdala v nem zhalost' i strakh*), whereas once that love has been obscured, he no longer responds empathetically to her suffering.[17] Although Chekhov mentions these Aristotelian concepts in a seemingly casual way, they appear to be central to "The Duel," especially to the moments of tragic recognition it describes.

In "Ward Six" Chekhov explores the mechanics of pity and fear on two levels: not only does he seek to arouse these emotions in his readers as they witness the suffering of the inmates, but he also makes pity and fear dynamic forces within the story, by having the main drama result from the fact that neither of the two protagonists can respond adequately when he witnesses the suffering of others. In Dr. Ragin, the capacity for experiencing fear and pity has atrophied, whereas in Gromov it has hypertrophied.

Already an inmate of ward 6 when the action begins, Ivan Dmitrich Gromov suffers from a "persecution mania." Although a series of personal misfortunes had left him in an unstable mental state, excessive fear, leading to his mental collapse and incarceration, was triggered when he found himself the chance witness to the misfortune of others. We are told that Gromov was going about his business one autumn day when "in one of the side streets, he came upon two convicts in chains accompanied by four armed guards. Ivan Dmitrich had often encountered convicts and they always aroused in him feelings of pity and discomfort, but this time he was strangely and unaccountably affected. For some reason he suddenly felt that he *too* could be clapped in irons and led in this same way through the mud to prison." At the sight of the convicts, Gromov realizes that he is exposed to similar dangers, and the result is fear. But his anxiety then develops into a persecution

complex that debilitates him and threatens to engulf all else, even his
pity for other people.

> At home he was haunted all day by these convicts and soldiers with
> rifles, and an inexplicable mental anxiety prevented him from reading
> or concentrating. He did not light his lamp in the evening and at night
> he was unable to sleep, but kept thinking that he too could be arrested,
> clapped in irons, and thrown into prison. He knew of no crime in his
> past and was confident that in the future he would never be guilty of
> murder, arson or theft, but was it not possible to commit a crime by
> accident, without meaning to, and was not calumny too, or even a
> judicial error, conceivable?

Gromov's feeling of "there but for the grace of God go I," his initial
sympathetic pity for the convicts, and the concomitant fear for himself
quickly give way to a nearly psychopathic self-pity as he imagines his
own arrest for a crime he did not commit. In a dangerous mental leap,
Gromov goes from a wise recognition that such misfortune is something
that could happen to him to the unhealthy delusion that it was hap-
pening to him, or was about to.

To a certain degree, Chekhov may be using Gromov's fear of judicial
error to draw attention to the prevailing lack of faith in Russian justice.
Indeed, in Sakhalin, Chekhov had learned of many cases of people
being convicted of crimes they did not commit.[18] Gromov's fears of
incarceration become a self-fulfilling prophecy when he ends up im-
prisoned in ward 6. From the Aristotelian point of view, were Gromov
nothing more than the innocent victim of the obviously flawed Russian
system, his situation would shock the reader but not evoke the deeper
emotions of fear and pity; in the *Poetics*, Aristotle argues that the
misfortune of a completely innocent man is more "shocking" than "fearful and pitiful."[19] Chekhov appears to make Gromov into something of
a tragic hero, one whose particular flaw may be seen as his tendency
to excess in his response to the world. In what may be a reference to
Aristotle's ethical ideal of the golden mean, we are told that, with
Gromov, "there was no middle ground" (*serediny zhe ne bylo*). Gromov's
tragic flaw lies in his immoderate response to the suffering of others.

In contrast, Dr. Andrei Efimych Ragin, who is in charge of the
ward, shut his eyes to the suffering he witnesses. At one point, Gromov
notes that heartlessness may be an occupational hazard afflicting judges,
physicians, and police, that is, people who "have an official, professional
relation to other men's suffering." Dr. Ragin's callousness may be related
to this phenomenon.[20] The doctor's indifference to suffering manifests
itself in his motto, "It's all the same" (*vsë ravno*). He elevates this
colloquial verbal tick to the status of a general philosophical view that
nothing matters. But the phrase literally means that it is all the same,

that all is equivalent, that everything is like everything else, that there is no difference between one thing and another. In other words, Ragin sees false similarities or equivalencies. When he asserts the similarity between a comfortable study and ward 6, between a frock coat and an inmate's smock, the doctor vilely abuses the capacity for contemplating likenesses that, according to Aristotle, is the tool of the philosopher.[21]

Dr. Ragin, in insisting that everything is equivalent, recalls the "philosopher" Chekhov refers to in *The Island of Sakhalin* when he writes of convicts that "if he is not a philosopher, for whom it is all the same where and under what conditions he lives, the convict can't, and shouldn't, not want to escape."[22] In Chekhov's lexicon, the term *philosopher* stands as a pejorative epithet for someone who has withdrawn into his mind. The blind assertion of similarities between disparate phenomena, such as Dr. Ragin practices, constitutes a disregard for the physical world and for life itself.

At the time he wrote "Ward Six," Chekhov had been reading the *Meditations* of Marcus Aurelius, who preached a mix of philanthropy and retirement within the self. "If you are doing what is right," claims Marcus Aurelius, "never mind whether you are freezing with cold or beside a good fire; heavy-eyed or fresh from a sound sleep."[23] In his long conversations with Gromov, Dr. Ragin echoes this notion of the equivalence of all physical states and the primacy of the inner world of the self. When Ragin presents Gromov with such platitudes as "In any physical environment you can find solace within yourself" or "The common man looks for good or evil in external things: a carriage, a study, while the thinking man looks for them within himself," Gromov counsels him to "go preach that philosophy in Greece, where it's warm and smells of oranges; it's not suited to the climate here." His point is that the doctor, in asserting the equivalence of all external things, uses his own comfortable existence as his point of reference. The more Gromov argues that there is a difference in climate between Russia and Greece, that there is a difference between being hungry and having enough to eat, that there is a difference between being beaten and not, the more it becomes apparent that Ragin's tragic flaw lies in his unwillingness to concede these differences.

For Chekhov, such differences were quite real, and philosophical pessimism such as Ragin's was anathema to him. In a letter of 1894, in which he reveals his views on some of the issues explored in "Ward Six," Chekhov directly suggests that his own commitment to progress results from the fact that differences between various physical states (differences of the kind ignored by Ragin) mattered to him. He writes: "I acquired my belief in progress when still a child; I couldn't help believing in it, because the difference between the period when they flogged me and the period when they stopped flogging me was enormous."[24] Life had schooled him in such a way that he strove to improve physical conditions in an attempt to alleviate suffering. Dr. Ragin, in maintaining that "it is all futile, senseless," and that "there is essentially no difference between the best Viennese clinic and [this] hospital," violates the values of the medical profession, since, from Chekhov's point of view, doctors ought to believe in material progress.[25]

In "Ward Six" Chekhov points out the root meaning of the doctor's indifference: as he ceases to perceive the differences among real phenomena, the world becomes one big, senseless simile where everything is like everything else, or one big, senseless tautology.[26] In keeping with this worldview, he fails to respond to the suffering around him. The phrase that he keeps repeating to Gromov, "What is there to fear?" (*chego boiat'sia?*), is the Aristotelian corollary of "It's all the same" (*vsë ravno*).[27] Dr. Ragin does nothing to alleviate the suffering he witnesses because he is indifferent to it; he feels no fear and consequently no pity. Whereas Gromov was overcome by manic fear and self-pity, Ragin shows an exaggerated indifference to the suffering of others. But for both, the net result is the same: incarceration in ward 6. Gromov suggests that Ragin fails to respond to the suffering of others because he has never suffered himself. According to Gromov, Ragin's acquaintance with reality (which for Gromov is synonymous with 'suffering) has remained theoretical. Having never been beaten as a child, having never gone hungry, the doctor has had no firsthand knowledge of suffering and no conception of what it is to need.

All this changes when Dr. Ragin himself becomes an inmate in ward 6. At first, as Nikita takes away his clothes, Ragin clings to his indifference: "'It's all the same [*vsë ravno*]...' thought Andrei Efimych [Ragin], modestly drawing the dressing gown around him and feeling that he looked like a convict in his new costume. 'It's all the same [*vsë ravno*]... Whether it's a frockcoat, a uniform, or this robe, it's all the same [*vsë ravno*]' ... Andrei Efimych was convinced even now that there was no difference between Byelova's house [his former residence] and Ward No. 6." But soon, the physical differences that the doctor had so long denied become apparent:

Nikita quickly opened the door, and using both hands and his knee, roughly knocked Andrei Efimych to one side, then drew back his fist and punched him in the face. Andrei Efimych felt as though a huge salty wave had broken over his head and was dragging him back to his bed; there was, in fact, a salty taste in his mouth, probably blood from his teeth. Waving his arms as if trying to emerge, he caught hold of somebody's bed, and at that moment felt two more blows from Nikita's fists in his back.

Ivan Dmitrich [Gromov] screamed loudly. He too was evidently being beaten.

Then all was quiet. The moon shed its pale light through the bars, and on the floor lay a shadow that looked like a net. It was terrible. Andrei Efimich lay still, holding his breath, waiting in terror to be struck again. He felt as if someone had taken a sickle, thrust it into his body, and twisted it several times in his chest and bowels. He bit the pillow and clenched his teeth with pain; and all of a sudden out of the chaos there clearly flashed through his mind the dreadful, unbearable thought that these people, who now looked like black shadows in the moonlight, must have experienced this same pain day in and day out for years. How could it have happened that in the course of more than twenty years he had not known, had refused to know this? Having no conception of pain, he could not possibly have known it, so he was not guilty, but his conscience, no less inexorable and implacable than Nikita, made him turn cold from head to foot.

Only when he himself experiences physical pain does Dr. Ragin know what fear is: He waited "in terror to be struck again." The question, "What is there to fear?" (*chego boiat'sia?*) is no longer a rhetorical one; one answer is pain. Only now does he sense his true kinship with Gromov and others, for now he understands the suffering that he had witnessed day in and day out for years (or which he would have witnessed had he gone to work every day as he was supposed to).

In this story, Chekhov explores the epistemology of suffering and seems to suggest that the surest route to an understanding of suffering is to experience it directly, for yourself. This is ultimately what happens to Dr. Ragin at the end of "Ward Six." But by the time Dr. Ragin gets an idea of what the inmates of ward 6 have endured day in and day out, he is about to die, having, in a sense, been destroyed by his realization, and he can do nothing about it.

Chekhov outlines a tragic situation for which there are many precedents. For example, what happens to Ragin is similar to what happens to King Lear, who takes pity on what he refers to as "houseless heads and unfed sides" only after he, too, finds himself homeless and hungry. Lear realizes that when he had been in a position to help those in need, he had "ta'en / Too little care of this!" If you want to know what suffering is like, then you should "expose [your]self to feel what wretches feel."[28] But the physical suffering of feeling what powerless wretches feel, combined with mental anguish, kills Lear. Like Lear, Ragin realizes that he had neglected both his professional and his human duties only when it is too late to do anything about them.

Although he presents tragic situations of this sort, Chekhov refuses to romanticize suffering. It may heighten consciousness, or as Ragin argues, it may indeed differentiate man's life from that of an amoeba, but at the same time it destroys the physical organism, and under such circumstances the enlightenment serves little practical purpose. An essential difference exists between the fear experienced by the witness of mimetic suffering and that experienced by the witness (and especially by the victim) of actual suffering. The latter debilitates, whereas the former, according to Aristotle, does not. As one critic puts it, "Tragic fear, though it may send an inward shudder through the blood, does not paralyze the mind or stir the senses, as does the direct vision of some impending calamity. And the reason is that this fear, unlike the fear of common reality, is based on the imaginative union with another's life. The spectator is lifted out of himself. He becomes one with the tragic sufferer and through him with humanity at large."[29] For the inmates of ward 6, fear stuns, paralyzes, and even kills. But the reader who "visits" ward 6 may, by being "lifted out of himself," learn from the fear witnessed through the medium of art. The reader may even be motivated to act on behalf of the sick and prisoners, thereby fulfilling what Chekhov referred to as "the chief commandment of Christian civilization."[30]

According to Aristotelian scholars, "the purpose of the catharsis of pity and fear is not to drain our emotional capacities so that we are no longer able to feel these emotions; instead it is to predispose us to feel emotion in the right way, at the right time, towards the right object, with the right motive, and to the proper degree."[31] The protagonists of Chekhov's story fail to undergo catharsis upon witnessing the actual suffering of others. The pity and fear Gromov experienced as he watched the convicts' suffering became pathological, developed into a mania, and found no outlet, whereas Ragin for years exhibited a pathological inability to feel pity and fear upon witnessing the suffering of others. He fears and pities only when the suffering becomes his own. But these emotions are not purged; on the contrary, they, combined with the physical pain they accompany, destroy the doctor.

Chekhov arouses fear and pity in his reader by making the suffering of others seem real and matter to the reader, who in this way is spared the actual trip to ward 6, spared actually putting on an inmate's smock, and, above all, spared actually being beaten by Nikita. To this end, Chekhov makes the fictional (mental) visit to ward 6 as vivid as possible. He concentrates on physical details, on the stench of the place that makes you feel as though "you've entered a menagerie," on the bars on the window, and so forth, lest the reader ever try to ignore the difference between a comfortable study and ward 6.

In trying to evoke fear and pity in the reader, Chekhov employs many similes, the simile itself being the poetic device that, by suggesting a physical image for something, "undoes the withdrawal from the physical world of appearances which characterizes mental activities."[32] Since "Ward Six" is about, among other things, the perils of withdrawing from the physical world into an abstract world of mental activity, the simile becomes a particularly important literary device. Chekhov uses the simile to rouse the reader and force him or her back into the physical world. He uses it as an antidote to the indifference resulting from withdrawal into one's self. In the passage describing the doctor's first beating and the tragic recognition it brings about within him, Chekhov uses a series of similes: the taste of blood in Ragin's mouth is compared to a salty wave breaking over his head, the pain of being beaten is compared to that of having a sickle thrust into his body; more interestingly, Ragin's conscience is compared to Nikita. Chekhov uses these similes to make what Ragin undergoes more vivid and real to the reader, who may never have been beaten and who may also be tempted to use ignorance as a moral subterfuge. "Ward Six" is affective and effective largely because Chekhov makes proper, judicious, and artistic use of the very faculty that is impaired in his two heroes, Gromov and Ragin, the faculty for contemplating similarities. Their respective disorders, which are two extremes of the same continuum, prevent them from experiencing fear and pity in a healthy, moderate, cathartic fashion.

Chekhov uses his literary skills, especially his artistic faculty for contemplating likenesses, to encourage his readers to empathize with the inmates of ward 6, to recognize the full horror of ward 6 by feeling that there is a kinship between them and the inmates.[33] He does not lose sight, however, of the fact that differences exist. One difference is that the fictional visitor to ward 6, unlike the inmate, may have the actual power, freedom, and/or strength to fight to eliminate senseless suffering. The inmate is locked in ward 6, but the reader is not. The reader should not, in Chekhov's words, simply "sit within [his] four walls and complain what a mess God has made of creating man."[34]

Echoes and Allusions

Joseph L. Conrad

Chekhov's "Volodya": Transformations of

Turgenev's "First Love"

IN LIGHT of the considerable Russian-language scholarship tying Anton Chekhov's works to those of Ivan Turgenev, it is
curious that no connection has yet been made between "Volodya" (1887)
and "First Love" (1860).[1] Numerous Western studies have illuminated
the Tolstoy-Chekhov link, but less attention has been paid to thematic
and stylistic similarities between Chekhov's works and those of Turgenev. Chekhov often read and discussed Turgenev's prose, yet he seems
never to have mentioned or alluded to "First Love." The present examination of the two stories will show that Chekhov must indeed have
begun "Volodya" with Turgenev's tale in mind. Whereas "First Love,"
however elegantly written, seems rooted in the middle of nineteenth-
century Russia, Chekhov's treatment of Turgenev's material increases
the importance of the story's primary themes for Chekhov's time and
for ours. His adaptation and inversion of the themes of first love and
death, and many lesser details, transformed the substance of Turgenev's
story from a wistful memoir into a significant probe of adolescent
psychology.

At first it may seem that "Volodya" and "First Love" are an unlikely
pair for comparison. Turgenev's novella is a largely autobiographical
reminiscence by a mature narrator, framing the story of his youthful
awakening to the emotions of love, jealousy, and passion; the resolution
of those emotions brings the narrator to a greater personal understanding of human relations and of the nature of love itself. Chekhov's om-
niscient narrator portrays a teenager's first sensations of sexual desire,
sensations that trigger emotions of shame, guilt, and despair: the story
focuses on these emotions and then culminates in the boy's suicide. This
emphasis makes Chekhov's story much more immediate for readers of
our time as it did for those of his own.

Numerous heretofore overlooked similarities suggest that Chekhov
utilized, adapted, and transposed features of Turgenev's tale when he

157

began "Volodya." Certain shared details beg examination. Turgenev's narrator, Vladimir Petrovich, was sixteen and spending the summer at his parents' dacha when he fell in love with a neighbor, Princess Zinaida, five years his senior. In many ways a typically Turgenevian heroine, she was an enigmatic, willful young woman.[2] She normally addressed her adolescent admirer as Monsieur Woldemar, but once, when introducing her younger brother to him, she said: "Here's a companion for you, Volodya. His name is Volodya, too."[3]

Here it may be useful to note that the names of the male protagonists in each story are significant. Vladimir, which is popularly derived from Russian *vladet'* + *mir*, suggests "rule in peace" and, perhaps by extension, "be in self-control." Vladimir Petrovich's surname is not indicated, but his patronymic is derived from Pyotr (Petr), which in turn is based on the Greek *petra*, "rock cliff." Thus, Turgenev's mature narrator is indeed appropriately named, for he is calm and reflective and has already weathered the storms of youth. When the youthful persona of Vladimir Petrovich is called Woldemar by Zinaida, the European form assigns him particular distinction among her admirers and focuses the reader's attention on him. Chekhov's use of the diminutive Volodya for his protagonist underscores the fact that those around him do not take him seriously and at first leads the reader to do likewise: it seems to be, after all, only a tale about a lad. The selection of title and name for his creation must have been intended to suggest irony, for his protagonist is able neither to live in peace with his environment nor to rule himself, and his situation turns out to be far more serious than the reader expects.

The coincidence of first names becomes still more important when we consider that Chekhov entitled the original version of his story "His First Love" (Ego pervaia liubov'); there he treated an eighteen-year-old's infatuation with Niuta, an older, and married, friend of his mother's. For the somewhat revised and expanded version published in his collection *Gloomy People* (Khmurye liudi, 1890), Chekhov lowered Volodya's age to seventeen (bringing it closer to Woldemar's sixteen), developed further the boy's confused emotions, and introduced the motif of suicide.

Similarities in titles, names, and ages are not the only details linking the stories. Both male protagonists are shy, insecure adolescents. Each is an only child, reared largely by his mother: Woldemar's father is cold and distant, and Volodya's father died some years prior to the events of the tale. Moreover, each boy is troubled by an impending examination. Yet instead of studying diligently, each prefers to sit outside—Woldemar in the garden and Volodya in a garden gazebo (*v besedke*)—where they dream of conquering the objects of their desire.

Each is also destined to experience the conflicting emotions of sexual attraction for the first time. Turgenev's treatment is almost ethereal. His mature narrator writes of his earlier, adolescent sensations of love and desire: "I remember, at that time the image of woman, the phantom of feminine love, almost never arose in definite outlines in my mind: but in all that I dreamed, in everything I felt, there was hidden the half-conscious, embarrassing premonition of something new, unspeakably sweet, and feminine... This premonition, this expectation, penetrated my whole body: I breathed of it, it flowed through my veins in every drop of blood... and it was soon to take place." Turgenev's narrator confesses that he found in Zinaida something "so enchanting, imperious, caressing, mocking, and dear" that he "would have given everything in the world at that moment" to have her attention.[4] Yet he is embarrassed before her and is somewhat offended that she treats him as if he were a child. As we shall see, Turgenev's description of Woldemar's youthful ardor differs considerably from Chekhov's treatment of Volodya's sensual experience, his probe of the boy's disturbed psyche, and the human loss represented by Volodya's suicide.

Here it should be noted that there is a previously unremarked sexual aspect to Woldemar's first love that was perhaps an important stimulus for Chekhov's story. While it may have remained sublimated for the young, inexperienced Woldemar, recognition of his sexual interest in Zinaida seems to be acknowledged by Vladimir Petrovich's description, which tells us that he was enchanted by her "downy, golden hair, her virginal neck, her sloping shoulders, and her tender, calm bosom." He confesses that he "would have gladly caressed every fold of her dress" (an early galley proof had "gladly kissed") and continues: "The tips of her shoes peeped from under her skirt: I could have knelt in adoration to those shoes!" (an earlier version had "to her feet"). His all-too-obvious interest was to prompt Zinaida to comment, "How you do look at me!" and to shake a finger at him in reproach.

The sight of Zinaida was not the only factor pleasing to Woldemar: other sensory perceptions were aroused during a game of forfeits when their faces were together under her white silk kerchief. The narrator remembers that both their heads "were suddenly plunged in a close, semitransparent, fragrant darkness; how near and how softly her eyes shone in this darkness," and he recalls "the burning breath of her parted lips and the glint of her teeth and how her hair tickled and set me on fire." Zinaida again noticed the effect she had on his awakening sexuality, but her immediate response was to "smile mysteriously and playfully [*lukavo*]" and to challenge him with a whispered "Well, what is it?"[5] The effect of so much sensory stimulation was immediate: he blushed and had difficulty breathing. As we consider their behavior from afar, Zinaida was apparently amused and was only gently teasing Woldemar; but he was transported to a state of ecstasy so that her strong, sharp blows on his fingers were both painful and pleasurable. Woldemar's emotional and sensory reactions suggest those of an aroused libido and lead us toward Chekhov's protagonist.

Vladimir Petrovich tells us that there were many new sensations (each of which was also to be experienced by Chekhov's Volodya): young Woldemar "languished" in her absence, thought of her "days on end," and was jealous yet felt unworthy; he "stupidly exaggerated" his own importance and felt an "insurmountable force" (*nepobedimaia sila*) draw him to her. Zinaida "enjoyed his passion," made a fool of him, "amused herself" with him, and "tormented" him. (All these actions were to be repeated by Volodya's own temptress.) Yet approximately from this point, Turgenev turns the reader's interest to Zinaida's own first love, for Woldemar's father, and soon reveals a third first love, that of Woldemar's father for Zinaida, which appears even more unexpectedly. Unhappily married, Woldemar's father has found love too late.

In composing "Volodya," Chekhov indeed seems to have appropriated details from Turgenev's "First Love."[6] Yet he inverted others; for example, Chekhov's Volodya is also spending time at a rented dacha, but his mother is an impoverished widow. Thus, contrary to the situation in "First Love," where Woldemar's mother was a wealthy member of the nobility and Zinaida's mother was of the impoverished gentry, Volodya is a guest of Niuta's rich cousin. He senses acutely that he and his mother are considered "poor relations." And like Woldemar, who had recently read Schiller's *The Robbers* (Die Räuber, 1781) Volodya is given to fancy; but instead of repeating Woldemar's conventionally early romantic notions, he is beset by dark, brooding thoughts.[7]

A number of relatively more important aspects, taken together, reinforce the suspicion that Chekhov had Turgenev's story in mind. For example, Volodya loathes Niuta's husband, much as Woldemar hated Zinaida's admirers, with the intense passion of Woldemar as he sought out his rival. Like Woldemar, Volodya is unduly ashamed and feels that everyone treats him like a child, yet he boldly seeks out an affair (*intrizhka;* the diminutive suggests that it will be common, even vulgar) with the older woman. Volodya's naïveté in pursuing that "little intrigue" leads directly to his destiny: like Woldemar, he would sacrifice everything to have the love object. And his first reaction to the sex act is that the experience is one for which he could give his whole life. Ironically, he does.

Chekhov supplies a realistic basis for Volodya's youthful emotional confusion. In contrast to the vague longings of Turgenev's Woldemar and his casual neglect of his studies, Volodya is beset by three specific problems, each of which increases the pressure on his transition from child to adult: he must pass an examination in mathematics the following day, or he will fail yet another year in high school; he is greatly disturbed by his mother's ingratiatory posturing before their wealthy relatives; and he is unsettled by the initial sensations of sexual arousal that he is experiencing. Unable to discuss his concerns with his mother (or anyone else), he is terribly alone. These are grave problems for a boy on the threshold of manhood, and they well indicate Volodya's adolescent disquiet, but the first two figure less prominently in the story than does his emergent sexuality.

Chekhov's treatment of Volodya's third problem is more realistically presented than Turgenev's description of Woldemar's daydreaming. In the second paragraph of Chekhov's first version we read: "Not even for a minute could the boy get rid of that strange new feeling that was oppressing and irritating him. A whole month had passed during which the thought of Anna Fedorovna [Niuta] would not go out of his mind." The narrator informs us that Volodya is aware of the difference between his sexual urge and the romantic dreams of previous literary heroes: "That desire was not at all like the pure, poetic love that he knew from novels: it was new and sweet, but he was ashamed of it and decidedly afraid of it as something so bad and dirty [nekhoroshii i nechistyi] that it was difficult to admit it even to himself."[8] Chekhov has increased the impact of these sensations on the reader by introducing the epithet nechistyi, which often suggests a situation or location lacking in protection from demonic spirits. While the devil may indeed be stalking Volodya, nechistyi would seem to be used here in the modern sense of "dirty" and "forbidden."

Chekhov's original portrayal of the emotional torment experienced by a young person when faced with these new sensations elevates his story to a far more meaningful exploration of the theme of first love and one with broader implications than those of Turgenev's lovely, yet personal, memoir. Likewise, the theme of death, which gives an elegiac cast to Turgenev's story, becomes a more compelling factor in Chekhov. Chekhov transposes the melancholy contemplation of inevitable death closing "First Love" into a stark demonstration of pointless suicide, which has an unsettling impact on the reader of his tale.

Let us examine Chekhov's treatment of the two themes in detail. The emotion-charged, earthy attraction of Niuta and her conscious seduction of Volodya are very different from the effect of Zinaida's youthful beauty on Woldemar and her role-playing as his queen to elicit his admiration. For example, Vladimir Petrovich remembers Zinaida as a "tall, well-built young woman in a striped pink dress with a white scarf on her head" and tells us that his "eyes devoured this graceful figure, the slender neck, the beautiful arms . . . the intelligent eye . . . the lashes and delicate cheek"; these are the features that captivated young Woldemar. For comparison, consider Chekhov's description of the sensual Niuta:

> She was full of motion, a loud and mocking woman, about thirty, healthy, full of figure, pink-complexioned, with round shoulders, a round, full chin, and with a constant smile on her thin lips. She was not pretty and not young—Volodya knew that well, but he could not tear his eyes from her when, having thrown both arms back to her neck, she would straighten her hair, bare her elbows with their dimples, or when playing croquet would shrug her round shoulders and move her smooth back, or, after a long laugh and a run up the stairs, would fall into the armchair and, breathing heavily, would move her nostrils and act as if her breasts were confined and [she were] out of breath.

Given nineteenth-century standards, this description borders on the erotic. Niuta does share some features with Zinaida (e.g., she is older than her admirer, and she is active, has a constant, often mocking smile, and has a healthy pink complexion and round shoulders), but she is a very mundane version of Turgenev's romantic heroine.[9]

Both Turgenev and Chekhov carefully selected names for their characters. And just as was the case for the male protagonists, those of the heroines indicate their personalities and respective functions: Zinaida Aleksandrovna Zasekina's given name is from the genitive singular form of the Greek "Zeus," that is, *zenos* (the equivalent Russian epithet would be *bozhestvennaia*, "divine") and is thus properly suggestive of the goddesslike role she plays before her entourage of somewhat older men, as well as of young Woldemar's devotion to her. Her patronymic stems from the Greek *aleks-*, "to defend," "ward off," and *aner*, genitive singular of *andros*, "man." At first she does indeed appear to be an advocate of men in her encouragement of their attentions, yet soon we see her ward off those would-be suitors. But by the last half of the story, when she has fallen in love with Woldemar's father, she stops defending herself altogether. Her family name, Zasekina, is perhaps from the Russian word *zaseka*, indicating a clearing in a forest or a barrier made of piled tree trunks; thus her name could signify an impediment to the happy love imagined by young Woldemar, a love that is abruptly trimmed when he learns the identity of his rival. A second possible origin of her surname is the Russian *zasech'*, "to flog," "to beat mercilessly (to death)"; indeed, Woldemar's father strikes her with his quirt when she pridefully tells him that he must separate from "that" woman (*de cette*), that is, his wife, Woldemar's mother. Given Turgenev's interest in finding just the right names for his protagonists (e.g., Rudin, Arkadi, Odintsova, and Bazarov), he must certainly have picked Zinaida's names with their lexical connotations in mind.

Chekhov's Niuta is a diminutive of Anna, which is derived (via the Greek "Anna") from the Hebrew "Hannah," *hanani*, meaning "grace," "lovely appearance," and "favored by God." If this was Chekhov's conscious choice, it must have been applied ironically, like the name of Volodya, for Niuta is a coarse woman, one who trifles with the boy's intensely developing sexual drive.[10] Moreover, her patronymic stems from the name Fedor, which in turn is from the Greek *theos + doron*, or "gift of God"; this patronymic reinforces Chekhov's irony. Her family name is not indicated, but she is identified as a cousin of the hostess, Lili Shumikhina, whose surname seems to be derived from the Russian *shum*, "noise," "din," with a third, figurative meaning of "sensation," "stir," which would befit the role she plays in consciously stirring up Volodya's emotions.

Sitting in a "dark corner of the gazebo," Volodya feels "an insurmountable desire [*nepobedimoe zhelanie*; the revised version has *sil'noe zhelanie*, and each variant recalls Woldemar's *nepobedimaia sila*] to see Niuta . . . to hear her laughter and the rustle [*shorokh*] of her dress." Confusion and feelings of inadequacy are suggested by his self-assessment: he "knows" that he is anything but handsome, for he has freckles and beady eyes, and he stoops and lacks a moustache, which would lend an aura of the heroic. Yet like Woldemar, who thought of himself as a knight coming to serve his ladylove, Volodya daydreams that he is "handsome, daring, witty, one who speaks and laughs louder than anyone else and is dressed according to the latest fashion."[11] It is at this point, "in the very heat of his daydreams," that Niuta suddenly appears before him, almost as if he had conjured her up.

Here Chekhov chooses to emphasize the boy's sensory perceptions. Volodya quickly becomes aware of Niuta's sensuality. Consider this description of his reaction to seeing her return from the bathhouse: "A sheet and a fluffy [*mokhnatyi*] towel were draped on her shoulders, and her wet hair, stuck to her forehead, peeked out from under her white, embroidered kerchief.[12] There came from her the damp, cool smell of the bathhouse and almond soap. Her nostrils and breasts were in motion from the walk; her face seemed more fresh and healthy than ever before. The upper button of her robe (this was the first thing that Volodya noticed) was unbuttoned, so that the boy could see her whole neck and even [the upper portion of] her breast."

As did Zinaida with Woldemar, Niuta reproaches Volodya for his mute staring and taunts him by asking if he likes her and why he doesn't court women or fall in love, and she exhorts him to "be a man!" Her emotional seduction of the boy continues as she offers: "Why don't you court me, for example? . . . You can learn with me, [even] practice [*repetirovat'*]." Overwhelmed by his new sensations, he can only respond with a stammered "I... I love you." When he seizes the opportunity to embrace her, she pauses, then frees herself, leaving him even more confused, as well as embarrassed. Introducing a device much favored by Turgenev (alas, used to the point of cliché in his novels and shorter prose), Chekhov lets Volodya overhear Niuta telling his mother about the incident. Though deeply offended and humiliated by the women's callous disregard of his new feelings, he is still enthralled, and we read that he "watched Niuta hungrily and waited" for another opportunity. But Chekhov's first version of the story ends abruptly when, out of frustration, Volodya reproaches his mother for her pretensions and posturing before Lili Shumikhina.

In the final version Chekhov concentrates on Niuta's physical seduction of Volodya, her overpowering effect on him, and his moment of ecstasy that is quickly followed by revulsion. The narrative heightens the emphasis on Volodya's sensory perceptions. Awakened in the middle of the night by his mother's request for medicine, he spies Niuta at his door "in that same robe in which she had gone to bathe." She languorously strokes her uncombed tresses; Volodya exclaims to himself, "How long and full [her hair] is!" Her presence has an unsettling effect on him. At first he is dizzy from the fumes of the medicine cabinet (ether, carbolic acid, and morphine), but watching her raised arms as she tends to her hair, he gazes at her in wonderment. In contrast to the ethereal effect of Zinaida on young Woldemar, the impression Niuta makes on Volodya is almost magical: "In her loose robe, sleepy, with her hair undone, by the meager light, . . . she seemed charming, luxurious, to Volodya... Enchanted, his whole body trembling, and remembering with enjoyment how he had embraced that wonderful body in the gazebo, he gives her [the morphine] and says: 'How beautiful you are.'" Older and less emotional than Volodya and in a mood for casual dalliance, she quickly checks to see if anyone is nearby and then comments, *sotto voce*, "Oh, these high schoolers." She enters his room, and we read of his reaction to what follows: "Then it seemed to Volodya that the room, Niuta, the dawn, and he himself all became fused into a single sensation of heightened, extraordinary, and never-before-experienced happiness for which one could give his whole life and go to eternal torment; but half a minute passed, and all that suddenly disappeared. Volodya saw only that fat, ugly face distorted by an expression of disgust [*gadlivost'*], and he himself felt revulsion at what had happened." Niuta's cruel response is to exclaim what a pitiful creature he is, an "ugly duckling." This causes him to think, "Indeed I am ugly [*gadok*]; everything is ugly [*vsë gadko*]."

Following Volodya's emotional agitation and its first exciting, then depressing, release, Chekhov increases the level of his frustration: the next morning Volodya's mood is marked by the thought of the examination he did not take and by hearing Niuta's now offensively loud laughter. Seeing her together with her black-browed and bearded husband, whom he detests (Is her husband also a devil's advocate?), Volodya is humiliated by the thought that she is mocking him and cares little for their shared experience. A brief scene shows how Volodya's frustration and anger turn against his mother. Her unfeeling lack of concern for her son's emotional well-being is demonstrated when, in response to Volodya's scathing accusation that she is an "immoral hanger-on with no soul," she quickly, and fearfully, warns that the "coachman will hear." Impervious to his condemnation, she fails to see that he is desperately seeking contact, comfort, and counsel.

Volodya, who daydreamed of fulfilled fantasies, is now burdened by uneasy contemplation of the disparity between the ideal and the real: "The heavier his soul became, the more strongly he felt that somewhere in this world some people had a life that was pure, noble in spirit, warm, exquisite, full of love, caresses, happiness, carefree."[13] But Chekhov, as if sensing that he is perilously close to sentimentality, redresses the situation by adding the comment: "He felt this and yearned for it so strongly that a passenger [in the train] stared at him intently and asked: 'You must have a toothache?'" Judging by the passenger's reaction, Volodya's face was grotesquely distorted, itself an indication of his disturbed psyche. Whereas Turgenev commonly used subtle gestures and looks to suggest a protagonist's emotional state, Chekhov introduces this almost bizarre detail and leaves his reader to make the connection. Nor does he spell out his intention, as did Tolstoy, in authorial explanation of facial expressions. Because of Chekhov's restraint, the reader witnesses the result of Volodya's adolescent sensitivity and yet can remain objective in assessing the boy's situation. We find a balanced presentation of Volodya's emotional turmoil and his inability to understand the coarseness of his surroundings.

Chekhov's final text explores Volodya's wounded psyche more completely than the early version and quickly brings the boy's torment to an end. In his mother's small communal apartment, Volodya's humiliation is compounded. Though described in sparing detail, their two rooms seem as crowded and dreary as any inhabited by Dostoevsky's impoverished families. The human closeness, caused by the presence of several boarders, ironically increases Volodya's sense of isolation. Finding no one interested in him or his problems, he goes into the other room to study. There he notices a newspaper on the desk and reads the title: *Figaro*. Chekhov does not indicate his thought, but given Volodya's state of mind it was perhaps "Finita la commedia." Volodya takes a loaded pistol from the desk drawer (the context suggests that he knew it was there). At that very moment he overhears his mother's voice from the next room saying in response to a boarder's comment that he, Volodya, is only behaving like a normal teenager: "No . . . he is too spoiled! . . . He has no one to control him, and I am weak and cannot do anything. . . . I am so unhappy!" The unwitting irony of that statement, given Volodya's sense of inadequacy and his wish for his mother's love, is too much to bear. He looks the pistol over, cocks it, and, on the second try, succeeds in ending his life: "Something struck Volodya with terrible force at the back of his neck, and he fell to the desk, face down amid the glasses and bottles. Then he saw his late father, in a top hat with a broad black ribbon, who had worn mourning clothes in Menton for some lady, suddenly grab him with both hands, and they both flew off into some very dark, deep abyss. Then everything became fused and disappeared." The reader is moved by the finality of this act and by a feeling of senseless loss.

The unexpected ending of Chekhov's story is stunning, but it is a matter of historical record that from the late 1860s through the 1880s there was a large number of teen suicides in Russia. This was a fact that caused Chekhov personal concern: the adolescent son of his friend and publisher, A. S. Suvorin, shot himself in May 1887 at about the same time as Chekhov composed the first version of his tale, which did not contain Volodya's suicide. Coincidentally, Chekhov was soon thereafter informed by a doctor in Taganrog that several pupils in the local high school had killed themselves that year out of "wounded vanity." And after his much respected supporter D. V. Grigorovich advised him in December 1887 to take up the theme of teen suicide, Chekhov revised his story accordingly. The historical and personal context of "Volodya" contributes to its sense of immediacy, whether or not the story is compared with "First Love." But considering the many other points of contact with Turgenev's tale, Volodya's suicide should not come as a surprise. The motif of death figures prominently in "First Love." Even that of suicide was already suggested in the text. Thus it may be that this motif, along with the alarming statistics of teen suicide in his day, led Chekhov's genius toward the somber ending of "Volodya."

In "First Love" the suicide motif appears when Zinaida asks one of her early admirers, the hussar Belovzorov, what he would do if she were his wife. He responds, "I'd kill myself." Later Dr. Lushin, another of Zinaida's erstwhile admirers, informs Woldemar that Belovzorov has "disappeared without a trace; they say that he has gone off to [serve in] the Caucasus," an action that could result in his death in battle. But in a earlier galley proof, we find, instead of the latter phrase: "He has shot himself. Yes, shot himself. Couldn't stand it either." As a master of understatement, Turgenev ultimately chose not to be so direct.[14] While one can only speculate, it is possible that Chekhov knew of Turgenev's earlier version.

In addition to the hint of Belovzorov's demise, "First Love" is marked by the deaths of two of the three principals. Soon after hearing of Belovzorov's disappearance, Woldemar had a "strange and terrible dream" in which he saw his father with the quirt in his hand; Zinaida cowering in a corner with a red welt, not on her forearm but on her forehead (suggesting punishment for adultery); and "behind them both, Belovzorov, all bloody, opening his pale lips and angrily threatening [his] father." Woldemar's father was to die of a stroke two months afterward. Although Zinaida's death was foreshadowed by a falling star just as Woldemar was about to discover her tryst with his father, it did not occur until some four years later, when the adult Vladimir Petrovich was informed by yet another member of Zinaida's early entourage that she was married (her surname was by now Dolskaya) and staying at a local hotel, the Demuth.[15] She died in childbirth only four days before he sought her out. His reaction to that sad news was to imagine her in the grave: "Those eyes, those curls—in a narrow box, in the damp, subterranean darkness, right here, not far from me, who was still living, and, perhaps, [only] a few paces from my father." That melancholy thought caused him to utter his soliloquy on the misguided nature of youth, which ends in the lament: "Oh, what I could have done if I had not lost my time in vain!"[16]

From these sentiments it is but a short distance to Chekhov's "Volodya." We have seen that his transformation of Turgenev's themes of first love and death has combined them with penetrating insight into adolescent psychology. He not only demonstrated a sensitive, naive teenager's confusion when confronted by awakening sexual urges, but as a doctor interested in then-new developments in psychiatry, he recognized and pointed to the need for positive human interaction: Volodya lacks anyone who could give him sympathetic counsel. His self-esteem is harmed by the apparent neglect of coarse and unfeeling women (his mother and his love object, Niuta). His isolation is emphasized by Niuta's callous seduction (she is one of Chekhov's memorable predatory females), by her humiliating responses to his fumbling approaches, by the absence of a trusted male figure (aside from Volodya's already deceased father, the only men in the story are Niuta's husband and a cigar-smoking French boarder who smells strongly of the perfumes from his factory), and by his mother's insensitive laughter at her son's awkwardness. Understandably, Volodya reacts in angry humiliation, with spite and self-hatred that ends in self-destruction. By ending his story abruptly, Chekhov emphasizes both the boy's tragedy and society's loss. The reader is first shocked and then involuntarily drawn to contemplation of the reasons for Volodya's decision.

In sum, Chekhov may have borrowed material found in Turgenev's personal reminiscence, but he developed it into a story dealing with one of those "evils of the day," teen suicide, which was a serious problem in Russian society of the 1870s and 1880s. Composed when he was only twenty-seven, "Volodya" demonstrates that Chekhov was already a perceptive observer, whose diagnosis of this particular "evil of the day" was strikingly accurate.

Andrew R. Durkin

Allusion and Dialogue in "The Duel"

THE CENTRAL characters in "The Duel" (Duel',
1891), the "humanist" Laevsky and the "scientist" von Koren, exist
in an atmosphere thick with literary and cultural allusion, from
Shakespeare through Pushkin, Lermontov, and Turgenev to Darwin,
Herbert Spencer, and Tolstoy's "Kreutzer Sonata." Indeed the conflict
that arises between Laevsky and von Koren can be read in part as a
struggle over which of them truly deserves the designation of hero, the
figure who defines the world of the literary work. The resultant cacophony of egos in large part derives from the fact that Laevsky and
von Koren, for all their apparent difference, in fact can be seen as two
phases of a dominant literary and cultural figure of the nineteenth
century, the romantic hero, characterized by L. Zvonnikova as suc-
cessively a follower of "the Romantic model of behavior" and "the
realistic movement" (in Lidya Ginzburg's terminology).[1] Each advances
a claim to the authority of his own position. Laevsky by appeal to
literary tradition, von Koren by scientific argument. In fact, "The Duel"
discredits both claims to authority, in part by juxtaposing to them an
alternative literary tradition that by implication may contain more of
value for the modern, postromantic man. The young deacon Pobedov
is connected with a literary mode and with values that serve as a
counterpoint to the tradition of which both Laevsky and von Koren
are products. This alternative mode of literature derives from Leskov
and posits both a hero and a literary form that differ sharply from
those of the "high" novel.

Although Chekhov's name has not often been linked with that of
Leskov, there is biographical evidence indicating Chekhov's esteem for
Leskov's works as well as Chekhov's interest in some of Leskov's works
at the time of composition of "The Duel." We know from Chekhov's
letters that he met Leskov in 1883, during a visit by Leskov to Moscow
with Nikolai Leykin, the editor of *Oskolki*, to which both Leskov and
Chekhov were contributors at the time. Chekhov describes his first
meeting with Leskov in a letter from late October 1883 to his brother

169

Aleksandr and relates how Leskov anointed Chekhov as a writer as Samuel anointed David.

> Along with Leykin there came my favorite writer [*pisaka*, a familiar term for a writer that could be translated as "scribbler"], the famous N. S. Leskov. The latter visited us, went with me to the Salon [*des variétés*] and to the Sobolev puppet booths [the houses of prostitution in Sobolev Alley]. He gave me his works with an autograph. Once I am riding with him at night. He turns to me half drunk and asks: "Do you know who I am?"[2] "I know." "No, you don't know... I am a mystic..." "I know that too..." He goggles his old eyes at me and prophesies: "You will die before your brother." "Could be." "I shall anoint thee with balm, as Samuel anointed David... Write." This fellow resembles an elegant Frenchman and at the same time a defrocked village priest. Quite a person, worth attention. When I'm in Petersburg, I'll visit him. We parted as friends.[3]

The semihumorous anointing was, apparently, the first time that Chekhov's talent was recognized by a representative of the previous generation of writers. Later, in February 1891, Chekhov sent copies of several works of Leskov's (along with many other books) to Sakhalin for use in the primary schools there. In the summer of the same year, when Chekhov was working on "The Duel," he ordered several works by Leskov (as well as works of other authors) from Posrednik, the publishing firm established by Tolstoy to provide inexpensive editions of serious literature for mass readership. Upon receiving the books, Chekhov wrote to the manager of the press, Gorbunov-Posadov, on September 4 (after the completion of "The Duel"): "I'm very grateful to you. The vast majority of the books are being read with interest. The things by Tolstoy and Leskov are particularly good. Epictetus is presented very well. The vignettes are good, particularly on "Conscience-stricken Daniel" and on the Pushkin fairy tale. In general, in outward appearance, and in inner content, and in spirit, the shipment produced the most joyful impression in me."[4]

What were possible reasons that Chekhov referred to Leskov as his "favorite writer" (*liubimyi pisaka*) and, more important, employed one of his works as a crucial subtext in "The Duel"? Apart from Leskov's linguistic inventiveness and humor, he had been a pioneer in moving away both from the novel as the hierarchically dominant genre and from the central figures typical of the Russian novel, namely members of the educated, Europeanized gentry or *intelligentsia*. Leskov developed (or returned to) forms in which clearly defined novelistic structure was replaced by episodic or open narratives. In addition, the typical Leskov character of the 1870s (as well as of his shorter works of the 1860s) is an exemplar of the "truly" Russian—a member of the clergy,

170

an Old Believer, a peasant, or a craftsman. Even longer works of the 1870s, such as *Cathedral Folk* (Soboriane, 1872) or *The Enchanted Wanderer* (Ocharovannyi strannik, 1873) are conceived as chronicle or picaresque rather than novel. Not only does Leskov break the mold of the novel with its coherent plot and tidy closure, but his characters speak in highly idiosyncratic, often substandard language, an indication of their own autonomous existence as well as of the social heterogeneity of Russia and by implication of all society. They are also often comic or ludicrous characters, such as Flyagin in *The Enchanted Wanderer*, or at least they seem so from the perspective of the Europeanized elite and its preferred literary forms and heroes. In fact, they offer a way out of the dead end of the novel, in Leskov's view a European form incapable of expressing the essence of Russian life.

In the 1880s Leskov undertook an even more radical experiment in a direction away from the novel; instead of depicting the Russian people in all their linguistic and social diversity, he adopted (and adapted) a preferred literary form of the people themselves, the parable. Drawing on the Prolog, a collection of early Christian and Russian parables and saints' lives arranged for daily reading, he composed a series of stylizations in this mode. They include "The Tale of the God-favored Woodcutter" (Povest' o bogougodnom drovokole, 1886), "The Tale of Theodore the Christian and His Friend Abraham the Hebrew" (Povest' of Fedore-khristianine i o druge ego Abrame-zhidovine, 1886), "The Beautous Aza" (Prekrasnaia Aza, 1888), and "The Legend of Conscience-stricken Daniel" (Legenda o sovestnom Danile, 1888), of which the last is the most important with regard to "The Duel."[5]

In keeping with his increasing sympathy with Tolstoyan views, one of Leskov's principal points in his selection and adaptation of these texts was to demonstrate the power of simple Christian faith and charity, outside the structures of the official Church that claims to act on the authority of the precepts of Christ. This point is made particularly forcefully in "The Legend of Conscience-stricken Daniel," which first appeared in *Novoe vremia* in 1888 and was included in the 1889 Suvorin edition of Leskov's works. In the late 1880s Chekhov was both a contributor to and a regular reader of *Novoe vremia*; he also owned a copy of the Suvorin edition of Leskov's works, which he later donated to the public library in Taganrog.

"The Duel" contains clear indications that what may be termed a popular, nonheroic element, linked primarily with Leskov, plays an essential role in the story. We know that in March 1891, when the composition of the story was under way, Chekhov wrote to his family during his first trip to Europe, requesting that they buy him a copy of a Russian folk print (*lubok*) with a depiction of a miracle of St. Varlaam, showing, according to Chekhov, St. Vaarlam "riding on a sleigh; in the distance on a balcony stands the bishop, and below, beneath the picture, is the [text of] the life of St. Varlaam. Buy it and put it on my desk for me" (March 20, 1891). Chekhov had in mind a depiction of a miracle attributed to St. Vaarlam of Khutynsk, who prayed for a brief frost in June to control worms that were destroying the crops; in anticipation of snow, the saint rode to the bishop in a sleigh, and on the appointed day, waist-deep snow fell. This exemplum of the mixture of unquestioning faith and seemingly ludicrous behavior posited on it is replaced in the final text of "The Duel" by the deacon's story about his uncle, a priest who takes his umbrella and leather coat with him when he goes out in the fields to pray for rain. This version also recalls Leskov's "Tale of the God-favored Woodcutter," in which the prayers of a humble woodcutter bring rain. In all three stories, the logical absurdity of faith, as well as its power, is emphasized.

The deacon is thus linked with popular faith by an anecdote that points to a legend about a Russian saint and to a tale from the Prolog as reworked by Leskov. The deacon's clerical background of course also suggests connections with Leskov's fictional world, as do his origins in the central Russian territory that is one of Leskov's favored locales. (Leskov himself was from this region, being a native of Orel.) In addition, the deacon displays a Leskovian absurdity, spending his time fishing (although fishing was the profession of Peter before he was called to be "a fisher of men"), playing a guitar and singing a seminarians' drinking song in mock–Church Slavonic, wholeheartedly enjoying children's party games while others are using them for cover for more sinister messages, and viewing everything in a comic light. Particularly in conversation with the hyperrational von Koren, the deacon often seems to be illogical or naive in the style of one of "God's fools."

Unlike Laevsky or von Koren, who are clearly conscious of the literary models that dictate their behavior, the deacon lacks the awareness of his literary antecedents that leads von Koren and Laevsky (as well as Nadezhda Fedorovna) to cast themselves and others in predetermined roles or to draw frames around experience. In keeping with his Leskovian absurdity, the deacon's most frequent reaction to the behavior or statements of those around him is laughter. The deacon is surrounded by an aura of laughter; in the first paragraph to give any hint of his character, words based on the root *smekh*, "laughter," occur six times:

> The deacon was very prone to laughter [*smeshliv*] and laughed [*smeialsia*] at every trifle to the point of getting a pain in his side or collapsing. It seemed that he liked to be among people only because they have their comic [*smeshnye*] sides and because one can give them

funny [*smeshnye*] nicknames. He called Samoilenko a tarantula, his orderly a drake, and was in rapture when von Koren once called Laevsky and Nadezhda Fedorovna macaques. He would look intently at people's faces, listen without blinking, and one could see how his eyes would fill with laughter [*smekhom*] and his face would become tense waiting for the moment he could let himself go and roll with laughter [*smekhom*].[6]

At first glance, the deacon would seem to be the ally of von Koren in the latter's denigration of Laevsky and Nadezhda Fedorovna, and von Koren himself doubtless feels that the deacon is a totally malleable disciple (von Koren attempts to recruit the deacon for his expedition, uses him as a secretary, and lectures to him, particularly in chapter 16). Certain aspects of the deacon's attitude toward others, however, distinguish it from von Koren's censorious mockery. Although the deacon also employs animal metaphors and finds von Koren's use of them amusing, there is an essential difference in the principle on which the deacon's metaphors are based. As his comparisons of the portly, close-cropped Samoilenko to a tarantula and of his tenor-voiced orderly to a drake suggest, the deacon's animal metaphors rely on visual, external resemblance and do not involve moral judgment. Even the metaphor the deacon appropriates from von Koren, Laevsky and Nadezhda Fedorovna as macaques, undergoes a translation. For von Koren, the metaphor is a condemnation, combining the traditional use of monkeys as an emblem of sexual license with pseudo-Darwinist prejudice concerning the evolutionary hierarchy of primates. For the deacon, however, an alternative association of monkeys as morally innocent, and hence as amusing imitators of human activity, may be operative; von Koren's comparisons of Laevsky to invertebrates, microbes, or mad dogs elicit no response from the deacon, for these comparisons lack potential for anything but a negative moral judgment. Finally, the deacon's most significant use of an animal metaphor similarly borrows from von Koren while simultaneously revaluing the comparison. In chapter 11, von Koren cites moles' underground fights to the death over territory as part of his argument concerning the universality and teleological necessity of the struggle for existence and the survival of the fittest; earlier, he also praised the weasel's apparently excessive and indiscriminate killing on the same grounds, turning Samoilenko's argument around. Von Koren has already asserted his willingness to apply the same principle to human conflicts. On the morning of the duel, as the deacon watches the preliminaries from his place of concealment, the word *moles* (*kroty*) flashes through his mind. To von Koren's emphasis on the strength and courage (or instinct) of moles in their combats, the deacon doubtless adds a more usually noted characteristic of the animals in question: their blindness.

In addition, there is a peculiarity about the deacon's laughter itself. During lunch at Samoilenko's, for example, the deacon twice starts to guffaw at von Koren's characterizations of Laevsky, and the true object and possible motivation of the deacon's laughter are often left unspecified and ambiguous. Von Koren takes the deacon's laughter as agreement but at the same time feels that such a reaction lacks appropriate seriousness of concern. In fact, it could be that the deacon's laughter is in part evoked by the very vehemence with which von Koren argues his case against Laevsky. In Bakhtinian terms, the deacon's laughter could be taken as an indication of the acceptance of von Koren's position as authoritative (the result von Koren himself of course desires and assumes), or it could be taken as a true reply, a dialogic response that treats von Koren's discourse as one among many and therefore relativized and without absolute authority. This is not to say that the deacon's perception of the comic aspects of people who take themselves very seriously is therefore the fully valid perspective. The deacon's reaction to the argument that leads to the challenge to the duel is laughter at Samoilenko's red face and agitated manner, and his expectations in going to watch the duel surreptitiously are of an amusing and bloodless spectacle that will serve as the subject of jokes and stories:

> The deacon began to consider this question [whether good people such as von Koren and Laevsky can be saved even if they are not believers], but he recalled what a funny [*smeshnaia*] figure Samoilenko had cut today, and this interrupted the course of his thoughts. He imagined how he would sit down under a bush and watch, and when tomorrow at lunch von Koren would start to boast, he, the deacon, would start to relate to him, laughing [*so smekhom*], all the details of the duel. . . .
>
> It would be so good to describe the duel in a comic light [*v smeshnom vide*]. His father-in-law would read it and laugh [*smeiat'sia*]; don't give his father-in-law anything to eat, just tell him or write to him something funny [*smeshnoe*].

The deacon's expectations of the duel as a purely comic event are of course shattered, although it is his intervention that changes the duel's potentially tragic outcome to an essentially comic one. Nevertheless, his perspective suggests the underlying foolishness of the entire episode.

The question of authority in discourse is directly raised, with explicit links to Leskov, in chapter 17, the discussion concerning science and the humanities, in which von Koren's rhetorical unassailability and authority over the plot are at their apparent peak. Von Koren bases his decision to eliminate Laevsky and his purportedly baneful influence on the principle of natural selection, arguing that when it

> "wishes to annihilate a sickly, scrofulous, degenerate tribe, then don't hinder it with your pills and quotations from a poorly understood Gospel.

In Leskov there is a conscientious Daniel, who finds a leper outside town and feeds him and keeps him warm in the name of charity and Christ. If that Daniel really loved people, then he would have dragged the leper farther from town and thrown him in a ravine and gone himself to serve the healthy. Christ, I hope, preached to us a love that was rational, sensible, and useful."

"What sort of person are you!" laughed the deacon. "If you don't believe in Christ, why do you mention him so often?"

Von Koren of course misses, or refuses to accept, the point of the emblematic incident in Leskov, itself a variant of the parable of the Good Samaritan, namely that true love of one's neighbor is the highest value in human existence, outweighing the instinct for self-preservation (Laevsky is coming to this conclusion by a different path at approximately the same time). It is important, however, that von Koren cites his source precisely; it is in fact one of the few occasions, if not the only one, in "The Duel" in which a character cites a work that is not clearly part of the *intelligentsia's* "required reading." In addition, von Koren refers to a precise incident in detail; characters in "The Duel" more usually recall a single motif (e.g., Karenin's ears) or make vague references (to the duels in *Hero of Our Times* and *Fathers and Sons*).

Von Koren's precision of citation, however, masks a more important omission or misreading with regard to Leskov's story. (Von Koren's failure or deliberate distortions as reader also raise the question of the accuracy of his "reading" of Laevsky, to this point seemingly authoritative.) Von Koren focuses on a relatively minor episode and overlooks the applicability to himself of the thematics of the main part of Leskov's story. The incident with the leper appears only in the final paragraphs of the story and has a clearly "added-on" character, occupying less than two pages out of a total of eighteen. In the longer, first part of the story, the Egyptian hermit Daniel inadvertently kills a pagan in self-defense while escaping captivity. Beset by his conscience, he seeks advice from various patriarchs, the pope, and a prince, but they all, despite or because of their doctrinal quarrels with one another, agree that Daniel has not only not committed a sin but has even performed a service for the Church and the state by killing one of their enemies. As the patriarch of Alexandria explains to Daniel:

"Why do you weary yourself and without reason disturb our serenity with trifles? You were in captivity by force, and you bear no sin for having killed an unbaptized barbarian."

"But my conscience tortures me—I recall the commandment by which it is not permitted to kill anyone."

"The killing of a barbarian is not included. That is not the same as the killing of a person, but equal to the killing of a beast."

The patriarch's comment to Daniel recalls von Koren's constant reduction of human behavior, and particularly that of his opponent Laevsky, to the level of animals and his willingness to rid the world of these harmful nonhumans. On the basis of science (or of pseudo science), von Koren is able to interpret as he sees fit Christ's command to love one's neighbor and justifies the same sort of murderous act the patriarch condones on religious grounds. In both cases the moral error arises from the desire to give one's own discourse full authoritativeness, ripping it out of the dialogic world of human languages and giving it the absolute power reserved for divine utterance. In Daniel's further searchings, Leskov points directly at the tendency of the limited discourse of an individual to take on the authority of absolute, divinely revealed truth:

> Daniel related everything to the prince and added how he had visited all the patriarchs and the pope, and what they had answered him.
> "Well then. Could it be that this did not relieve you?" inquired the prince.
> "No, things became even more difficult."
> "Why?"
> "Because, o prince, I began to think: May the words of men not hide from our eyes the Word of Christ, for then justice [*spravedlivost'*, "fairness"] will depart from men and the law of Christian love will be to them as if unknown. I fear temptation and do not seek further instruction from the consecrated but have come before you and beg punishment for the death of a human being."

This contradiction between the falsely authoritative language of the individual and the real authority of moral (and natural) truth is dramatized in "The Duel" at the moment of greatest tension, the duel itself. The complexity of intersecting lines at this moment requires that the passage (the end of chapter 19 and the beginning of chapter 20) be cited at length:

> "Hurry up and shoot!" thought Laevsky, and he felt that his pale, trembling [a mark of crisis in Chekhov] face must be arousing even greater hatred in von Koren.
> "Now I'll kill him," thought von Koren, taking aim at Laevsky's forehead and already fingering the trigger. "Yes, of course, I'll kill..."
> "He'll kill him!"—a desperate shout was heard somewhere very close by.
> Just then the shot rang out. Seeing that Laevsky was still standing in his place and had not fallen, everyone looked in the direction from which the shout had come and saw the deacon. Pale, with damp hair that had stuck to his forehead and cheeks, all wet and dirty, he was standing on the opposite bank [of the stream] in the corn and was smiling oddly and waving his wet hat. Sheshkovsky started laughing from joy, then burst into tears and walked off to one side...

20

A short while later von Koren and the deacon met near the footbridge. The deacon was upset and breathing heavily and avoided looking von Koren in the eyes. He was ashamed of being afraid and of his dirty, wet clothes.

"It seemed to me as though you wanted to kill him..." he muttered. "How contrary that is to human nature! How unnatural that is! [*Do kakoi stepeni eto protivoestestvenno!*]

This is the first time that von Koren's thoughts are directly reported, but at this moment of his complete certainty in the correctness of his own action and in the inevitability of a plot development that will confirm him as the unquestioned hero, his position is suddenly revealed as erroneous and limited. His own inner monologue is appropriated and made public by the deacon, and this recontextualization and "publication" function as a serious parody, in which von Koren's false authoritativeness is replaced by the full weight of moral truth.

The fact that the deacon's words are not attributed to any speaker ("a desperate shout") further enhances their suprapersonal, absolute authoritativeness. The participants in the duel, as well as the reader, are surprised by a disembodied voice that calls things by their right names. When the speaker is finally identified, he presents a strange mixture of the prophetic man of God in his clerical garb and the man of nature, rising wet and muddy from his hiding place. Chekhov has of course held the deacon "in reserve" until this moment; the deacon has played no direct role in the complex relations among the other characters that constitute the intrigue of "The Duel," a plot in which even a minor character such as Acmianov has played a pivotal part. Now, however, the deacon, seemingly naive and unable to counter adequately von Koren's weighty arguments in favor of the philanthropy of murder, has delivered the simple truth that confounds the fictive logic of von Koren's rationalizations. The deacon himself has of course had a deeper look into human nature; what he had expected to be a comedy has been something quite different in which he has been morally obligated to participate. His early direct look at the faces of others is replaced by a reluctance to look von Koren in the eyes. All that remains of his habitual laughter is a weak smile, and his laughter is shifted to Sheshkovsky, who both laughs and cries at the release of tension, suggesting the ambiguous nature of the tragicomedy in which they have all participated.

That religious and moral doctrine on the one hand and true science and logic on the other concur in the condemnation of murder is suggested by the deacon's comments to von Koren: "How contrary [or "repellent," *protivno*] that is to human nature! How unnatural that is!"

The first statement recalls the arguments of natural law ethics, while the second (*protivoestestvenno*) suggests something contrary to man's biological nature itself. Von Koren's sophistic opposition of religion and science, in favor of the latter, dissolves in the face of a single, stubborn truth: the deliberate killing of another human being is murder.

Paul Debreczeny

"The Black Monk": Chekhov's Version of Symbolism

THE VISION of Andrei Kovrin, hero of "The Black Monk," suggests that there is a higher reality, an "eternal truth" as he puts it, that is accessible only to outstanding individuals endowed with clairvoyance. Such an assumption was to be the central tenet of Russian symbolism, especially after 1901, when Aleksandr Blok conceived his Beautiful Lady, inspired by Vladimir Solovyov's vision of the Divine Sophia.[1] In this essay I would like to suggest that "The Black Monk," written in 1893 and first published in January 1894, anticipates the fusion of symbolism and mysticism by some eight or ten years.[2]

How much of a symbolist movement was there in Russia by 1893, and how much did Chekhov know about it? First, it can be safely assumed that Chekhov was aware of French symbolism: not only had he traveled in France and read French authors, but he must also have seen Zinaida Vengerova's essay "Symbolist Poets in France," published in volume 9 of *Evropeiskii vestnik* for 1892. Second, some essays appearing in the press, by Akim Volynsky (Flekser) and Nikolai Minsky (Vilenkin) for example, signaled the emergence of a Russian symbolist movement. Especially interesting from our point of view is Minsky's 1890 essay *In the Light of Conscience: Thoughts and Dreams about the Purpose of Life,* of which Chekhov had a copy.[3] Here Minsky advocated a Nietzschean individualism, calling for the creation of a new man who would be above the common herd. As Bernice Rosenthal has pointed out, Nietzsche's cult of the individual with heightened aesthetic and philosophical sensitivities had a profound influence on the first outstanding representative of Russian decadence, Dmitry Merezhkovsky, and on the development of Russian symbolism in general.[4] When the Black Monk tells Kovrin that "if you want to be healthy and normal, go and join the herd," and when Kovrin himself recognizes that he has suffered from "megalomania," Chekhov's arrow seems to aim either at Schopenhauer, from whom Nietzsche had borrowed many of his ideas, or at Nietzsche himself.[5]

Dmitry Merezhkovsky had actually not reached his fully Nietz-

179

schean phase before Chekhov's story was published, but his 1890 drama *Sylvio* did portray a bored Renaissance prince who wanted to fly as an eagle and become a superman. In his "Acropolis" (1891), too, Merezhkovsky called for a new Parthenon, to be created by "God-like men on earth."[6] Further, his 1892 collection of poems, *Symbols*, showed the influence not only of Nietzsche but also of the French symbolists and contained his translation of Edgar Allan Poe's "The Raven," which was to become part of the symbolist canon. The poem in the volume that comes closest to Chekhov's theme of communication with transcendental beings is "Vera," which tells the story of a young woman who commits suicide but subsequently establishes spiritual union with her beloved one, providing him with inspiration to carry on a useful life.

There can be no doubt that Chekhov followed Merezhkovsky's work closely. They were both associated with the journal *Severny vestnik*, on whose pages Merezhkovsky reviewed Chekhov's volumes *In the Twilight Hours* (1887) and *Short Stories* (1888).[7] The two met personally in Venice in March 1891, and from then on we see Chekhov referring to his younger contemporary in several letters, describing him as an intelligent and appealing person, although poking fun at his "high-flown strivings" and criticizing his drama *The Storm Has Passed* (1893).[8] In December 1892—just the winter before Chekhov started working on his "Black Monk"—Merezhkovsky gave his lectures "Reasons for the Decline of, and New Trends in, Contemporary Russian Literature," about which Chekhov read newspaper reports. In January 1893, when the lectures were published as a brochure, Merezhkovsky presented Chekhov with a copy, inscribing it, "To Anton Pavlovich Chekhov, from a devoted friend and admirer of your talent, D. S. Merezhkovsky."[9]

It is quite possible, in my opinion, that Kovrin the visionary was trying to do just what Merezhkovsky described in his concluding lecture as "a leap across the abyss into *that realm, those shores;* a leap to the frontiers of free divine idealism."[10] Furthermore, the Black Monk's words about a genius accelerating by whole centuries mankind's progress toward attaining "the kingdom of eternal truth" seems to echo Merezhkovsky's assertion that "the sudden spark, the radiant lightning of national consciousness, which people await and long for, at times for centuries, flares up only in the tempestuous and fecund atmosphere created by genius."[11]

At the time Chekhov was working on his story, Vladimir Solovyov was not generally thought of as a symbolist, but both his poetry and his theological writings were clearly pointing toward symbolism. He seems to be present in "The Black Monk" not only by virtue of his ideas but as a personality too. His poem "Three Visions," describing his encounters with Sophia, the Divine Wisdom, did not appear in print until 1898, but the encounters themselves had occurred in 1875 and were widely talked about, along with tales of his occult interests and other eccentricities.[12] Most relevant to our discussion is Solovyov's alleged assertion that "in all the decisive instances of his life he acted according to the directions and advice of the spirit of a certain Norman woman of the 16th or 17th century, who appeared to him when he wished."[13] Which of the rumors about Solovyov actually reached Chekhov is impossible to say, but living as he did among the leading cultural circles of Russia, he could hardly fail to miss at least some of them.[14] Further, it was a well-known fact that Solovyov had an extremely delicate and nervous constitution and that he had left his teaching position at the university.[15] All of this makes him a likely prototype for Chekhov's Kovrin.

More important, the lyrical poems Solovyov published from the late 1870s through the early 1890s are replete with visions akin to that of Kovrin. "We obtain eternal truth / With a prophet's secret clairvoyance," he writes in an 1878 lyric. He has visions of past poets, who come to him "Having flown, as on a swan's wings, / Over the dual barrier of space and time," much like the Black Monk. In one poem even the location of a vision is similar to that described by Chekhov: "The rays of the sun play above the wild Tosna, / The bank is steep and high... / I see the familiar old pines."[16] Like Kovrin before his death, Solovyov's lyrical persona feels dejected when deprived of his vision and longs for its return:

It was only a dream. After your dreary awakening
You will be waiting with languid melancholy
For another glimpse of the heavenly vision,
For another echo of the sacred harmony.[17]

The ideas conveyed in Solovyov's poetry find full theoretical expression in his long essay "The Meaning of Love," published in installments in the journal *Problems of Philosophy and Psychology* from 1892 through 1894. According to Solovyov's theory, matter represents "the other," created by God to oppose his own spirituality, and the historical process involves a gradual integration of this nondivine material chaos into the divine cosmos. The integrative process is observable even at the inorganic level of nature, as witnessed by the pull of gravity and by a mysterious optical phenomenon called "ether," which, Solovyov says, holds the universe together but has so far eluded definition by scientists.[18] This kind of pseudo-scientific argument, showing some traces of Schopenhauer, anticipates Kovrin's optical theories about the periodic reappearance of a mirage.

Even more important from the point of view of our discussion is

181

Solovyov's claim that at the human level the force that will eventually bring the nondivine chaos into harmony with the divine cosmos is the physical and spiritual union between man and woman. If that union is purely physical, it does not recognize the individuality of the persons involved and therefore remains at the animal level. If it is purely spiritual, it fails to engage matter, which needs to be infused with spirit. On the rare occasions when love, both spiritual and physical, is fully achieved, we get a glimpse into the future, which Solovyov describes as "a gleam of otherworldly happiness, an infusion of otherworldly joy."[19] It is not by accident, it seems, that Kovrin is filled with love for Tanya just after he has had his first conversation with the Black Monk, that is, when he is at his most spiritual. His declaration of love represents the unification of the spirit with the flesh, and he experiences just the kind of otherworldly joy that Solovyov refers to. "I am happy," Kovrin says. "Tanya, dear Tanya, you're such an appealing person. Dear Tanya, I am so glad, so glad!"

The kind of love Solovyov describes is achieved only by exceptional people at the present stage of historical development. "It may be," he writes, "that it will take thousands of years before love attains its full expression." He advises that for the time being a person of heightened spiritual awareness should "take part in the general historical process as consciously and actively as possible."[20] That future stage of development, which Solovyov calls "heavenly kingdom," seems to be just what the Black Monk holds up before Kovrin. "A great, brilliant future awaits you, human beings," says the Black Monk. "And the more men like you there are on earth, the more quickly this future will come about. Without men like you serving the highest principles, leading conscious and free lives, humanity would be worthless. In the normal course of development it would have to wait a long time for the fulfillment of its earthly history. But you will lead it into the kingdom of eternal truth a few thousand years ahead of time—this is your noble service." At the present time, in Solovyov's view, we only glimpse the future in flashes of happiness, which makes some people think that the future is just an illusion. But, writes Solovyov, "Even if I, standing on this side of the transcendental world, perceive a certain ideal object only as the figment of my imagination, this does not mean that that object lacks full reality in another, higher sphere of being."[21] Similarly, when Kovrin questions the Black Monk's existence, the latter explains to him that "I exist in your imagination; and since your imagination is part of nature, I also exist in nature." Finally, Solovyov states that the flashes of happiness we attain in love are transitory; they will be replaced by discord or dullness in the lives even of those who have attained the utmost spiritual development under the present historical circumstances, which is why the Russian Orthodox Church regards marriage as "martyrdom."[22] No term could describe Kovrin's marriage more appropriately.

Working on his story, Chekhov might not have had in mind particular passages from Merezhkovsky or Solovyov, but it does seem that he was alluding to the incipient symbolist movement at least in a general sense.[23] If that is so, then what was his purpose? It goes without saying that allusions to symbolism do not make Chekhov a symbolist any more than including Lensky's elegy in chapter 6 of *Evgeny Onegin* made Pushkin a sentimentalist. The question is to what use Chekhov put the elements taken from symbolism.

Chekhov's own well-known explanation of "The Black Monk," in his letters of December 18, 1893, to A. S. Suvorin and of January 15, 1894, to M. O. Menshikov, was that is represented a medical case history, a *historia morbi*, and that the subject studied was megalomania. The vision of the Black Monk, he repeated to family and friends, was his own.[24] Taking Chekhov's statement at face value, we can relate "The Black Monk" to the group of his stories known as clinical studies or experimental narratives.[25]

As in "An Attack of Nerves" (1889), Chekhov seems to have chosen a mentally unstable young man for his hero and placed him in a stressful situation as an experiment. It is Chekhov the physician who emphasizes that in childhood Kovrin looked angelic and carried himself with his late mother's graceful delicacy. When we first meet him, he is overworked, suffers from insomnia, and drinks too much. He has come to the country estate of his adopted father, Pesotsky, to take a rest on the advice of his physician friend. It turns out, however, that the Pesotskys, father and daughter, are the wrong company for a person needing relaxation.

Tanya loves her father and is deeply involved with his orchard, but this is not enough for him: he demands total devotion, to the exclusion of any personal aspirations on her part. "Of course," she says about the orchard, "it's all very nice and useful but sometimes I want something else, to break the monotony." That "something else" is just what her father fears. "Here I am," he says, "writing articles and exhibiting at shows and winning medals... They say Pesotsky grows apples as big as a man's head and that he's made a fortune with his orchard. In other words, Kochubey is rich and renowned. But I ask you: what is the point of it all? The garden is indeed beautiful, a showpiece... . . . But what's the point of it? What's its purpose?" The reference to the hero of Pushkin's *Poltava* is telling, for Kochubey fell upon bad days owing to his daughter's passion for another man. "The secret of my success," Pesotsky continues, "is not that it's a big garden, with lots of gardeners, but that I love the whole business, do you follow? I love it, perhaps more than I love myself." But if his personal identity is so intimately bound up with the orchard and if his business is so successful, then why is he so anxious about it? Seeing a farmhand tie a horse to an apple tree throws Pesotsky into a hysterical fit, and his horticultural articles, instead of calmly reporting his success, turn out to be "torrents of venomous animadversions" against academic botanists. Quite clearly, it is not the garden that is making him so tense, but the person whose complete devotion to the garden he demands, Tanya. "What if she should marry, God forbid?" he whispers with a frightened look. "This is my point! She'll marry, have children, and then the last thing she'll care about will be the garden." Tying her to the orchard, it transpires, is just an excuse for tying her to himself. One is reminded of "Rappaccini's Daughter" (1844) by Nathaniel Hawthorne, whose heroine is also isolated from the outside world by the magic garden her father created. Tanya responds to her father by an ambivalent mixture of affection and the desire to break away. Their covertly incestuous relationship finds expression in hysterical quarrels.

The curious suggestion Pesotsky eventually makes is that the only man Tanya could marry without being severed from the garden is Kovrin. The illogic of the suggestion is glaring, for that city dweller, deeply involved in his intellectual pursuits and totally ignorant of horticulture, is the least likely person to continue Pesotsky's business. Sensing this himself, Pesotsky adds that Kovrin would provide him with a grandson whom the old man would bring up to be his successor. This suggestion is even more incongruous, not only because the frail, highly strung Kovrin scarcely resembles a stud to be hired for breeding but also because, only a minute earlier, Pesotsky was saying that raising children would be the very thing that would take Tanya away from the garden. What compels Pesotsky to advance such an obviously specious argument? In my opinion the only answer can be that he regards Kovrin as his son ("I love you as my own son") and subconsciously hopes that if this almost-son of the family marries Tanya, the incest can somehow be perpetrated. It is suggested that Tanya is willing to accept Kovrin for the same reason: "You know," she says, "that my father adores you. Sometimes it seems to me as though he loved you more than me."

As soon as fantasy turns into reality, however, neither father nor daughter can accept the interloper. Even though Tanya had imagined all along that she would marry her adopted brother, when she heard his actual proposal she "was quite stunned; she stooped, shrank, and suddenly seemed to have aged ten years." Similarly, her father, even though he has proposed the match to Korvin in the first place, gets into a rage when he is told about the engagement and rides off whipping his horse, making Tanya weep for the rest of the day. Kovrin never is able to drive a wedge between father and daughter: it is characteristic that Pesotsky is present when Kovrin gets carted off to the psychiatrist and that in the letter he receives from Tanya just before his death she complains about how he had driven her *father* to the grave.

Why does Kovrin let himself be dragged into such an unhealthy family relationship? The narrator implies that the mentally unstable young philosopher, brought up by Pesotsky (who no doubt contributed to his instability), just cannot resist the pull of a mutually destructive, neurotic entanglement. "He felt," we read, "that this weeping, trembling girl's nerves were reacting to his own half-sick, overwrought nerves like iron to a magnet." And as V. B. Kataev has pointed out, Kovrin is as detached from his own real feelings as Pesotsky and Tanya are from theirs: when he feels elation after his enounter with his phantom, he mistakes this for the ecstasy of love.[26] If we read the story this way, Kovrin's hallucination is no more than a symptom of his mental deterioration, which lands him in Tanya's arms. The hero, weak by disposition, succumbs to a destructive environment.

"The Black Monk" is more complex than that, however. Before Kovrin's "cure," it is emphasized, he was "an unusual person," who had "made himself a brilliant career." He had earned a master's degree and was teaching psychology at the university, and when he worked at his philosophical studies he felt that "every vein in his body was pulsating and throbbing with pleasure." His hallucinations increase his mental powers and his general appeal as a person. After Kovrin's first meeting with the Black Monk, Tanya and her guests find that he has "a radiant, inspired look about him" and that he is "most interesting." The happiness the Black Monk brings him is emphasized at every step. As a result of their encounters, he feels he is a special person, capable of great deeds, and his work is inspired. His philosophical writings of that fecund original period are so impressive that the trajectory of his career soars high for a while even after his hallucinations are discovered. No wonder he complains of having been cured:

> Why, why did you subject me to a cure? All those bromides, idleness, warm baths, supervision, the petty worry over every sip I swallow, every step I take—all this will turn me into a complete idiot. I was going crazy, I did have megalomania, but I was bright and cheerful, even happy. I was interesting and original. Now I have grown more rational and stable, but I am just like anybody else, a mediocrity. Life bores me... Oh, how cruelly you have treated me! I did have hallucinations, but what harm did they do to anybody? I am asking you: what harm did they do?

Read this way, "The Black Monk" appears to be as much an indictment of psychiatric practices as a study of a mental patient. We are once more reminded of "An Attack of Nerves," whose ending implies that psychotherapy is useful for keeping a sensitive person's social conscience under control. Anticipating Freud, Chekhov seems to be saying by Kovrin's story that a neurosis may be adaptive and should not be tampered with unless it is altogether incapacitating. In other words, people need personal myths to live by; crazy visions, as long as they nurture the soul, are better than sober drabness. Responding perhaps to Merezhkovsky's statement that "symbols are the divine aspect of our spirit," which have to arise from the depth of the soul spontaneously, Chekhov emphasizes that Kovrin's symbol is a projection of his own inner self.[27] "I am a product of your inflamed imagination," the Black Monk tells the hero, which also confirms what Joseph Conrad has suggested in his recent study, that Kovrin extracted his vision from the depths of a collective subconscious.[28] Conrad sees the Black Monk as an evil tempter. Advocating knowledge as he does, the monk is indeed playing Mephistopheles to a Chekhovian Faust; but from the point of view of mythmaking, it is immaterial whether the mythic figure created is evil or benevolent. Either way it lends meaning to the universe and helps to provide the individual with a sense of purpose.

How anxious Kovrin was to see himself as part of a larger creation can be seen in his fondness for personifying nature. "So much space, freedom, and tranquillity here," he thinks to himself on the riverbank just before he encounters the Black Monk for the first time. "The whole world seems to be looking at me with bated breath, waiting for me to understand it." The contrasting images of the orchard, the flower garden, and the somber park, acquiring personalities of their own, play their parts as the dialectic of human conflicts is acted out. Kovrin's initial happiness corresponds to spring and early summer—the natural backdrop for romance and fulfillment—but the archetypal seasonal expectation is ironically reversed when the summer, even before the wedding, turns into a "very hot and dry one, so much so that they had to keep watering every tree."[29] Nature completely changes her personality by the second summer, when Kovrin, cured from his hallucinations, visits the riverbank. "The somber pines with their shaggy roots," he reflects, "which had seen him here the previous year looking so young, joyful, and lively, no longer talked in whispers but stood motionless and dumb, as though they didn't recognize him." Having lost touch with the purpose of the universe, Kovrin makes one last, desperate attempt to join forces with it before he dies. "The bay, which seemed to be alive," we read, "looked at him with its many light blue, dark blue, turquoise, and flame-colored eyes and beckoned him." This final attempt at personifying nature brings on the last appearance of the Black Monk. Chekhov may be saying, anticipating anthropologists of our century, that Kovrin's predicament—his alienation from a natural universe—is a symptom of an industrial civilization and that in some other cultures, indeed in earlier periods of Russian history, he and his hallucinations would have been perfectly acceptable.

Such a reading of the story, however, is also fraught with problems. Kovrin's visions made him happy and productive, but even if he had not been thrown into the psychiatrist's clutches, he could not have maintained his feverish way of life for long. Moreover—and this is Chekhov's ultimate irony—Kovrin did not die of a mental illness. "He had hemorrhages in the throat," we read. "He would spit blood, with considerable loss once or twice a month, which left him extremely weak and drowsy." He himself realizes that he is suffering from the same disease that killed his mother—tuberculosis. Under these circumstances it seems almost entirely irrelevant whether he received the right psychiatric treatment or not.

It is not surprising that the two leading populist critics of Chekhov's time, A. M. Skabichevsky and N. K. Mikhailovsky, both found the story incomprehensible. "The reader cannot draw any conclusion from all this," wrote Skabichevsky.[30] "What does the story mean?" asked Mikhailovsky. "What is its message? . . . Is the Black Monk a benevolent genius who comforts weary people with dreams and visions about the role allotted to 'God's chosen' . . . or is he an evil genius who seduces people by cunning flattery into a world of sickness and misfortune?"[31] If Chekhov had nothing else in common with the symbolists, he and they certainly drew the same kind of critical response. "It was precisely Chekhov," writes A. P. Chudakov, "who made the critics finally assemble a full arsenal with which to attack new artistic trends at the end of the century."[32] Among the critics, those of a populist orientation were most apt to show astonishment over the incomprehensibility of Chekhov's stories. He himself thought that critics of that persuasion had descended from Dmitry Pisarev, whom he detested for his comment on Pushkin's *Onegin*. If Chekhov shows an anxiety of influence, it has to do with the *narodnik* trend of the last decade of the nineteenth century. By origin and education he should have belonged to it, but he disliked the smug self-assurance of its representatives, who imagined they knew all the answers to questions of aesthetics and morality. Under the circumstances, he seems to have felt an urge to *épater le narodnik*. I submit that Chekhov, in his gentle way, was as fond of baffling his critics as were Valery Briusov or Zinaida Hippius.

Chekhov, I repeat, was no symbolist, but rather like Pushkin in the early part of the century, he responded to every new trend, absorbing it into his own art. What brings "The Black Monk" close to symbolism are not just allusions to Merezhkovsky and Solovyov, and not just the kind of critical response the story was designed to elicit. Much more significantly, what brings the story close to symbolism is the overall effect Chekhov was aiming at. Like the symbolists, he suggests and implies, rather than declares, and he creates an emotional state rather than attempting to convey a definite thought.[33] "In poetry," wrote Merezhkovsky, "what is not stated, what only gleams through the beauty of a symbol, is much more effective than a thing embodied in words."[34] The "meaning" of "The Black Monk" may be difficult to sum up in social or philosophical terms, but if its details—the smoke-filled orchard at dawn, the fairyland of the garden, the mysterious riverbank with its pine trees, the fever of Kovrin's sleepless nights, his intellectual excitement, his sense of being special, and his experience of falling in love with all its dire consequences—forever linger on in the reader's memory, then it certainly is an effective work of art.

Svetlana Evdokimova

"The Darling": Femininity Scorned and Desired

"ALL MEN are scoundrels, and all women are charming creatures," concluded one of Chekhov's contemporaries after reading "The Darling" (1899). "This is a mockery offensive for a woman," complained another.[1] The way the story was received by Chekhov's contemporaries not only reveals the readers' uncertainty about the role of the woman in society and about the masculine ideal of femininity but also testifies to the inherent ambiguity of the story itself.

When the story first appeared in print, several critics believed that Chekhov's plan was to mock a dependent and unemancipated woman, who had no opinions of her own but was capable only of repeating the words of her husbands, her lover, and even a schoolboy. Critics blamed Olenka for submissiveness. Maxim Gorky supported this negative interpretation: "Like a grey mouse, the Darling anxiously darts about, a sweet, gentle creature who is capable of loving so much and so submissively. One can slap her in her face, and even then she will not dare to let out a moan, the gentle slave."[2] Others, among them Tolstoy, perceived this character as the very embodiment of femininity, as a true ideal of womanhood: "The soul of Darling, with her capacity for devoting herself with her whole being to the one she loves, is not ridiculous but wonderful and holy."[3] Tolstoy not only admired "The Darling," but he proclaimed that, although Chekhov's intent was to curse the heroine, against his will he blessed her.

It is obvious that both Tolstoy and Gorky, to take only two examples, manipulated their interpretations of the text to emphasize one characteristic of the heroine at the expense of others; indeed, they assimilated "The Darling" to their own mythopoetic systems. Thus, when Tolstoy included Chekhov's story in his *Readings for Every Day of the Year* (Krug chteniia), he even went so far as to cut out sentences and passages from Chekhov's text that did not accord with his interpretation.[4] He eliminated Olenka's dreams and all sensual details from Olenka's portrait in order to make his interpretation of the heroine as a "holy soul" more convincing. Gorky, by contrast, was so concerned with the fate

189

of abused and submissive Russian women that he ignored the facts that Olenka is not a victimized wife, that she is not abused, neglected, or misunderstood, that she is financially independent, and that no one in the story ever tries to give her a slap in the face. No matter how interpreters manipulate Chekhov's text, clearly Olenka generates both positive and negative feelings. As Tolstoy himself aptly pointed out about "The Darling," "This is a pearl that similar to litmus paper may produce different effects."[5] Let us analyze the grounds that the text offers for such contradictory interpretations, the sources of the heroine's ambiguity, and the mythopoetic paradigm that lies at the core of Olenka's character and characterization.

"Dushechka," translated traditionally as "The Darling," is a story of a young woman, Olenka (nicknamed *dushechka*, which means "little soul" and is a term of endearment commonly used to address a woman), and of her four loves: two husbands, a lover, and a little schoolboy, Sashenka. The story is constructed as a cyclical, cumulative repetition of the same situation: affiliation and separation. Each time Olenka engages in a relationship, she identifies herself completely with the person she loves, to the extent of assimilating all his thoughts and opinions. Each time she stays alone, she loses all interest in life, all opinions, and she almost ceases to exist.

In his book *The Phoenix and the Spider* Renato Poggioli, inspired by Tolstoy's definition of the heroine as the one who does "what is loftiest, best, and brings man nearest to God—the work of loving," made an attempt to interpret the story as a new version of the myth of Psyche.[6] The very title of the story "Dushechka," a diminutive form of *dusha* (soul, or Psyche), suggests this parallel. In addition, this title brings to mind Bogdanovich's poem *Dushenka*, which is a free version of La Fontaine's *Les amours de Psyché et de Cupidon*. La Fontaine's tale, in turn, goes back to Apuleius's account of the myth of Cupid and Psyche in *Metamorphoses*. The perception of Olenka as a modern, Russified Psyche, however, is misleading.

The myth of Cupid and Psyche comprises a number of key motifs that are absent in Chekhov's story: Psyche marries outside her community (in folklore variants the girl often marries a monster); she violates the taboo against seeing her husband; she wanders in search of a lost lover, who is Cupid himself; and finally she is happily reunited with him. In Apuleius's version of the myth, Psyche in the end gives birth to a daughter, Pleasure. The heroine of Chekhov's story is the very opposite of Psyche. Olenka marries local residents, violates no taboo, commits no mistake, stays in her own house all the time, and is not happily reunited with her beloved; instead, her last love for a little boy, Sashenka, is full of troubles. Unlike Psyche, Olenka is barren, unable to conceive children with any of her lovers despite her obvious desire to become a mother; while married to her second husband, Pustovalov, Olenka prays to God to give her children.

Whereas the legendary Psyche marries outside her community, that is, into the other world, and then searches for her lost lover, Olenka seeks nothing, never crossing the boundaries of her domestic universe. In this respect she is much closer to Gogol's "old-fashioned landowners" or to the Manilovs in *Dead Souls* (this couple, we may recall, called each other *dushen'ka*) than to the curious and venturous heroine of Apuleius's tale. Like Gogol's old-fashioned landowners, Olenka lives in a secluded world, physically and emotionally limited to her home territory. She seeks her happiness nowhere but in her own house, never leaving the place "where she had lived since childhood, and which was bequeathed to her in the will."[7] Significantly, all Olenka's men come to live in her house: her first husband, Kukin, the veterinarian Smirnin and his son, Sashenka, are all her tenants; Pustovalov, Olenka's second husband, is her neighbor, but he also moves into Olenka's house after their marriage. Olenka has no contacts with the external world, contacts that would take her beyond her familial realm. Father, husbands, a lover, a boy whom she loves as her own son—all of them form one constellation of "relatives." Even Olenka's maiden name is Plemiannikova (from *ple-miannik*, "nephew," that is, a person belonging to one *plemia*, "tribe").

The external world beyond her courtyard brings Olenka nothing but troubles. The description of Olenka's marital bliss is immediately followed by the scene in which Olenka receives a telegram informing her of Kukin's death. This news is preceded by "an ominous knock" on her garden gate, that is, by a transgression of the boundary line separating Olenka from the outside world: "Late on Palm Sunday evening, an ominous knock suddenly was heard at the gate. Someone was banging at the door as though hammering on a barrel: bang! bang! bang! . . . 'Open up, I beg you,' said someone behind the gates in a deep, hollow voice. 'A telegram for you.'" This "ominous knock" brings to mind the man with a little hammer from Chekhov's story "Gooseberries." Chekhov was working on this story at approximately the same time as he was writing "The Darling." In "Gooseberries" Chekhov writes: "Behind the door of every contented, happy man there ought to be someone standing with a little hammer, who would keep reminding him by his knocking that there are unhappy people and that happy as he himself may be, life will sooner or later show him its claws. Disaster will strike—sickness, poverty, losses—and nobody will see him or listen to him, just as now he neither sees nor listens to others."

191

At the very end of "The Darling," just when Olenka is happy again, she is again reminded of the external world by "a loud knock" on the gate:

> Suddenly a loud knock was heard at the gate. Olenka wakes up and is breathless from fear. Her heart is pounding. Half a minute later, there is another knock.
>
> "A telegram from Kharkov," she thinks, beginning to tremble all over. "Sasha's mother wants him in Kharkov. Oh, goodness me!"

This time the alarm is a false one, but the knock on the gate is a warning. It is obvious that Olenka's last love, too, will abandon her.

The interpretation of the character of the "darling" as Psyche is based on emphasizing only one characteristic of Olenka—her capacity for love—the characteristic that Tolstoy praises so much in his essay. This selfless aspect of Olenka's love makes Tolstoy declare that Chekhov's heroine is an "example of what woman can be in order to be happy herself and to make those happy with whom her fate is united." Tolstoy goes on to develop his thought: "What would become of the world, what would become of us men if women had not that faculty and did not exercise it? Without women doctors, women telegraphists, women lawyers and scientists and authoresses, *we* might get on, but without mothers, helpers, friends, comforters, who love in man all that is best in him—without such women it would be hard to live in the world."[8]

The ideal of femininity Tolstoy puts forth in his essay is clearly what femininity is for men, or more precisely what it is for Tolstoy; it is defined as "complete devotion to the beloved," literally, "the complete giving up of self to the one you love" (*polnoe otdanie sebia tomu, kogo liubish'*).[9] For Tolstoy the ideal of femininity is, in fact, the annihilation of woman's individuality and of her existence as separate from that of man. As opposed to Tolstoy, Chekhov questions this ideal and points to the ultimate danger of Olenka's "complete giving up" to those she loves. The self-abnegating nature of Olenka's love is epitomized in the scene when the "darling" follows the boy down the street to school:

> "Sashenka, dear," she calls after him.
>
> He looks back, and she stuffs a date or a caramel candy into his palm. When they turn into the street near the grammar school, he feels ashamed that a tall, stout woman is following him, so he turns around and says:
>
> "Go home, Aunty. I'll make my own way now."

Olenka gives Sasha something—a date or a caramel—he does not need. Moreover, the boy wants to "make [his] own way" and perceives Olenka's complete devotion as an assault on his autonomy.

The nature of Olenka's love and character is far more reminiscent of another mythological figure than of Psyche. This is the Greek nymph Echo. In Ovid's account of the myth in his *Metamorphoses*, Juno becomes angry with the nymph Echo for distracting her with chatter, while the rest of the nymphs run off to Jupiter. As punishment, Juno deprives Echo of the ability to initiate discourse, enabling her only to repeat the last syllables of words uttered in her presence. Thus, upon falling in love with Narcissus, she is forced to use his words even for her own declaration of love, as she has no words of her own. When she seeks to embrace Narcissus, he pulls away, saying: "I'll die before I yield to you." She then merely repeats the last part of his sentence: "I yield to you" (*Metamorphoses* 3.391–92). She offers him what he does not need—herself. Her love is rejected, and Echo runs off into the woods and, finally, into rocky caves. In these hollow spaces she withers away with longing for Narcissus, first shrinking to a skeleton and then to only a voice. With no sounds to reverberate, this voice is not heard, and Echo practically ceases to exist; she is reborn, however, each time someone speaks words to echo.

Olenka mirrors the archetypal image of Echo. Like Echo who returns only fragments of speech, Olenka echoes the world around her, but she creates a reduced version of it. People, names, objects, feelings—everything is small and described in diminutive terms: Olenka, Vanichka, Vasichka, Volodichka, Sashenka, little cat (*koshechka*), little window (*okoshko*). Olenka even uses adjectives in diminutive form: *slavnen'kii, khoroshen'kii, umnen'kii, belen'kii*. And of course, Olenka herself is not *dusha* but only *dushechka*. She is not Psyche but only a faint, diminutive echo of Psyche.

Not only does Olenka repeat her men's words, but her very existence is reduced to a form of repetition. Like Echo, she has nothing of her own; she completely lacks any sense of an autonomous self. When she embarks upon a new love, she merges completely with the object of that love. While married to Ivan Kukin, the manager of an open-air theater, she identifies herself as "Vanichka and I" and echoes all his views: "Whatever Kukin said about the theater and the actors she repeated." Exactly the same occurs with Pustovalov, the veterinarian Smirnin, and even the boy Sashenka. Olenka's lack of self is not limited, however, to her lack of opinions. Not only does she not have her own conscious life, but she has no subconscious life of her own either. Even while asleep, she dreams about her husband's business: while married to Pustovalov, the manager of the local lumberyard, she has visions of timber, planks, and boards in her dreams.

Olenka's story, like Echo's, follows a sequence of births and deaths. Olenka is reborn each time she has the opportunity to merge her life with someone else's and to repeat someone else's "word." And Olenka dies an intellectual and spiritual death whenever she is deprived of that opportunity, losing all capacity for judgment and opinion. Like Echo, who shrivels up in the rocky caves after being spurned by Narcissus, Olenka withers away in her empty courtyard when her loves die or leave her: "Now she really was alone. . . . She got thinner; she lost her looks. And the passersby in the street would no longer look at her, as they used to before, and would no longer smile at her. . . . She would gaze blankly at her empty yard. She would think of nothing. She would want nothing. And afterward, when night came, she would go to bed and would dream of her empty yard. She would eat and drink as if against her will."

By contrast, in those moments when Olenka is full of love, she physically fills out as well: "Looking at her full [*polnye*] rosy cheeks, her soft white neck with a dark mole on it . . . men thought, 'Yes, you'll do!'" After Olenka's marriage to Kukin, her fullness (*polnota*) is stressed again: "He feasted his eyes on that neck and those plump [*polnye*], healthy shoulders." During this marriage, the narrator notes, "Olenka grew fuller [*polnela*] and beamed with happiness." And when Olenka finds her last love in Sashenka, she is described again as "a tall, stout [*polnaia*] woman."

The opposition full-thin (*polnyi-khudoi*) is further developed in the story into the opposition full-empty (*polnyi-pustoi*). In "The Darling," emptiness and thinness are observed to accompany the periods of Olenka's spiritual emptiness and solitude: "When she was with Kukin and Pustovalov, and later with the veterinary surgeon, Olenka could explain everything, and she would give her opinion on any possible subject, but now her mind and her heart were as empty as her yard." Love for the little boy brings Olenka back to life, once again inspiring her with opinions "after so many years of silence and emptiness [*pustoty*] in her thoughts."

Yet Olenka's fullness turns out to be ambiguous. When Smirnin reappears, bringing his son with him, Olenka's empty courtyard, a metaphor for her soul, is filled with dust: "On a hot July day, toward the evening, when the town herd of cattle was being driven along the street and the whole yard was filled [*napolnilsia*] with dust clouds, someone suddenly knocked at the gate." These dust clouds will inevitably dissipate, though, and the courtyard will become empty again. Likewise Olenka's fullness is always temporary. It is, in fact, itself a cloud of dust. She is doomed to stay forever empty in her empty yard, waiting for someone to come and to give her fullness of being, if only for a brief moment. Such is the fate of the Greek nymph Echo, hiding in hollow caves and waiting for those she can echo in order to become Echo, that is, in order to exist at all.

Given the typological similarity between the Darling and Echo, one can understand why Chekhov's story generated such contradictory responses from its readers. For the myth of Echo itself engendered different and often contradictory interpretations, in part because, in addition to the canonical and better-known tale of Echo and Narcissus discussed above, there exists a distinctly different version of the myth— the tale of Echo and Pan. In this tale, recounted in Longus's *Daphnis and Chloe*, Echo is a wood nymph and an excellent musician. She is a virgin who avoids the company of all males. Pan becomes angry with her because she rejects his advances and because he envies her musical skills. He therefore takes revenge on her by sending shepherds to rip her body apart. The pieces of Echo's body are then flung all across the earth, but they still sing and imitate all sounds as the nymph did before. "Pan himself they imitate too when he plays on the pipe," says Longus in his account of the myth.

Whereas the myth of Echo and Narcissus centers on Echo's reverberative sounds and repetitive language, the fable of Echo and Pan emphasizes the musical and, therefore, creative aspect of Echo. Hence two strands of interpretation—one positive and one negative—derive from the two conceptualizations of this figure. As John Hollander points out in his book *The Figure of Echo*, "in general it is in the milieu of Pan that Echo becomes a credential voice, associated with truth." It is this tradition, then, that led to the adoption of Echo as the symbol of poetry itself. By contrast, the negative readings of Echo arise from Echo's hollowness and repetitiveness, the qualities associated with the other Echo, the spurned lover of Narcissus. Thus Hollander concludes, "Pan's Echo is lyric, Narcissus' is satiric."[10]

The ambiguity of Olenka's character and the differences among its interpreters lie precisely in that Olenka can be seen as both a satiric and a poetic character. The story, indeed, contains both lyrical and satiric overtones. As one Chekhov scholar has noted, at the end of the story the narrator's tone shifts from the satiric to the lyrical, as, for example, in the following passage: "For this little boy, to whom she was not related in any way, for the dimples in his cheeks, for his school cap, she would have given her whole life; she would have given it gladly and with tears of tenderness. Why? Who can tell why?" Here the narrator's irony gives way to lyrical pathos.[11]

Tolstoy, indeed, perceives Olenka poetically. It is no coincidence that in his defense of the Darling, Tolstoy alluded to "the god of poetry": Chekhov "wanted to ridicule this woman, but the God of poetry took over, and he portrayed her charm and self-sacrifice"; Chekhov, "like Balaam, intended to curse, but the God of poetry forbade him to do so and commanded him to bless." To stress the poetic element of the story, Tolstoy repeatedly refers to Chekhov as a poet. In his afterword to "The Darling" the word *poet* is used five times. In this essay Tolstoy juxtaposes the comic and the poetic in the story. He insists that even though there are many comic elements in "The Darling" and many characters are indeed ridiculous, the heroine herself is not laughable: "Kukin's name is ridiculous, and so even is his illness and the telegram announcing his death. The timber dealer with his sedateness is ridiculous, and the veterinary surgeon and the boy are ridiculous; but the soul of Darling, with her capacity for devoting herself with her whole being to the one she loves, is not ridiculous but wonderful and holy."[12] Thus, the very qualities of Olenka that lend themselves to satire—her dependence, her lack of self—Tolstoy interprets poetically. But while poeticizing the heroine, Tolstoy disrupts Chekhov's text, as Pan did the body of Echo. Fascinated with "The Darling," Tolstoy nevertheless does violence to the text: desiring to possess it, he appropriates "The Darling" and reproduces it in his own *Krug chteniia.* But he eliminates some passages from Chekhov's text; that is to say, he "tears it to pieces." Pan's desire leads to destruction. Incidentally, Tolstoy concludes his afterword to "The Darling" with a story that reveals the connection between desire and destruction: "At the other end of the riding school a lady was learning to ride. I thought of how to avoid incommoding that lady and began looking at her. And looking at her, I began involuntarily to draw nearer and nearer to her, and although she, noticing the danger, hastened to get out of the way, I rode against her and upset her; that is to say, I did exactly the opposite of what I wished to do, simply because I had concentrated my attention upon her." Tolstoy uses this anecdote to illustrate his point that the outcome of Chekhov's story contradicts its intent: "The same thing has happened with Chekhov but in an inverse sense."[13] Best of all, however, this anecdote illustrates Tolstoy's own attitude toward "The Darling": he "concentrated his attention upon her," and as a result he "upset her."

If Tolstoy in his reading of "The Darling" follows the tradition associated with Pan's version of the Echo myth, then satire-oriented readers, such as Gorky, deny the heroine any poetry, scorning her as did Narcissus. They view Olenka as the embodiment of the negative woman–Echo type, emphasizing her vacuity and dependence. I suggest that both types of readings are valid and can be explained by the story's archetypal connections to the same complex myth, that of Echo. In both myths Echo is punished for her creativity either as a storyteller or as a musician, and her autonomy is not tolerated. In both cases Echo's physical being is ultimately destroyed either as a consequence of Narcissus's scorn or as a result of Pan's desire. It is the tale of Echo and Narcissus, however, that most clearly conveys the dynamics between

196

scorn, desire, and destruction associated with the myth of Echo. As Julia Kristeva mentions in her essay on Narcissus, "Narcissus encounters a prefiguration of his doubling in a watery reflection in the person of the nymph Echo."[14] Indeed the figure of Echo in this tale is not limited to the role of a rejected lover and points to the ambiguous nature of Narcissus's attitude toward his own mirror image: Narcissus rejects an acoustic reflection of himself (Echo, or a reflected sound) but falls in love with his visual reflection (reflected light). As the desire for one's reflection leads to destruction, Narcissus's rejection of Echo could be interpreted as an attempt at self-preservation. Hence, we see the inherent tension of Narcissus's love for himself: the reflection of self is both spurned and desired. The way Chekhov portrays the Darling in his story suggests the same tension between desire and scorn of one's own mirror image that is revealed in the myth of Echo. What Tolstoy thought to be a disparity between the outcome of the story and its intent is, in fact, equally present in "The Darling": the author both "blesses" the heroine and "curses" her. He is both attracted to a woman-Echo and scorns her, as he sees the inherent danger of Echo's love and of the love for Echo.

The Parodic and the Prosaic

Laurence Senelick

Offenbach and Chekhov; or, La Belle Elena

> Daudet declares that there's a fine book to be
> written: *The Century of Offenbach*, asserting
> that this whole era is descended from him,
> his joking, his music.
> —Edmond de Goncourt, *Journal*
> (January 5, 1887)

VERY LITTLE attention has been paid by literary historians to Chekhov's dramatic antecedents. There are the standard references to Turgenev's *A Month in the Country* and discussions of shared themes in Ostrovsky, but no one has yet carried out the tedious research on the numerous, mediocre Russian vaudevilles, society dramas, and *pièces à thèse* that Chekhov took in as playgoer and reviewer throughout his lifetime. Even if intensive spadework were done in this arid field, it would probably not explain, except by contrast, Chekhov's singularity as a playwright. As the poet Aleksandr Blok wrote, Chekhov is in drama *sui generis*, seemingly without origins and without successful epigones.

A modern critic has attempted to define an outstanding comic genius in the theater by referring to his "mixture of scepticism and compassion for humanity. . . . Nothing escapes his irony, particulary not what he loves." The critic continues, "He . . . nuances the feelings of his characters so well that each becomes a reduced model of humanity, rather than a stereotype."[1] These are not statements about Chekhov but are instead a French writer's analysis of Jacques Offenbach. The similarities of approach between the German-born composer and the Russian writer are not entirely coincidental, for, as I hope to demonstrate, Chekhov from an early age imbibed the Offenbachian perspective, which he found appealing. It served as an early and abiding influence on his artistic developement.

The nature of history, including literary history, is to gravitate to high seriousness and to grant more significance to the solemn than to the gay. *Il penseroso* is rated higher than *L'allegro*. In Chekhov's lifetime, his reputation suffered somewhat from his refusal to subscribe to earnest factions, and well into the twentieth century critics pontificated that his irrepressible facetiousness, his dramatic irony, and his penchant for "small forms" would relegate him forever to the limbo of minor writers. In this respect too, Chekhov has much in common with Offenbach, whose talents were not always taken seriously because they served the causes of comedy, raillery, and sex. One of the few nineteenth-century thinkers to acknowledge Offenbach's greatness was Nietzsche, who wrote in *The Will to Power:* "If one understands genius in an artist to be the highest freedom under the law, divine lightness, frivolity in the most difficult things, then Offenbach has far more right to the name 'Genius' than Wagner. Wagner is difficult, ponderous: nothing is more alien to him than the moments of high-spirited perfection such as this harlequin Offenbach achieves five, six times in each of his buffooneries."[2] *Mutatis mutandis*, something similar might be said of Chekhov.

For more than a decade, the most popular play on the Russian stage was Offenbach's *opéra bouffe, La belle Hélène.* Its premiere staging in Russian as *Prekrasnaia Elena* in the 1868–69 season achieved a record-breaking forty-two consecutive performances. Indeed, if one checks the repertory lists of the imperial theaters in St. Petersburg for the period between the operetta's first appearance in French in 1859 and the ending of the imperial dramatic monopoly in the capitals in 1881, *La belle Hélène* chalks up a remarkable 132 performances. It beats out Gogol's *Inspector General* and Griboedov's *Woe from Wit*, the two most eminent works of Russian drama to that time; even *Hamlet* was later to be presented far less often than Offenbach's *La Périchole* and *Orphée aux enfers.*[3] These successes were repeated in Moscow, occasioning a rhyme:

When *La belle Hélène*
Suddenly appears...
Everything around is dropped:
Katkov, tariffs and treasons
And the disease of famine.[4]

The significance of these performances and those taking place in provincial playhouses all over the empire lies in their introduction of eroticism into the Russian theater. The very first Petersburg performance of *La belle Hélène* at the Michael Theater in 1866 starred a French singer, Devéria, who portrayed an openly seductive Hélène, alluring and appealing to the guardsmen in the pit. On her lips the words "Tell me, Venus, what do you find so amusing / in making my virtue take a tumble" became a pressing invitation, far more sensual and capitulating than had been the interpretation by the role's creator in Paris, Hortense Schneider.[5] Offenbach's exhilarating music, exemplified by the cancan in *Orphée,* and the unbridled gaiety of his plots acted as a stimulant, almost an aphrodisiac. Throughout the Western world, Offenbach was considered to have a liberating effect. In his autobiographical novel, *The Son of a Servant*, the Swedish dramatist August Strindberg recalled how seeing *Orphée aux enfers* at the Royal Theater in Stockholm when a college student undermined many of his youthful inhibitions and enabled him to take a cynical view of the hidebound traditions that were repressing him.[6] In particular, it put a fresh slant on the classics and their hold on modern literary efforts. The extent of this liberation seems to have been greatest in those societies whose theaters were most fettered by state censorship or middle-class morality: England, America, Austria, and Russia.

Confronted by the overwhelming popularity of Offenbach, the Russian intellectual establishment set its face against this epidemic of licentious high spirits. Among the Slavophile faction, M. P. Shchepkin found the whole genre "untalented, insignificant, and cynical," and the playwright Ostrovsky denounced it as immoral and alien, distracting the populace from the need for a native repertory.[7] The most bizarre expression of this conservative distaste was N. K. Mikhailovsky's article of 1871, "Darwinism and Offenbach's Operettas," in *Otechestvennye zapiski* (Notes of the Fatherland), which saw the comic operas as separate tenets of philistine liberalism converging and gathering momentum to legitimate the worst aspects of bourgeois culture. He considered the development of operetta "an historical atavism," awakening base, immoral principles in man. Farfetched and naive as this parallel was, it recognized that Offenbach's main appeal was to a burgeoning middle class, eager to throw over the trammels of exclusivist "high art."[8] On the liberal side, the journalist A. S. Suvorin (who was a liberal early in his career, though he later became a hardshell reactionary) condemned Offenbach and operetta for mocking those things that decent people take seriously. Sometimes Suvorin would admit the comic opera's force as a political phenomenon; at other times he would dismiss its significance as a social factor. Like the rest, he complained that Offenbach's derisiveness was anti-idealistic.

Fiction as well found Offenbach a convenient point of reference. In *Anna Karenina* (1875–77), a sidelight on Vronsky's character is provided when he confesses to regular attendance at *opéra bouffe:* "I do believe I've seen it a hundred times, and always with fresh enjoyment. It's exquisite! I know it's disgraceful, but I fall asleep at the opera, yet I sit out the *opéra bouffe* to the last minute and enjoy it." When he attempts to describe the leading actress to a lady of society, she refuses to hear about such a "horror," despite the fact that everyone already knows about such "horrors." Operetta lacks the propriety of grand opera, and Tolstoy uses this fact to comment on the social hypocrisy of his characters. Later, the landowner Svyazhsky, whose advanced principles run counter to his ordinary life, is characterized as someone who would sell his estate to hear *La belle Hélène.*

Shchedrin in his masterpiece *The Golovlyov Family* (Gospoda Golovlëvy, 1876) used Offenbach as a metonym for social corruption and personal degradation. When his heroine, Anninka, runs away from home and goes on the stage, it is with vague goals of "sacred art," but "she stripped herself bare in *La belle Hélène,* played the drunken Périchole, sang every conceivable indecency in *La grand duchesse de Gérolstein,* and was even sorry that it was inadmissible to show *la chose* and *l'amour* on the stage." Eventually, her acting in these pieces becomes so obscene that "even the uncritical provincial audience" is sickened by it.[9] The way Anninka is cast and costumed in Offenbach's works during her theatrical progress is used by Shchedrin to chart her moral decline.

Strikingly, Chekhov never mentions Offenbach in these tones of opprobrium, partly because he found such anti-idealism congenial, and partly because he was inoculated during his formative years. One of the leading propagandists for operetta in the provinces had been a Taganrog landowner and retired military officer, Grigory Stavrovich Valyano. Having run through an enormous legacy, in 1869 he founded the first playhouses exclusively for operetta in Taganrog and in nearby Rostov, where he served not only as impresario but also as an actor, director, and translator and maintained a high level of quality in both musical and dramatic performances. Through his connections in Paris and Vienna, he was able to introduce a new repertory of comic opera into theaters both in the capitals and in the provinces, before financial reverses reduced him to a mere player in other people's troupes.[10]

As an adolescent, Anton Chekhov was an inveterate playgoer at the Taganrog theater. According to his brother Ivan, the first play he saw there was *La belle Hélène.*[11] At the age of twelve he might also have attended a farcical takeoff, *In Pursuit of La belle Hélène* (V pogoniu za prekrasnoi Elenoi, by V. A. Krylov, 1872), in the civic theater's new building. Later, particularly between 1876 and 1879 when his parents were in Moscow and his theatergoing increased under the aegis of his uncle Mitrofan, Chekhov had the opportunity to enjoy Offenbach's *Barbe bleue, Les brigands, La princesse de Trébizonde,* and *La Périchole,* as well *Hélène* itself.[12] Chroniclers tell us that all the coachmen, peddlers, and organ-grinders in the empire were singing the Russian lyrics to "Quand j'étais roi de Boéotie" from *Orphée.* The young Chekhov may well have joined them.[13]

The versions of Offenbach that Chekhov saw had been considerably Russified. Most of the political allusions and wordplay had been replaced by heavy-handed, conventional references to the usual laughingstocks of the Russian vaudeville. Audiences at *Orphée* roared when the actor Gorbunov came on wearing a heavy peasant coat over his costume as Mercury, and it was common for whoever played Vanka Styx (originally John Styx, a barb at the Parisian taste for English domestics) to lard his aria with topical verses about a quick ride down Nevsky Prospect or getting the better of Siberian merchants.[14] One of the chief adapters was the extraordinarily prolific Viktor Krylov, who appears in Chekhovian biography as the hack who offered to rewrite *Ivanov* for a share of the profits, in order to make it conform to traditional stage practice. Despite the sea-changes he and others made to the librettos of Meilhac, Halévy, and Crémieux, however, Offenbach's music remained untouched, and the overarching high spirits, infectious sensuality, and socially leveling nature of the dramatic situations persisted.

Chekhov, like Strindberg, was liberated from the grip of the classics by Offenbach's irreverent treatment of gods and heroes. During his childhood, educational reforms intended to make it more difficult for minorities and lower orders to rise in society had intensified the Greek and Latin curricula. As a consequence, schoolmasters and Latin grammar remain shorthand for blinkered and narrow-minded pedantry throughout Chekhov's work. Whenever he does make a classical allusion, it is almost never to Homer or Virgil but to Offenbach's perversion of mythology. Chekhov seems well aware that he was thus aligning himself with the unwitting confusion of a Russian public whose classical background was so shaky that its most vivid images of ancient Greece came from the operetta stage. In his satire "From the Notebook of Ivan Ivanych," written between 1883 and 1886 (an unintentional counterpart to Flaubert's *Dictionnaire des idées réçues*), a disquisition on the harm caused by women offers as its prime historical example: "The Trojan War broke out on account of Belle Hélène."[15]

Chekhov's familiarity with Offenbach deepened during his journalistic apprenticeship in Moscow; his letters are studded with quotations from Offenbach songs. In 1883 he complains that he can't finish a story because a hurdy-gurdy is churning out *La belle Hélène* under his window.[16] Through his brother Nikolai, who worked as a scene painter for the impresario Mikhail Lentovsky, Chekhov had free access to Lentovsky's various enterprises, including his enormously popular operetta theater, the Bouffe, and his "Fantasy Theater" in Hermitage Park. His repertory abounded with Offenbach from 1878 on and included a revival of *La belle Hélène* in 1885. Chekhov's attitude toward Lentovsky was mocking but affectionate; he appreciated the man's good sense, amiability, and ingenuity, but in his theatrical gossip columns Chekhov teased Lentovsky's fondness for sensational effects. When Chekhov reviewed a Lentovsky production of *The Rich Baker's Wife* (La Boulangère a des écus, 1880) or the lavish six-hour *Trip to the Moon* (1883) or *Geneviève de Brabant* (1883), his criticism was directed not so much at the operas themselves but at the lack of proportion in devoting such vast resources to light entertainment. Chekhov described the spectacular *Trip to the Moon* (whose coauthor of the Russian libretto was Chekhov's newspaper colleague L. I. Gulaev) as "grandiose and pompous as a wedding coach, and as highfalutin as a million ungreased wheels."[17] In another feuilleton, Chekhov set Offenbach's ghost to haunt the manager Kuznetsov, who mixed *opéra bouffe* with national folk opera, and garbled the macaronics of a performance whose principals are French but whose chorus sings in Russian: "Bez zhenshchin, sans femmes, bez femm-shchin, sans zhen-femmes."[18]

Chekhov's attitude toward these operettas is part of his attraction-repulsion to the theater in general. While he preserves his precocious fondness for these works, he also demonstrates a new awareness of the tawdriness and lewdness they promote on both sides of the footlights. The ebullience expressed in the music and lyrics is often neutralized by the coarseness of the largely male audience and the squalor of backstage intrigue. Chekhov's earliest stories, located in many cases in a theatrical milieu ("Fairy Tales of Melpomene," he characterized them), refer regularly to Offenbach, and the operetta stage runs through his humorous prose as a sustaining stream of local allusion, providing a bohemian alternative to the petit-bourgeois life that he otherwise portrays. Offenbach is also shown to be a Russian cliché for European culture. In Chekhov's parody of conservative officialdom, "Goose Conversation" (October 1884), the old geese view the West as "the land of operetta! Operetta, you'll agree, is a good, even an indispensable thing"; they complain that by flying south instead of west they have never had a chance to hear Hélène's famous aria. In "My Guide to Housekeeping" (1886) the tyrannical husband forces his wife to play excerpts from Offenbach as an aid to digestion after a heavy meal. A description of holiday crowds in the week following Easter ("Krasnaia gorka," March 1885) points out that while some plebeians sing Russian folk songs, semisophisticated hotel servants and bootblacks yelp (*lupiat*) the number about cautious husbands from *La belle Hélène*. (The song in question explains to the inopportune Ménélas that a well-bred husband will always inform his wife exactly when he is to return home and is characterized ironically by Chekhov as "a mixture of heathen outlook and humanitarianism.") Valets who fancy such fare seem an early sketch for Yasha in *The Cherry Orchard* with his longing for Paris. In June 1885 Chekhov drew on *Barbe bleue* for two pieces: "Boots," in which a man given the wrong boots at an inn inadvertently reveals that the actor playing Bluebeard is sleeping with the wife of the actor playing

King Bobèche and is chased at gunpoint for his pains; and "My Wives," a rather misogynistic conceit in which Raoul Bluebeard justifies his uxoricides by delineating the insufferable nature of his spouses.

Thereafter, Chekhov no longer refers directly to Offenbach in the stories, no doubt because he had become immersed in a sphere of experience wider than the limited bohemian milieux of greenroom, press room, and consulting room. He was taking himself more seriously as an author. The new care in his writing did not require the instant flavor of ribaldry he could achieve by dropping Offenbach's name. Yet at the end of his career, in one of his last, great stories, Chekhov was to return to his metonymic use of operetta as a token for the man-in-the-street's idea of European sophistication. In 1897 Chekhov saw *La belle Hélène* for the last time, in the original French at the Biarritz Casino.[19] Revivals at three different Moscow theaters in 1898 were covered in *Novosti dnia*, a paper Chekhov read regularly. This may have jogged his recollection of the provincial performances of his youth, for in "The Darling" (Dushechka, 1899) the impressionable Olenka's first husband runs a summer musical theater. The couple lament the general failure of the public to comprehend art, especially its refusal to come and see Hervé's *Petit Faust* and Offenbach's *Orphée* at their house. This reprise of Chekhov's mockery of philistine taste is more affectionate, less sardonic, than in his earlier writings.

An Offenbachian correlative of greater importance to the fabric of meaning occurs in Chekhov's one-act play *Swan Song* (Lebedinaia pesnia, 1887–88), based on the short story "Calchas" (Kalkhas, November 1886), whose title bears a special message to an Offenbach aficionado. In both variants of this "Laugh, clown, laugh" scenario, the veteran actor Svetlovidov traces the decline in his fortunes back to the moment when his fiancée watched him play "a vulgar, slapstick part" and refused to marry him unless he left the stage. As it happens, he is dressed in the costume of Calchas, the wily oracle-monger in *La belle Hélène*, a role he has just played at his benefit performance. This costume was a garishly decorated tunic, short enough to reveal the actor's superannuated legs; in the story (where he is fifty-eight) and, more effectively because visually in the play (where his age is increased to sixty-eight), this garb serves as an ironic counterpoint to the old ham's plaints and his quotations from *Hamlet, Lear, Othello*, and Griboedov. It not only vividly supports his claim that he is relegated to playing crude farce but also undercuts the self-pity that is a pitfall for anyone assuming the role of Svetlovidov. The classical quotations do not appear in the story but were provided by Chekhov in the one-act play as a showcase for the popular actor Davydov, who played leading roles in Offenbach in the provinces. To have a celebrated comic bemoaning his state as a comic while wearing a comic costume must have produced a vividly Pirandellian hall-of-mirrors effect in the original production.

Offenbach's Calchas is a fraud who appropriates the offerings to the gods for his own uses and interprets the oracles to suit the occasion. Svetlovidov's fraud lies in the false faces his profession makes him wear; despite his maudlin tale of the past, he seems to exist only when he is reciting his lines. His very *nom de théâtre*, Bright Aspect, is a sorry misnomer. Just as Offenbach's high priest moves between high-flown addresses to divinity and a very colloquial idiom, Svetlovidov shuttles back and forth between rhetorical verse imprecations and a fruity, vernacular Russian packed with more homely curses. The relation of the Offenbachian character to Chekhov's play is so crucial that it is pointless, as some critics have done, to identify Calchas as a character in Shakespeare's *Troilus and Cressida*—a play never performed in the nineteenth century, least of all on the tsarist stage—and equally pointless for Svetlovidovs in modern productions to come on wearing Roman togas.[20]

Lines, themes, and characters from Offenbach's operettas pervaded Chekhov's imagination. Much richer, however, was Offenbach's influence on Chekhov's playwriting after this stock of operettic allusion had been absorbed into his literary subconscious, whence he could draw on it more intuitively. The character of Elena Andreevna, first presented in *The Wood Demon* and then rewritten in *Uncle Vanya*, is an updating, even a sort of parody of La Belle Hélène as she appears in Offenbach. The belle Hélène drawn by Meilhac and Halévy was not intended, says the French critic David Rissin, as a personal depiction of any one woman in society but summed up "the great bourgeoises in general, indeed even the bourgeoisie in its entirety."[21] She is not portrayed as a temptress or even as inordinately susceptible, but sees herself rather as the passive pawn of history. Hélène complains that the hand of fate weighs heavily on her, because of her scandalous parentage and her standing as the most beautiful woman in the world. "I wish I could have been a peaceful middle-class housewife, married to some nice merchant from Mitylene," she sighs. Ménélas is "a good and excellent man"; she tried to love him but couldn't.[22] When the shepherd Pâris arrives and informs her that he is entitled to the most beautiful woman in the world, she is caught in a dilemma, knowing that she fits that description but has an obligation to remain a respectable wife. Her plight suggests that the system of gods and men requires the debauch of women, even against their will.

In the second act, Hélène sings her famous "Invocation à Vénus":

T'wards husband's honor we're well meaning
And seek to guard it at all cost,

But unt'ward circumstances intervening,
Despite ourselves our honor's lost...
Take the example of my mother!
When the great swan was drawing near
(Which, as you know, became my father),
What should she think she had to fear?
Venus, please tell why does it divert you
In this way to topple my virtue?

Ah! wretched queen for all our beauty!...
That gift of heaven's heavy odds!
To fight off men was once my duty,
My duty's now to fight off gods.
I fight on bravely to confound all
Temptations, but to no avail...
For if Olympus wills my downfall
Sooner or later I shall fail.[23]

Much of the song's success comes from the chorus and its operative word *cascader*, "to tumble," "to take a spill," "to go an a spree," which marvelously captures Hélène's insouciant erotism tinged with impudence. Its image of physical imbalance works as a metaphor for the imminent loss of moral equipoise. This scene is the key episode in *La belle Hélène*, for the aria, like the best operatic songs, expressed not so much external events as what is transpiring in the mind of the character. In a novel and yet accurate manner, Offenbach shows us a sensual and unsatisfied woman struggling against the fatality of her nature. When she finally decides to kick over the traces, the action can (and must, if it has any resonance) symbolize liberation not only from sexual but from all socially ordained morality. Offenbach's originality comes in his depiction of the conflict from the woman's point of view.[24] (Hélène in fact continues to repulse Pâris; Pâris bribes Calchas, who pretends to send her sweet dreams. In this ostensible vision, she is willing to succumb to the shepherd's advances, and by act III, yielding wholly to fate, she allows him, in the disguise of a priest of Venus, to carry her off to Cythæra.)

In Chekhov's comedy *The Wood Demon* (1890), Offenbach's burlesque of the Homeric abduction is doubly burlesqued, a relation made clear in the dialogue. When, in the denouement of act IV, the mill owner Dyadin returns Elena Andreevna to her husband the professor, it is with the words: "Your Excellency, I was the one who made off with your wife, as once a certain Paris did the beautiful Helen." His words, *prekrasnaia Elena*, are, in fact, the title of Offenbach's operetta in Russian, and Dyadin goes on to garble another of Chekhov's favorite plays: "It was I! Although pockmarked Parises don't exist, still, friend

209

Horatio, there's more in earth than is met with in your philosophy." Not only is this rural Russian Paris ugly and middle-aged, but he is also an acknowledged cuckold. Chekhov's Helen is abducted by a substitute Menelaus.

Elena did not appear in the original cast list of *The Wood Demon*, which Chekhov drew up for his intended collaborator, Suvorin, in October 1888, but the playwright had already experimented with the character of a tempted wife in his short story "A Misfortune" (Neschast'e, 1886). Like Offenbach's operetta, this narrative is essentially constructed in three acts. In the first, Sofya Petrovna, a notary's wife who thinks herself "an ordinary woman," halfheartedly resists the open-air advances of the lawyer Ilin, although she is sorely drawn by his insistence that he loves her because she is "so beautiful." In the second, during a card party that seems to correspond to the game of goose played in act II of *La belle Hélène*, Sofya Petrovna is confident of her "unassailable virtue"; she flirts and lets herself be tempted in the frivolous atmosphere, much as Hélène allows herself to be wooed in the false dream. Sofya's discordant feelings emerge in her own central aria, as she sings melancholy ballads for her guests "nervously, with a certain half-tipsy fervor," yet sensing that something bad will happen. In act III, she comes to a decision while the strains of a tenor are heard outside her window. When her husband proves to be listless and tendentious in the face of her imminent betrayal, she walks out, calling herself immoral but driven by something "stronger than her shame, and reason, and fear."

Contemporary critics remarked on the originality of portraying the conflicted feelings of a young married woman of the *intelligentsia* torn between desire and duty, without noting that Chekhov seems to have used the Offenbachian model to effect a parody of *Anna Karenina* on a bourgeois plane. Characteristically, whenever Chekhov experiments with a new genre or theme, he parodies it. As in Offenbach, the husband remains a caricature, and the ardent seducer is drawn somewhat sketchily, but the warring factions within the woman's psyche occupy our attention and raise the farce to a higher level. That Chekhov should relate them to musical utterance is also a telling detail.

Elena Andreevna, as she is limned in *The Wood Demon*, is, like Sofya Petrovna, also placed in a summertime, dacha ambience that provides the leisured break from routine that is the middle-class equivalent of court life and the seaside resort in *Hélène*. Her character is handled somewhat differently than it will be in *Uncle Vanya*. Whereas in *Vanya* her conjugal faithfulness is a subject broached by Voinitsky and Astrov and overheard by Waffles, in *The Wood Demon* her looks and her fidelity are debated among male guests. In other words, this earlier Elena is a topic for smoking-room commentary, which creates a *louche* aura around her even before her first entrance. Her own worldliness is rather greater in her earlier avatar: she comments that love letters are a futile strategem; they may be received but go unread. This is surely the voice of experience. She also shares La Belle Hélène's insistence on her virtue; Voinitsky, objecting to her indolence and sluggishness, adds, "So much virtue that, pardon me, it makes me sick to look at it." She has the bad dreams and presentiments of a classical heroine and the tendency to see her circumstances as exemplary: "I have no will of my own. I'm cowardly, inhibited, and I keep thinking that, if I were to be unfaithful, all wives would follow my example and leave their husbands." This heightening of personal experience into a universal example recalls the prototype of Helen of Troy, the paradigmatic unfaithful wife who brought disaster in her wake.

Chekhov ordinarily avoids the epic or the grand gesture. So Offenbach's satiric leveling of mythological tropes is matched by Chehov's thwarting of theatrical expectation. As we have seen, the abduction is caricatured and aborted, and Elena remarks on her voluntary return to the professor, "Do you think she will turn her freedom to any good use? Don't worry... She will come back... She has already come back." She wryly accepts a "woman's lot," to grow stale in household routine, and lacks the courage to make the final break. In other words, Helen chooses to go back to Menelaus before any harm is done; as in Giraudoux, "The Trojan War will not take place." Chekhov outdoes Offenbach in ironic bathos: Offenbach had suggested that respectable women of the Second Empire needed a good deal of persuasion to give in to their sensual feelings, but when they did, the result was cataclysmic. Chekhov suggests that respectable women of the Russian Empire are so alien to their own sensual nature that they remain inhibited and bound to a life they know is stifling.

When he came to convert *The Wood Demon* to *Uncle Vanya*, Chekhov typically omitted many of the more blatant statements, including Elena's fear of setting an example for all wives. Some of her worldliness is pared away, but it will return highly amplified in *The Cherry Orchard*, reappearing as Ranevskaya in her Parisian gowns. Still, Voinitsky's speech about immorality is unchanged in *Uncle Vanya* and is virtually a synopsis of Pâris's arguments in *La belle Hélène:* "To be unfaithful to an old husband you can't stand—that's considered immoral; but to try to stifle one's poor youth and living feeling—that's not immoral."

By reducing the cast of *The Wood Demon* to the tight family circle of *Uncle Vanya*, Chekhov has set Offenbach's triangle in the foreground of the work. Both cynosure and catalyst, Elena is, like Hélène, a respectable middle-class wife, anxious to preserve her virtue even when

211

assailed by alluring temptation. She disclaims responsibility for the sexual attraction she exerts on the men around her and protests that their attentions are a nuisance. Her complaint that men cannot look at a woman with an old husband without desiring her echoes Hélène's grievances. The professor, her elderly spouse, is less complaisant, more dictatorial, than Ménélas, but he too is a feeble, somewhat comic valetudinarian. The Greek connection is underlined when Waffles asks him if he knows a certain Lakedaimonov. It's a natural assumption, one cuckold calling to a putative colleague, since Menelaus was king of Sparta, otherwise known as Lacedæmonia. (In *Wood Demon*, the name was the less burlesque Novosyolov.)

Moreover, the Elena of *Uncle Vanya* is given her own version of the invocation to Venus, a solo aria in act III. Here, prompted by Sonya's hopeless love for Astrov, she allows herself to fantasize what it would be like to give herself to a man like him. She ruminates on Vanya's insistence that she has *rusalka*'s (water nymph's) blood and should give in to her desires once in her life; she wonders if he is right. (This seems to me very close to Hélène's sorry awareness that she is the offspring of Leda and the Swan, that her nature springs from that lustful miscegenation.) Vanya had urged Elena "to hurry up and fall in love with some water sprite up to your ears—and plop headfirst into the millrace," a choice of words that has two Offenbachian echoes. The Swedish tourist Baron Gondremarck in *La vie parisienne* sings that he intends to plunge into Parisian pleasures *jusque là*, a phrase that became proverbial; and plopping headfirst into a millrace seems a homely version of Hélène's *cascader*. Both Hélène and Elena end their arias on a querulous and conscience-stricken note, followed by the entrance of the feared but longed-for seducer, Pâris/Astrov.

In both Offenbach and Chekhov, the pressing suit of the intruder is interrupted by another intrusion in a farcical key by a husband or husband-surrogate. Chekhov distributes some of Ménélas's functions to Vanya, who longs to be Elena's mate and always addresses her as Hélène. In Offenbach, when Ménélas bursts into the bedchamber to find his wife in the arms of Pâris, no scene of melodramatic jealousy ensues: Hélène inquires about his trip, and the hapless king is informed by her and by his royal colleagues that respectable husbands always send an advance message giving the time of their return. In Chekhov, Vanya's inopportune stumbling upon Elena and Astrov's kiss is a similar damp squib: instead of an explosion of jealousy or shame, there is Astrov's trivial chat about the weather and, later, his mocking reference to "Uncle Vanya and his bouquet of roses," while Vanya stammers, "Huh? Well, yes . . . fine . . . Hélène, I saw it all, all." Ménélas tries to make a scene: "I'm not an ordinary husband; I'm an epic husband, I am! I want people to be talking about this case four thousand years from now." This absurd megalomania seems echoed in Vanya's cry, "I could have been a Dostoevsky, a Schopenhauer," a statement whose very absurdity breaks into his consciousness a moment later.

It may be stretching my point too far to try to demonstrate that the final chorus in *La belle Hélène*, with its reiterated "Va pour Cythère, va, va, va," is echoed in the motiflike "They've gone" in the last act of *Uncle Vanya*. Nevertheless, Chekhov may be trying for a *reductio ad absurdum* by sending his Helen, not with her lover but with her husband, not to Cythæra, the haunt of Venus, but to Kharkov, a town that in Chekhov always stands for the most sleepy and dismal backwater, the terminus of unfulfilled lives.

The chief value of Offenbach's inspiration for Chekhov is in providing a dramatic treatment of adultery that was neither slapstick nor hysterical. In most plays by Chekhov's contemporaries that deal with transgressing wives or women contemplating an illicit affair, the tone is melodramatic, neurasthenic, charged with overwrought emotions. The women are either impossibly sensual Messalinas or guilt-ridden Niobes. Without moralizing, *La belle Hélène* offered a critical means of depicting a wife who, faced with temptation, has to come to terms with her own nature.

The mainspring of all Offenbach's plots is frustration: villains are few, and a character suffers defeat when his own desire, usually for sex or power, collides with that of others. In grand opera, these individual conflicts engender desperate actions in the characters and strong emotions in the spectators. But in Offenbachian operetta, these conflicting desires generate an impression of absurdity. The futility of the characters' striving stirs up a different kind of emotion in them and in the spectators: lucid laughter in face of unreconciled contradictions.

Chekhov, I would submit, shares a similar viewpoint and a similar technique, particularly in his drama, in which frustrated desire is a leitmotiv. The clash of velleities rarely leads to effective or culminating action but exhibits ridiculous inconsistencies that result only in laughter or futile despair. Unlike Offenbach, Chekhov does not reverse moral values; his approach to Offenbach's diminution of epic and melodrama is to expose the conventionality of emotional posturing and to dissolve tragic aspirations in an acid bath of triviality. Offenbach settles his situations in a riot of high spirits, a musical finale that takes refuge in frivolity, in the face of everything. Working in a more realistic mode, Chekhov can have recourse to this manic anarchy only in such farces as *The Wedding* or *The Jubilee*. In his major plays, the finales are open-ended, unresolved, more often watered with tears than with champagne. Having learned to whistle Offenbach's tunes, Chekhov rearranged them for a chamber orchestra.

Gary Saul Morson

Uncle Vanya as Prosaic Metadrama

> Solyony: I have never had anything against
> you, Baron. But I have the temperament
> of Lermontov. [*Softly*] I even look like
> Lermontov... so they say...
> —Chekhov, *The Three Sisters*

THEATER OF THEATRICALITY

IT MIGHT be said that the fundamental theme of Chekhov's plays is theatricality itself, our tendency to live our lives "dramatically." In Chekhov's view, life as we actually live it does not generally conform to staged plots, except when people try to endow their lives with a spurious meaningfulness by imitating literary characters and scenes. Traditional plays imitate life only to the extent that people imitate plays, which is unfortunately all too common. There are Hamlets in life primarily because people have read *Hamlet* or works like it. The theater has been realistic only when people have self-consciously reversed mimesis to imitate it.

Such reverse mimesis is typical of Chekhov's major characters. His plays center on histrionic people who imitate theatrical performances and model themselves on other melodramatic genres. They posture, seek grand romance, imagine that a tragic fatalism governs their lives, and indulge in utopian dreams while they neglect the ordinary virtues and ignore the daily processes that truly sustain them. Such virtues— the prosaic decencies in which Chekhov deeply believed—are typically practiced by relatively undramatic characters who do not appreciate their own significance.[1] In the background of the play and on the margins of its central actions, truly meaningful prosaic life can be glimpsed.

Because histrionics is Chekhov's central theme, his plays rely to a great extent on metatheatrical devices. Those devices show us why the world is *not* a stage and why we should detect falsity whenever it seems to resemble a play. Metatheatricality is most obvious in *The Sea Gull*, Chekhov's first major dramatic success. Indeed, Chekhov's use of the technique in this play borders on the heavy-handed. We have only to

214

recall that one major character, an actress, behaves as theatrically with her family as she does on the stage; that her son is a playwright who devotes his life to romantic longing and *ressentiment*; that an aspiring young actress tries to reenact the romance of a famous novel by sending its author a quotation from it; that citizens from *Hamlet* suffuse the action; and, of course, that a play-within-a-play provides the point of reference for all other events. *Uncle Vanya* dispenses with much of this overt machinery while still maintaining the metatheatrical allusions it was designed to create. In effect, the internal play expands to become the drama itself. Like a committee of the whole, *Uncle Vanya* becomes in its entirety a sort of play-within-a-play.

As a result, the work reverses the usual foreground and background of a drama. In most plays, people behave "dramatically" in a world where such behavior is appropriate. The audience, which lives in the undramatic world we all know, participates vicariously in the more interesting and exciting world of the stage. That, indeed, may be one reason people go to the theater. In *Uncle Vanya* the characters carry on just as "dramatically" as anyone might expect from the stage, but they do so in a world that seems as ordinary and everyday as the world of the audience. Consequently, actions that would be tragic or heroic in other plays here acquire tonalities of comedy or even farce. Chekhov never tired of reminding Stanislavsky and others that his plays were not melodramas but precisely (as he subtitled *The Sea Gull* and *The Cherry Orchard*) comedies. Chekhov gives us dramatic characters in an undramatic world in order to satirize all theatrical poses and all attempts to behave as if life were literary and theatrical. Histrionics for Chekhov was a particularly loathsome form of lying, which truly cultured people avoid "even in small matters."[2]

Chekhov's toying with the dramatic frame may be seen as a particularly original use of a traditional satiric technique. Like his great predecessors in parody, he transforms his main characters into what might be called "generic refugees."[3] That is, he creates characters who would be at home in one genre but places them in the world of another. So Don Quixote, Emma Bovary, and Ilya Ilych Oblomov become comic when forced to live in a realistic world rather than the chivalric adventure story, the romantic novel, or the idyll of which they dream. *War and Peace* places its epic hero, Prince Andrei, in a novelistic world where epic heroism is an illusion; *Middlemarch* confers refugee status on Dorothea in its Prelude about how she, like Saint Theresa, needed an "epic life" to realize her potential but, in the nineteenth century, could find only prosaic reality. As these examples show, this technique does not preclude an admixture of sympathy in the satire.

Chekhov's main characters think of themselves as heroes or heroines from various genres of Russian literature, which is ironic, of course, because they are characters in Russian literature. Having read the great authors, they, like many members of the *intelligentsia*, plagiarize significance by imitating received models. Here it is worth observing that the Russian term *intelligentsia* does not mean the same thing as the English word *intelligentsia*, which underwent a shift in meaning when borrowed from the Russian. In Russian, an *intelligent* (member of the intelligentsia) was not necessarily an intellectual, and not all intellectuals were *intelligenty*. A member of the *intelligentsia* was identified as such by a particular way of living—bad manners of a specified sort were important—and above all by a complex of attitudes, including militant atheism, an opposition to all established authority, socialism, and a mystique of revolution. Prosaic virtues were regarded as unimportant, if not harmful, and a taste for the grand and dramatic was cultivated. *Intelligenty* were expected to adopt one or another grand system of thought that purported to explain all of culture and society and promised an end to all human suffering if a given kind of revolution should take place; the function of the *intelligentsia* was to adopt the right system and make sure its recommendations were put into practice. To do so, solidarity—what Chekhov despised as intellectual conformism—was needed. If by *intellectual* we mean someone characterized by independence of thought, we can see how it was easily possible for an intellectual to be an "antiintelligentsial" and for an *intelligent* to be antiintellectual. A member of an *intelligentsia* "circle," even if he never read a book, would be considered an *intelligent* more readily than Leo Tolstoy, who expressed utter contempt for this whole complex of beliefs and lived a manifestly nonintelligentsial life.

Not surprisingly, this dominant tradition of the *intelligentsia* generated a countertradition of thinkers who rejected its fundamental premises. Tolstoy's masterpieces, *War and Peace* and *Anna Karenina*, explicitly attack all grand systems of thought, all attempts to find hidden laws of history, and, consequently, all prescriptions for universal salvation. For Tolstoy, and the countertradition generally, it is not the dramatic events of life that matter, either for individuals or for societies, but the countless small, prosaic events of daily life.

It was above all this aspect of Tolstoy's thought that had the most profound influence on Chekhov, who, as we have seen, constantly expressed the deepest skepticism about the intelligentsial mentality and valued everyday virtues. Invited to join one *intelligentsia* circle, Chekhov responded with an accusation of hypocrisy and a restatement of his most cherished values—honesty and simple acts of kindness, for which "you've got to be not so much the young literary figure as just a plain human being. Let us be ordinary people, let us adopt the same attitude *toward all*, then an artificially overwrought solidarity will not be needed."[4] In the twentieth century this countertradition—the kind of thought I call prosaics—has been represented by that remarkable anthology of essays by disillusioned *intelligenty, Landmarks: A Collection of Essays on the Russian Intelligentsia* (1909); by Mikhail Zoschenko; and by the literary and cultural critic Mikhail Bakhtin.[5]

Both Chekhov and Tolstoy understood that the prestige of the *intelligentsia* cast a shadow on educated society as a whole and predisposed people to adopt grand roles drawn from literature. Chekhov's characters imagine that they are heroes or heroines in a genre suffused with romance, heroism, great theories, and decisive action, or else they try to play the lead roles in tragic tales of paralyzing disillusionment and emptiness. They consider themselves to be either heroes or "heroes of our time." But their search for drama unfolds in Chekhov's universe of prosaics.

In its examination of histrionics, *Uncle Vanya* is in a position to exploit metatheatrical devices. *Uncle Vanya* is theater about theatricality, and so its main characters are continually "overacting." One reason the play has proven so difficult to stage in the right tonality— as critics and directors have constantly noted—is that the actors must overact and call attention to their theatrical status but without ceasing to play real people who truly suffer. They must not over-overact. Their performance must allude to but not shatter the dramatic frame.

When we watch *Uncle Vanya*, we do not see actors playing characters. We see characters playing characters. They labor under the belief that this role-playing brings them closer to "true life," but in fact it does the opposite. The audience contemplates real people—people like themselves—who live citational lives, that is, lives shaped by literary role-playing, lives consisting not so much of actions as of allusions. We are asked to consider the extent to which our own lives are, like the title of this play, citational.

TURGENEV'S GOUT

> If criticism, the authority of which you cite,
> knows what you and I don't, why has it kept mum
> until now? Why doesn't it disclose to us the truth
> and immutable laws? If it had known, believe me,
> it would long ago have shown us the way and we
> would know what to do. . . . But criticism keeps
> pompously quiet or gets off cheap with idle,
> worthless chatter. If it presents itself to you as
> influential, it is only because it is immodest,

insolent, and loud, because it is an empty barrel
that one involuntarily hears. Let's spit on all this.
—Chekhov, letter to Leontiev-Shcheglov,
March 22, 1890

Chekhov places members of the *intelligentsia* at the center of his
play because they are especially given to self-dramatization and because
they love to display their superior culture. As they cite novels, criticism,
and other dramas, Chekhov shapes his metaliterary satire of histrionics
and intelligentsial posing.

Old Serebryakov, we are told at the very beginning of the play,
was a former theology student and the son of a sexton. These are just
the roots one would choose if one's goal was to display a typical member
of the *intelligentsia*. A professor of literature, he peevishly demands
that someone fetch his copy of the poet Batyushkov, looks down on
those with fewer citations at their disposal, and tries to illuminate his
life with literary models.

He makes even his illness allusive: "They say that Turgenev developed angina pectoris from gout. I'm afraid I may have it."[6] At the
beginning of his speech to the assembled family in act III, he first asks
them "to lend me your ears, as the saying goes [*Laughs*]." As is so often
the case in Chekhov's plays, the line is more meaningful than he knows,
for the speech he has prepared, like that of his Shakespearean model,
is made under false pretenses. Appropriately enough, he continues his
game of allusions by citing Gogol's famous play—"I invited you here,
ladies and gentlemen, to announce that the Inspector General is
coming"—evidently without having considered that its action concerns
confidence games. Like *Uncle Vanya*, *The Inspector General* involves
multiple layers of role-playing, mutually reinforcing poses, and self-
induced self-deceptions. In his last appearance of the play, the professor
proposes to transform its action into yet another occasion for professional
criticism: "After what has happened, I have lived through so much,
and thought so much in the course of a few hours, that I believe I
could write a whole treatise for the edification of posterity." It is hard
to decide whether to call this line pathetic or repulsive, but in either
case it ought to disturb us professionals more than it has.

If the old professor projects ill-considered confidence in his merely
citational importance, then Voinitsky, who has at last understood such
falsities, can only create new ones. He realizes that for most of his life
he has been content with a vicarious connection to the professor's vicarious connection to literature, but all he learns from his disillusionment is that the professor was the wrong intermediary.

Given our own views of the professor, we may take at face value

Voinitsky's denunciation of his work as an uncomprehending and momentarily fashionable deployment of modish but empty jargon. But that only makes Voinitsky's desire for a better connection with literature even more misguided. Filled with all the self-pity, impotent rage, and underground *ressentiment* of a disappointed member of the *intelligentsia*, he regrets that he is too old to surpass the professor at his own game. Chekhov brilliantly merges despair and slapstick humor—we seem to check ourselves in midlaugh—when Voinitsky declares: "My life is over! I was talented, intelligent, self-confident... If I had had a normal life, I might have been a Schopenhauer, a Dostoevsky..." To put it mildly, the choice of Dostoevsky as an example of someone who lived "a normal life" suggests a rather odd (but intelligentsial) understanding of normality. And we are aware of Dostoevsky's penchant for describing the very mixture of megalomania and self-contempt that Vanya so pathetically displays.

As if to mock both Voinitsky's precarious connection to literature and his self-indulgent pleas for pity, Chekhov has the ridiculous and truly pitiful Telegin interrupt the scene of confrontation. Telegin insists on his own incredibly vicarious link to scholarship:

> TELEGIN [*embarrassed*]: Your Excellency, I cherish not only a feeling of reverence for scholarship, but of kinship as well. My brother Grigory Ilych's wife's brother—perhaps you know him—Konstantin Trofimovitch Lakedomonov, was an M.A....
>
> VOINITSKY: Be quiet, Waffles, we're talking business.

In Telegin's pathetic "perhaps you know him" and in the truly Gogolian name Lakedomonov we may perhaps detect another allusion to *The Inspector General*. In Gogol's play, Pyotr Ivanovich Bobchinsky would feel his life were worthwhile if the powers that be knew of his mere existence:

> BOBCHINSKY: I humbly beg you, sir, when you return to the capital, tell all those great gentlemen—the senators and admirals and all the rest— say, "Your Excellency or Your Highness, in such and such a town there lives a man called Pyotr Ivanovich Bobchinsky." Be sure to tell them, "Pyotr Ivanovich Bobchinsky lives there."
>
> KHLESTAKOV: Very well.
>
> BOBCHINSKY: And if you should happen to meet with the tsar, then tell the tsar too, "Your Imperial Majesty, in such and such a town there lives a man called Pyotr Ivanovich Bobchinsky."
>
> KHLESTAKOV: Fine.[7]

Telegin is a Bobchinsky for whom professors have replaced admirals.

Voinitsky seems unaware that he treats Telegin with the same disregard that he so resents in the professor's treatment of him.

Voinitsky is undoubtedly correct that his mother's "principles" are, as he puts it, a "venomous joke." As he now sees, she can only repeat received expressions "about the emancipation of women," without being aware that her own behavior verges on an unwitting counterargument. Her actions also suggest unconscious self-parody as she, presumably like so many shallow members of the *intelligentsia*, constantly "makes notes on the margins of her pamphlet." This stage direction closes act I, and the phrase is repeated by a number of characters, so by the time the stage directions repeat it again at the very end of the play, we are ready to apply Voinitsky's phrase about the professor—*perpetuum mobile*— to her as well. Her first speech concerns these insipid pamphlets that she imagines to be, in Voinitsky's phrase, "books of wisdom."

Her devotion to intelligentsial concerns has led her to idolize the old professor; she alone remains unaware that he is not what he pretends to be. But it is not so much her vacuity as her small, incessant acts of cruelty to her son that deprive her so totally of the audience's sympathy. As her son regrets his wasted life, she reproaches him in canned phrases for not caring more about the latest intellectual movements: "You used to be a man of definite convictions, an enlightened personality." We may imagine that Voinitsky's rage at the professor's proposal to deprive him of the estate is fueled to a significant extent by resentment of his mother, who repeats, as she has evidently done so often, "Jean, don't contradict Aleksandr. Believe me, he knows better than we do what is right and what is wrong." Even the professor, who has utter contempt for her, is not so intolerable as she is. Perhaps he senses, as we do, that as Telegin is a paltry double of Voinitsky, so Maria Vasilievna farcically duplicates him.

IDLENESS AND THE APOCALYPSE OF SQUABBLES

Elena Andreevna, the professor's young wife, and Astrov, the doctor who is summoned to treat him, each combine prosaic insight with melodramatic blindness. Though they often fail to live up to the standards they recommend, they do glimpse the value of everyday decency and ordinary virtues. They even understand, more or less, the danger of histrionic behavior, cited self-pity, and grand gestures, all of which nevertheless infect their own speeches. For this reason, Chekhov can use these speeches to enunciate the play's central values while simultaneously illustrating the consequences of not taking these values seriously enough.

Elena comes closest to a Chekhovian sermon as she fends off Voinitsky in act II:

> ELENA ANDREEVNA: Ivan Petrovich, you are an educated, intelligent man, and I should think you would understand that the world is being destroyed not by crime and fire, but by hatred, enmity, all these petty squabbles... Your business should be not to grumble, but to reconcile us to one another.
>
> VOINITSKY: First reconcile me to myself! My darling...

Elena is absolutely right: life is spoiled not by grand crises or dramatic disappointments but by "petty squabbles." It is all the more ironic, then, that in praising prosaic virtues she cannot avoid images of catastrophe and the rhetoric of apocalypse. Characteristically, her choice of words strikes Voinitsky most: "All that rhetoric and lazy morality, her foolish, lazy ideas about the ruin of the world—all that is utterly hateful to me."

Perhaps Chekhov intended Elena as an allusion to Dorothea Brooke, although Elena lacks Dorothea's unshakable integrity. Elena married the professor, just as Voinitsky worked for him, out of an intelligentsial love. Her speech about petty squabbles suggests that she has reflected on his daily pettiness and self-centered petulance, which he explicitly justifies as a right conferred by his professorial status. And so Elena, who has studied music at the conservatory, requires and does not receive permission to play the piano.

Elena understands that something is wrong, but not what would be right. We first see her in act I ignoring, almost to the point of the grotesque, the feelings of Telegin:

> TELEGIN: The temperature of the samovar has fallen perceptibly.
>
> ELENA ANDREEVNA: Never mind, Ivan Ivanovich, we'll drink it cold.
>
> TELEGIN: I beg your pardon... I am not Ivan Ivanovich, but Ilya Ilych... Ilya Ilych Telegin, or, as some people call me because of my pock-marked face, Waffles. I am Sonichka's godfather, and His Excellency, your husband, knows me quite well. I live here now, on your estate... You may have been so kind as to notice that I have dinner with you every day.
>
> SONYA: Ilya Ilych is our helper, our right hand. [*Tenderly*] Let me give you some more tea, Godfather.

If these lines are performed as I think Chekhov meant them, one will detect no reproach, no irony, in Telegin's voice. He has so little self-esteem that he expects to be overlooked, and so he reminds people of his existence—or of his brother's wife's brother's existence—sincerely, out of a sense that he is too insignificant to be remembered even when he is constantly present. Chekhov uses Telegin as a touchstone for the basic decency of other characters: is it worth their while to be kind to someone who is obviously of no use to anyone? In this scene, Elena fails the test, and Sonya, who calls him Godfather, passes it. Voinitsky, we remember, calls him Waffles, a nickname that only the pathetic Telegin could possibly accept and even repeat.

Elena does not work but, rather, as Astrov observes, infects everyone around her with her idleness. The old nurse speaks correctly when she complains that many of the household's ills derive from the visitors' disruption of old habits, habits related to work. A schedule, arrived at over the course of decades and carefully calibrated so that the estate can be well managed, has been replaced by a purely whimsical approach to time: Marina is awakened to get the samovar ready at 1:30 in the morning.

The *intelligentsia* may view habits as numbing, but from the standpoint of prosaics, good or bad habits more than anything else shape a life. Attention, after all, is a limited resource, and most of what we do occurs when we are concentrating on something else or on nothing in particular, as the sort of action and dialogue in Chekhov's plays makes clear. And yet it is the cumulative effect of all those actions, governed largely by habit, that conditions and indeed constitutes our lives. Moreover, habits result from countless earlier decisions and therefore can serve as a good index to a person's values and past behavior. That, indeed, is one reason Chekhov emphasizes them so much and one way in which he makes even short literary forms so resonant with incidents not directly described. Chekhov's wiser characters also understand that attention can be applied to new problems that demand more than habit only if good habits efficiently handle routine concerns. They keep one's mental hands free.

Relying on beauty, charm, and high ideals—she really has them— Elena does not appreciate the importance of habits, routine, and work. For her, life becomes meaningful at times of high drama, great sacrifice, or passionate romance. That is to say, it can be redeemed only by exceptional moments. Consequently, when those moments pass, she can only be bored. Sonya tries to suggest a different view. She values daily work and unexceptional moments, but Elena cannot understand:

ELENA ANDREEVNA [*in misery*]: I'm dying of boredom, I don't know what do do.

SONYA [*shrugging her shoulders*]: Isn't there plenty to do? If you only wanted to. . . .

ELENA ANDREEVNA: For instance?

SONYA: You could help with running the estate, teach, take care of the sick. Isn't that enough? When you and Papa were not here, Uncle Vanya and I used to go to market ourselves to sell the flour.

ELENA ANDREEVNA: I don't know how to do such things. And it's not interesting. Only in idealistic novels do people teach and doctor the peasants, and how can I, for no reason whatever, suddenly start teaching and looking after the peasants?

SONYA: I don't see how one can help doing it. Wait a bit, you'll get accustomed to it. [*Embraces her*] Don't be bored, darling.

Elena significantly misunderstands Sonya. Given her usual ways of thinking in literary terms, she translates Sonya's recommendations into a speech from an "idealistic novel." That, presumably, is why she ignores the possibility of helping with the estate and singles out teaching or doctoring the peasants. She imagines that Sonya offers only a ridiculous populist idyll.

If that were what Sonya meant, Elena's objections would be quite apt. Her misunderstanding allows Chekhov to make a characteristically prosaic point about meaningful activity. In the Russian countertradition, the dynamics and significance of work—daily, ordinary work—figure as a major theme. Elena's only idea of work corresponds to a view that Levin learns to reject in *Anna Karenina*—work "for all humanity"—and she correctly rejects that choice as work "for no reason whatever." What she cannot understand is the possibility of a different sort of work that would be meaningful: prosaic work.

Thinking like a member of the *intelligentsia*, she believes that either meaning is grand and transcendent or else it is absent. Her mistake in marrying the professor has convinced her that transcendent meaning is an illusion, and so she, like Voinitsky, can imagine only the opposite, a meaningless world of empty routine extending endlessly. But Sonya's actual recommendation, like the sort of daily work Levin describes as "incontestably necessary," implicitly challenges the very terms of Elena's, and the *intelligentsia*'s, dialectic.

Sonya recommends taking care of the estate *because it has to be done*. She can draw an "incontestable" connection between getting the right price for flour and making the estate operate profitably or between not allowing the hay to rot and not indulging in waste, which is troubling in itself. Like Tolstoy, Chekhov had utter contempt for the *intelligentsia*'s (and aristocracy's) disdain of efficiency, profitability, and the sort of deliberate calculation needed to avoid waste. That is one reason the play ends with the long-delayed recording of prices for agricultural products.

When Elena characterizes caring for peasants as a purely literary pose, Sonya replies that she does not see "how one can help doing it."

For Sonya, it is not a literary pose, and it serves no ideology but is part of her more general habits of caring for everyone. High ideals or broad social goals have nothing to do with her efforts on behalf of others, as we see in this very passage when she responds not with a counterargument but with a sympathetic embrace of the despairing Elena.

Sonya understands that both work and care require habits of working and caring. One has to know how they are done, and they cannot just be picked up "suddenly," as Elena correctly observes. Elena has the wrong habits, and that is her real problem. What she does not see is that she needs to begin acquiring new ones, which is what Sonya is really recommending.

WASTE BY OMISSION

> those graceful acts,
> Those thousand decencies that daily flow.
> —Milton, *Paradise Lost*

Least of all does Elena need romance, which is what Astrov offers. Like Elena and Voinitsky, he is obsessed with the vision of a brief, ecstatic affair in a literary setting. You are bound to be unfaithful sometime and somewhere, he tells Elena, so why not here, "in the lap of nature... At least it's poetic, the autumn is really beautiful... Here there is the plantation, the dilapidated country houses in the style of Turgenev." He might almost have said in the style of Chekhov. When this pathetic attempt at seduction fails, Astrov intones "Finita la commedia," a line that, interpreted literally, does correctly characterize his desire for romance as comic, if not farcical. When he repeats "Finita!" soon afterward, the possibility of farce grows stronger.

Astrov constantly looks for literary or theatrical images to explain his life. "What's the use?" he asks at the beginning of the play. "In one of Ostrovsky's plays there's a man with a large moustache and small abilities. That's me." In fact, these self-pitying allusions make him a good example of the "more intelligent" members of the *intelligentsia* as he describes them:

ASTROV: . . . it's hard to get along with the intelligentsia—they tire you out. All of them, all our good friends here, think and feel in a small way, they see no farther than their noses: to put it bluntly, they're stupid. And those who are more intelligent and more outstanding, are hysterical, eaten up with analysis and introspection... They whine. . . . [*He is about to drink*]

SONYA [*stopping him*]: No, please, I beg you, don't drink any more.

224

Of course, this very speech exemplifies the *intelligentsia*'s indulgence in self-pitying self-analysis. Astrov whines about whining, and what's more, he knows it. But this self-knowledge does him no good for reasons that Chekhov frequently explores.

Some self-destructive behavior can be modified by an awareness of what one is doing, but not the sort of introspection that Astrov describes. On the contrary, the more one is aware of it, the more that awareness becomes a part of it. (Perhaps that is what Karl Kraus meant when he said that psychoanalysis is the disease that it purports to cure.) The more Astrov blames himself for whining, and for whining about whining, the more he whines about it. This sort of introspective self-pity feeds on itself; so does alcoholic self-pity, which is why Chekhov has him drink while complaining.

To persuade him not to drink, Sonya reproaches Astrov for contradicting himself. "You always say people don't create, but merely destroy what has been given them from above. Then why, why, are you destroying yourself?" And in fact, Astrov has spoken powerfully about waste and the need for prosaic care; his speeches are the closest Chekhov comes to a Tolstoyan essay or to one of Levin's meditations.

Astrov's lectures on what we would now call "the environment" sound so strikingly contemporary that it is hard to see them in the context of Chekhov's play. In a way not uncommon in literary history, their very coincidence with current concerns provokes critical anachronism or the interpretation of them as detachable parts. It is worth stressing, therefore, that Astrov does not object to any and all destruction of trees. "Now I could accept the cutting of wood out of need, but why devastate the forests?" he says. "You will say that . . . the old life must naturally give place to the new. Yes, I understand, and if in place of these devastated forests there were highways, railroads, if there were factories, mills, schools, and the people had become healthier, richer, more intelligent—but, you see, there is nothing of the sort!" The chamber of commerce might well concur.

What bothers Astrov, what bothers Chekhov, is waste. And waste results from the lack not of great ideals but of daily care. The forests disappear for the same reason that the hay rots. After Sonya offers her breathless paraphrase of Astrov's ideas, Voinitsky, with his clothes still rumpled and his bad habits showing, refuses to see the point:

VOINITSKY [*laughing*]: Bravo, bravo! .. All that is charming, but not very convincing, [*to Astrov*] and so, my friend, allow me to go on heating my stoves with logs and building my barns with wood.

ASTROV: You can heat your stoves with peat and build your barns with brick . . . . The Russian forests are groaning under the ax . . . wonderful landscapes vanish never to return, and all because lazy man hasn't sense enough to stoop down and pick up fuel from the ground.

What destroys the forests, and what destroys lives, is not some malevolent force, not some lack of great ideas, and not some social or political evil. Trees fall, and lives are ruined, because of thoughtless behavior, everyday laziness, and bad habits, or, more accurately, the lack of good ones. Destruction results from what we do not do. Chekhov's prosaic vision receives remarkably powerful expression in these passages.

Astrov and Sonya also give voice to that vision when they describe how the ruin of forests is not just an analogue for but also a cause of needlessly impoverished lives. To paraphrase their thought: the background of our lives imperceptibly shapes them, because what happens constantly at the periphery of our attention, what is so familiar that we do not even notice it, modifies the tiny alterations of our thoughts. Literally and figuratively, our surroundings temper the "climate" of our minds. Like good housekeeping and careful estate management, unwasted forests subtly condition the lives unfolding in their midst.

Where Sonya, and especially Astrov, go wrong is in their rhetoric, which, like Elena's, becomes rapidly apocalyptic or utopian. They intone lyrical poetry celebrating prosaic habits and praise undramatic care with theatrical declamation:

SONYA: If you listen to him [Astrov], you'll fully agree with him. He says that the forests . . . teach man to understand beauty and induce in him a nobility of mind. Forests temper the severity of the climate. In countries where the climate is mild, less energy is wasted in the struggle with nature, so man is softer and more tender; in such countries the people are beautiful, flexible, easily stirred, their speech is elegant, their gestures graceful. Science and art flourish among them, their philosophy is not somber, and their attitude toward women is full of an exquisite courtesy...

. . . .

ASTROV: . . . maybe I am just a crank, but when I walk by a peasant's woodland which I have saved from being cut down, or when I hear the rustling of young trees which I have planted with my own hands, I realize that the climate is somewhat in my power, and that if, a thousand years from now, mankind is happy, I shall be responsible for that too, in a small way. When I plant a birch tree and then watch it put forth its leaves and sway in the wind, my soul is filled with pride, and I... [*seeing the workman who has brought a glass of vodka on a tray*] however... [*Drinks*]

They expect a lot from trees. The doctor and his admirers show enthusiasm in the sense Dr. Johnson defined the word: a vain belief in private revelation. Sonya's enthusiasm reflects her love for Astrov, but what does

226

Astrov's reflect? In his tendency to visionary exaggeration, in his millenarian references to the destiny of all mankind, we sense his distinctly unprosaic tendency, in spite of everything, to think in the terms of drama, utopias, and romance—and to drink.

Notes

Introduction

1. D. S. Merezhkovsky, "Chekhov i Gor'kii," in *Polnoe sobranie sochinenii*, vol. 14 (St. Petersburg, 1914), 66; D. S. Mirsky, "Chekhov and the English," *Monthly Criterion* 6, no. 14 (Oct. 1927):298.

2. Sergey N. Bulgakov, *Chekhov kak myslitel'* (Kiev, 1910), 8 (the book was first published in 1904, immediately after Chekhov's death); M. Kurdyumov, *Serdtse Smiatennoe* (Paris, 1934), 11.

3. A. P. Chekhov, *Polnoe sobranie sochinenii i pisem*, 30 vols. (Moscow, 1974–83), *Pis'ma* 2:177.

4. For a discussion of some of these questions, see Savely Senderovich, "Towards Chekhov's Deeper Reaches," in *Anton Chekhov Rediscovered: A Collection of New Studies with a Comprehensive Bibliography*, ed. Savely Senderovich and Munir Sendich (1987; East Lansing, Mich., 1987), 1–8. See, too, Senderovich's essay "A Fragment of Semiotic Theory of Poetic Prose (The Chekhovian Type)," *Essays in Poetics* 14, no. 2 (1989):43–64. A brief discussion of the characteristics of Chekhov's prose can be found in Z. S. Papernyi's "Pushkin v proze," originally published in 1973 and reprinted in Papernyi's book *Strelka iskusstva* (Moscow, 1986), 85–97. Other studies on Chekhov's poetics include Aleksandr P. Chudakov, *Chekhov's Poetics*, trans. Edwina Cruise and Donald Dragt (Ann Arbor, Mich., 1983), and idem, *Mir Chekhova* (Moscow, 1986); Jan van der Eng, Jan M. Meijer, and Herta Schmid, *On the Theory of Descriptive Poetics: Anton P. Chekhov as Story-Teller and Playwright* (Lisse, 1978); Nils Åke Nilsson, *Studies in Chekhov's Narrative Technique: "The Steppe" and "The Bishop"* (Stockholm, 1968); Thomas Winner, *Chekhov and His Prose* (New York, 1966); and Peter Bitsilli, *Chekhov's Art: A Stylistic Analysis*, trans. Toby Clyman and Edwina Cruise (Ann Arbor, Mich., 1983).

5. Letters to K. N. Leontiev, September 21, 1860, and February

11, 1855, in Ivan Turgenev, *Polnoe sobranie sochinenii i pisem*, 30 vols. (Moscow, 1960–68), *Pis'ma* 4:135, 2:259.

6. "Vospominaniia Ars. G. (I. Ia. Gurliand)," *Teatr i iskusstvo*, no. 28 (1904).

7. Kornei Chukovsky, *O Chekhove* (Moscow, 1967), 3, 4, 6, 7, 13, 15.

8. V. I. Nemirovich-Danchenko, "Gostepriimstvo Chekhova," quoted in Papernyi, *Strelka iskusstva*, 168; letter of November 30, 1901, in *Perepiska A. P. Chekhova i O. L. Knipper*, ed. A. B. Derman, vol. 2 (Moscow, 1936), 114; Chekhov, *Pis'ma* 10:136.

9. Letter to G. I. Rossolimo, October 11, 1899, in Chekhov, *Pis'ma* 8:284.

10. The remark is made by Gurov in the story "The Lady with the Dog" (Dama s sobachkoi), sec. 4.

11. I have omitted Bunin's sketch of Chekhov's life from the memoirs printed in this collection.

12. In several of his letters Chekhov refers to January 16 as his birthday. Chekhov once told Bunin that the deacon at his baptism had mistakenly dated his birth a day late. January 17, however, was accepted by Chekhov and his family as the day of his birth.

13. In a letter to A. I. Ertel, dated March 4, 1893, Chekhov writes, too, of his "fear of the public and of publicity," which he calls "foolish and ridiculous but nonetheless unconquerable." See Chekhov, *Pis'ma* 5:181.

14. Aleksei Suvorin, Chekhov's close friend and associate for many years, spoke of Chekhov as a "sensitive being, proud and independent. Deeply within there lay an element of selflessness." Quoted in Papernyi, *Strelka iskusstva*, 174.

15. Chekhov, *Sochineniia* 17:102.

16. Chekhov, *Pis'ma* 8:278.

17. Letter to Chekhov, July 15, 1888. See *Perepiska A. P. Chekhova*, ed. with commentary by M. P. Gromov et al. (Moscow, 1984), 321.

18. See also Chekhov's stories "Because of Little Apples" (1880) and "A Trifling Occurrence" (1886), in which the drama of the Fall provides an ironic subtext to the narratives. I discuss "Because of Little Apples" in my essay "Chekhov's Garden of Eden; or, The Fall of the Russian Adam and Eve," *Slavica Hierosolymitana: Slavic Studies of the Hebrew University* 4 (1979):70–78. My discussion of this story appears also in chapter 4 of my study *Dialogues with Dostoevsky: The Overwhelming Questions* (Stanford, Calif., 1993), 83–94.

19. Letter to B. A. Sadovsky, May 28, 1904, in Chekhov, *Pis'ma* 12:108. Chekhov is commenting on a poem sent to him by Sadovsky.

Chekhov writes that he admires the poem's "form" but adds with respect to the poem's "content" that "one does not feel conviction in it." He says, "In general there is no logic to the acts of your hero, whereas in art, as also in life, nothing accidental takes place."

20. Chekhov, *Pis'ma* 5:20.

21. Letter to S. P. Diaghilev, December 30, 1902, in Chekhov, *Pis'ma* 11:106. "It is necessary to believe in God," Chekhov wrote to another correspondent, "but if there is no faith, don't replace it with chatter, but search, search, search alone, one-on-one with one's conscience"; letter to V. S. Miroliubov, December 17, 1901, in *Pis'ma* 10:142.

22. Letter to M. O. Menshikov, January 28, 1900, in Chekhov, *Pis'ma* 9:29. See also Chekhov's letter to S. P. Diaghilev dated July 12, 1903, where he writes: "I have lost my faith long ago and only look with perplexity on every believing intellectual" (*Pis'ma* 11:234). Elsewhere he writes: "About Russia I'll say nothing, but the *intelligentsia* at present is only playing at religion and, chiefly, from nothing better to do" (*Pis'ma* 11:106).

23. Northrop Frye, *The Great Code: The Bible and Literature* (New York, 1983), xi. There is a long history of commentary on Chekhov's religious beliefs. See, for example, Merezhkovsky, "Chekhov i Gor'kii," 91–99. For a recent discussion of Chekhov's views on religion, see Ludolf Müller, "Der Glaube bei Čechov—Čechovs Glaube," in *Anton P. Čechov: Werk und Wirkung*, pt. 1, ed. Rolf-Dieter Kluge (Wiesbaden, 1990), 573–87.

24. For some recent studies that touch on the religious and mythopoetic subtext in Chekhov, see Savely Senderovich, "Chudo Georgiia o zmie: Istoriia oderzhimosti Chekhova odnim obrazom," *Russian Language Journal* 39, nos. 132–34 (1985):135–225. See also a shorter version in English of the same piece: "Anton Chekhov and St. George the Dragonslayer: An Introduction to the Theme," in *Anton Chekhov Rediscovered*, ed. Senderovich and Sendich, 167–87. See also my articles "'If I Forget Thee, O Jerusalem': An Essay on Chekhov's 'Rothschild's Fiddle,'" and "'The Betrothed': Chekhov's Last Testament," both in *Anton Chekhov Rediscovered*, 35–49, 51–63; "'A Woman's Kingdom': A Drama of Character and Fate," *Russian Language Journal* 39, nos. 132–34 (1985): and "Chekhov's Garden of Eden." See, too, Willa Chamberlain Axelrod, "Russian Orthodoxy in the Life and Fiction of A. P. Chekhov," Ph.D. diss., Yale University, 1991, pp. 158–98.

25. Merezhkovsky, "Chekhov i Gor'kii," 93, 98.

26. Letter to E. M. Shavrova, April 6, 1892, in Chekhov, *Pis'ma* 5:47.

27. Chekhov, *Sochineniia* 17:33–34.

28. V. V. Rozanov, *Legenda o velikom inkvizitore F. M. Dostoev-skogo* (1894; Berlin, 1924), 18.

29. The Russian text reads: "Natura—dura, sud'ba—indeika, i zhizn'—kopeika." I avail myself of Vladimir and Nicholas Nabokov's English version of this saying in their translation of Lermontov, *A Hero of Our Time* (New York, 1958), 169.

30. See my article, "'A Woman's Kingdom,'" 1–11.

31. Richard Selzer, "Chekhov: Doctor and Patient," *A.R.T. Inquiries: American Repertory Theatre News* 12, no. 2 (Jan. 1992):10. Chekhov's letters (still bowdlerized in the latest Russian edition by the editors) suggest some contrary evidence.

32. In this connection, see Conrad's "Sensuality in Čexov's Prose," *Slavic and East European Journal* 24, no. 2 (Summer 1980):103–17.

33. Leo Tolstoy, "An Afterword, by Tolstoy, to Chekhov's Story, 'Darling,'" in *What Is Art? and Essays on Art*, trans. Aylmer Maude (London, 1938), 325.

34. Renato Poggioli, *The Phoenix and the Spider* (Cambridge, Mass., 1957), 124, 126.

35. The concept was developed in Morson's book on Tolstoy, *Hidden in Plain View: Narrative and Creative Potentials in "War and Peace"* (Stanford, Calif., 1987), and then extended in *Mikhail Bakhtin: Creation of a Prosaics* (Stanford, Calif., 1990), coauthored with Caryl Emerson.

36. For a complete version of Morson's essay, see his "Prosaic Chekhov: Metadrama, the Intelligentsia, and *Uncle Vanya*," *TriQuarterly* (Winter 1990–91):118–59.

37. Chekhov, *Pis'ma* 8:101.

Do You Need My Biography?

Vladimir A. Tikhonov wrote Chekhov that he wanted to publish a photograph of the writer in the monthly journal *Sever*. He requested some biographical information to accompany the picture. Chekhov responded to Tikhonov's request in a letter of February 22, 1892. The excerpt printed here was translated by Robert Louis Jackson, from A. P. Chekhov, *Polnoe sobranie sochinenii i pisem*, 30 vols. (Moscow, 1974–83), *Pis'ma* 4:362–63. The physician to whom Chekhov refers is Grigorii A. Zakharin, a professor of medicine at Moscow University.

In Memory of Chekhov

Ivan Bunin, "Pamiati Chekhova," in *Pamiati A. P. Chekhova* (Moscow, 1906), 61–80. Bunin's essay on Chekhov was based on a speech he delivered at a memorial gathering in honor of Chekhov organized by the Society of Lovers of Russian Literature (Obshchestvo Liubitelei Rossiiskoi Slovesnosti) on October 24, 1904. The essay, printed here with some abridgement, was translated by Stephen Frauzel and Leslie Jackson.

Chekhov's Name Drama

This essay was translated from Russian by Stephen Frauzel and Leslie Jackson. Chekhov's letters quoted herein can be found in A. P. Chekhov, *Polnoe sobranie sochinenii i pisem*, 30 vols. (Moscow, 1974–83), *Pis'ma*, 12 vols.

"At Sea"

1. See editors' commentary, "Primechaniia," in A. P. Chekhov, *Polnoe sobranie sochinenii i pisem*, 30 vols. (Moscow, 1974–83), *Sochineniia* 4:517. All citations of Chekhov's works and letters are from this edition; translations are mine, unless otherwise indicated.

2. The Russian title, "V more," was accompanied by the subtitle "Rasskaz matrosa" (A Sailor's Story) in the version published in the second Marks edition of Chekhov's collected works in 1903; *Sochineniia* 2:530.

3. *Moskovskii listok* had just replaced a pseudonym used by Chekhov's brother Aleksandr with "A. Chekhov," misleading Chekhov's Moscow readership into taking the attached story as Chekhov's, while *Novosti dnia* had published a story Chekhov submitted under a pseudonym—a story, wrote Chekhov, that "I would have been ashamed to send to *Oskolki* [Leykin's paper]"—under Chekhov's real name.

4. See the editors' commentary in Chekhov, *Pis'ma* 9:532.

5. This may be plot structure par excellence. See, for instance, Ross Chambers, who claims that "all narratives are necessarily seductive, seduction being the means whereby they maintain their authority to narrate"; *Story and Situation: Narrative Seduction and the Power of Fiction* (Minneapolis, 1984), 218. See also Peter Brooks, *Reading for the Plot: Design and Invention in Narrative* (New York, 1984), and "The Idea of a Psychoanalytic Criticism," *Critical Inquiry* 13, no. 2 (1987):334–48.

6. R. G. Nazirov, "Chekhov i Giugo: Polemicheskoe prodolzhenie," *Filologicheskie nauki* 6, no. 4 (1983):21–25. References to Hugo's novel that follow rely on *Toilers of the Sea*, trans. Isabel Hapgood (New York, 1881).

7. Nazirov, 25–26, 22, 24.

8. M. Smolkin, "Shekspir v zhizni i tvorchestve Chekhova," in *Shekspirovskii sbornik*, ed. A. Anikst (Moscow, 1967), 80. See also Eleanor Rowe, *Hamlet: A Window on Russia* (New York, 1976), 107–13.

9. *Hamlet* I.i.147–49, from *The Riverside Shakespeare* (Boston, 1974), 1143. All subsequent citations of *Hamlet* are from this edition.

10. See the discussion in Smolkin, 80–84.

11. Sigmund Freud, *The Interpretation of Dreams*, trans. and ed. James Strachey (New York, 1965), 294–300.

12. See the editor's commentary in Chekhov, *Sochineniia* 1:530, 532.

13. J. Laplanche and J. B. Pontalis, *The Language of Psychoanalysis*, trans. Donald Nicholson-Smith (New York, 1973), 335.

14. This is in accordance with Freud's observations regarding the inability of the unconscious to operate according to either/or logic or to express it in dreams; *Interpretation of Dreams*, 351–52.

15. See Laplanche and Pontalis, 281–82.

16. See Sigmund Freud, "Instincts and Their Viscissitudes," trans. Cecil M. Baines, in Sigmund Freud, *General Psychological Theory*, ed. Phillip Rieff (New York, 1963), 93–96.

17. Cited in Carolina De Maegd-Soëp, *Chekhov and Women: Women in the Life and Work of Chekhov* (Columbus, Ohio, 1987), 39.

18. For a concise discussion of the Oedipus complex, which includes key references, see Laplanche and Pontalis, 282–87.

19. N. I. Gitovich, *Letopis' zhizni i tvorchestva A. P. Chekhova* (Moscow, 1955), 74.

20. The phrase belongs to Peter Rudnytsky, *Freud and Oedipus* (New York, 1987), 49.

21. T. L. Shchepkina-Kupernik, "O Chekhove," in *A. P. Chekhov v vospominaniiakh sovremennikov*, ed. N. I. Gitovich (Moscow, 1986), 235–36.

22. See editors' commentary in Chekhov, *Sochineniia* 1:586. See De Maegd-Soëp for a treatment of Chekhov and women; see also the penetrating remarks in Savely Senderovich, "Anton Chekhov and St. George the Dragonslayer: An Introduction to the Theme," in *Anton Chekhov Rediscovered: A Collection of New Studies with a Comprehensive Bibliography*, ed. S. Senderovich and M. Sendich (East Lansing, Mich., 1987), 167–87.

23. See, for example, Freud's treatment of the issue in "The Passing of the Oedipus-Complex," trans. Joan Riviere, in Sigmund Freud, *Sexuality and the Psychology of Love*, ed. Philip Rieff (New York, 1963), 176–82.

24. In the words of Harold Bloom, these are "as cases akin to what

Freud called the family romance"; *The Anxiety of Influence: A Theory of Poetry* (New York, 1973), 7.

25. In a letter to Suvorin on November 25, 1892, Chekhov contrasted his own generation of authors with its more impressive predecessors, stating of the former, "If you lift up the skirts of our muse, all you see is a flat area," while of the more virile elders he wrote, "They have a certain goal, like the ghost of Hamlet's father."

26. See also "First Debut" (1886), in which a young lawyer suffers through his first case as a defense attorney. His more experienced adversaries trounce him, but they say that he did a fine job and shows promise, "only he wrongfully implicated Hamlet in his speech."

"The Enemies"

1. Beverly Hahn, *Chekhov: A Study of the Major Stories and Plays* (Cambridge, Eng., 1977), 80, 90, 89.

2. V. Yermilov, *Chekhov, 1860–1904* (Moscow, 1949), 128, 129.

3. Yermilov's work evoked some sharp rebuttals. See, for example, E. A. Pokusaev, "Ob ideino-khudozhestvennoi kontseptsii rasskaza A. P. Chekhov 'Vragi,'" in *Ot "Slova o polku Igoreve" do "Tikhogo Dona": Sbornik statei k 90-letiiu N. K. Piksanova* (Leningrad, 1969), 183–90.

4. Dostoevsky, *Polnoe sobranie sochinenii*, 30 vols. (Leningrad, 1972–90), 15:202.

5. Hahn, 85.

6. For a recent article stressing the evangelical message of Chekhov in "The Enemies," see V. B. Kataev, "'Vragi: Interpretatsiia epokhi perestroiki," in *Teatr*, no. 1 (January 1991):114–19.

"Doma"

1. I refer to such stories of 1887 as "The Beggar" (Nishchii), "The Meeting" (Vstrecha), and "Good People" (Khoroshie liudi).

2. For the list of Tolstoy's favorites, see the letter of Tolstoy's son, I. L. Tolstoy, to Chekhov, printed in A. P. Chekhov, *Sobranie sochinenii*, 12 vols. (Moscow, 1960), 2:577. As a rule, the story "At Home" is mentioned or briefly discussed in connection with Chekhov's stories about children. For the latest example of such discussion, see Emma Polotskaia, *Puti chekhovskikh geroev* (Moscow, 1983), 39–41. No analysis of this story has yet been attempted.

3. Seryozha in *Anna Karenina* is upset by the fact that grown-ups "push him away" from themselves; they do not answer his need

for love and emotional involvement and prefer the dry language of duty. Seryozha, who wants to be caressed and loved, especially on the occasion of his name day, is severely criticized by his father during their class. Significantly, Seryozha is reprimanded for forgetting the lesson from the Old Testament, the part of the Bible associated with law in the Russian literary tradition. Likewise, in Chekhov's story, the father literally pushes his son away from the embrace and lectures him on the legality of stealing tobacco, thus trying to translate the language of love into that of law. Furthermore, both children began to muse on death in response to their fathers' demands and questioning. Seryozha in *Anna Karenina* fails to recall the patriarchs of the Old Testament because he starts meditating on the immortality of Enoch. Similarly, Chekhov's Seryozha fails to follow his father's formal and dry reasoning and ponders on the whereabouts of his dead mother instead. The legalistic formalism of their fathers is hardly a substitute for the pain of separation that these children confront.

4. A. P. Chekhov, "Doma," in *Polnoe sobranie sochinenii i pisem*, 30 vols. (Moscow, 1974–83), *Sochineniia*, vol. 6. Translations from the story are mine.

5. Seryozha is presented here as a riddle that his father has failed to solve. Reinhard Kuhn in his book *Corruption in Paradise: The Child in Western Literature* (Hannover, 1982) claims that children in Western literature are often portrayed in this manner, that is, like enigmatic creatures whom grown-ups fail to understand. See the first chapter of his book, "The Enigmatic Child."

6. The failure of Evgeny Petrovich, a lawyer, to take upon himself the emotional demands of domestic life is, perhaps, not surprising. Throughout his oeuvre Chekhov illustrates the inadequacies of lawyers and teachers who fulfill their responsibilities in a formal manner. In Chekhov's story "The Court Investigator" (Sledovatel', 1887), for example, the title character complains of his wife's death, failing to see that his own lack of love drove her to suicide.

Although attacks on lawyers seem to be universal, the Western tradition attacks the law's propensity to corrupt language and truth (see, for example, Richard Weisberg, *The Failure of the Word: The Protagonist as Lawyer in Modern Fiction* [New Haven, 1984]), while in Russia the law is often seen as undermining love. The eleventh-century Russian text "Sermon on Law and Grace" (Slovo o Zakone i Blagodati) established an opposition that can be found in the polemical writings of the Slavophiles as well as in the works of Dostoevsky, Tolstoy, and Chekhov.

7. The setting of the tale, that is, the description of a garden and a palace, bears a resemblance to Hans Christian Andersen's fairy tale

"The Nightingale" (1843). Andersen's tale with its musings on the power of art and its opposition between art and artificiality provides a curious subtext to the problematics of Chekhov's story.

8. Emma Polotskaya, for example, resorts to the aesthetic explanation of the success of the father's tale. She attributes this success to the artistic nature of the child: "It is the artistic nature of Seryozha that explains the secret of the unusually strong impression that the fairy tale . . . has made upon Seryozha" (40). There is nothing inherently wrong with such a view, but as I will try to show, there are deeper reasons behind the success of the tale than its artistry or the artistic nature of Seryozha.

9. Wayne C. Booth, *The Company We Keep: An Ethics of Fiction* (Berkeley, 1988), 483–84.

10. When Serezha recalls his dead mother, "sadness and something resembling fear appeared in his large, unblinking eyes." His reaction to the father's tale is described thus: "The whole tale had made a deep impression on Serezha. Once more sadness and something resembling fear crept into his eyes."

"The Bishop"

Nils Åke Nilsson, *Studies in Chekhov's Narrative Technique: "The Steppe" and "The Bishop"* (Stockholm, 1968), 62–75. Nilsson divided his discussion of "The Bishop" into two parts: "'The Bishop': Its Theme" and "'The Bishop': Its Lyricism." The first part of his discussion is given here slightly abridged. Several of the author's notes have been omitted or abridged. Translations are provided for the texts from which Professor Nilsson quotes in Russian.

1. S. N. Shchukin says in his *Recollections of Chekhov* that Chekhov told him that "The Bishop" was an old story that he had rewritten. A. P. Chekhov, *Polnoe sobranie sochinenii i pisem*, ed. S. D. Balukhaty et al., 20 vols. (Moscow, 1944–51), *Sochineniia* 9:616.

2. See, however, especially the article by Peter Bicilli in *Godoshnik na sofiiskiia universitet: Istoriko-filologicheski fakultet* 38 (translated into English in Peter Bitsilli, *Chekhov's Art: A Stylistic Analysis*, trans. Toby Clyman and Edwina Cruise [Ann Arbor, Mich., 1983], which contains some interesting views on the story. G. Berdnikov, in his *A. P. Chekhov* (Moscow, 1961), 451–53, pays less attention to it, but he gives the story its proper place among Chekhov's later works; on the whole the Soviet critics seemed to be rather reluctant to mention the story, apparently because it contains a sympathetic portrait of a priest.

3. See my article "Intonation and Rhythm in Čechov's Plays," in *Anton Čechov, 1860–1960: Some Essays*, ed. T. Eekman (Leiden, 1960),

reprinted in *Chekhov: A Collection of Critical Essays*, ed. Robert Louis Jackson (Englewood Cliffs, N.J., 1967).

4. Compare the use of "for some reason" (*pochemu-to*) in "The Betrothed," Chekhov's last story. There it is clearly used to stress the point of view of the heroine.

5. Bicilli recognizes only a present and a past, which influences his view on the idea of the story (110). Berdnikov instead stresses the importance of this line of spring and future (452).

Passage from Great Saturday to Easter Day in "Holy Night"

1. A. P. Chekhov, "Sviatoiu noch'iu," in *Polnoe sobranie sochinenii i pisem*, 30 vols. (Moscow, 1974–83), *Sochineniia* 5:92–103. All translations are mine. I prefer the literal translation "Holy Night" over the usual "Easter Eve," which focuses on Easter Day and does not acknowledge the importance of Great Saturday.

2. Stillness signifies Christ's rest in the tomb. Darkness represents both the sorrow of burial and the disappearance of Christ before the Resurrection. Waiting represents the expectation of new life.

3. The midnight service implicitly begins shortly after the bells ring at the monastery and a cannon shot is heard. During the Goltva crossing, a rocket of light pierces the darkness and a Procession of the Cross begins. These events signal that the midnight service is coming to a close and matins are imminent. In addition, during the Goltva crossing, the novice monk Ieronim refers to a verse that "they will soon sing at matins." And as the ferry arrives at the monastery's shore, he says, "Now they will begin to sing the Easter canon."

4. Golgotha, the site of Christ's Crucifixion and, in Russian tradition, the site of his burial and Resurrection, represents Christ's passage from death to life. See S. V. Bulgakov, *Nastol'naia kniga dlia sviashchenno-tserkovno-sluzhitelei* (Kharkov, 1900), 555.

5. *Velikii sbornik I–III* (Prague, 1950), 800. All translations from this Old Church Slavonic service book are mine.

6. Ibid., 800, 796.

7. *Akafistnik* (Brussels, 1978), 82.

8. "Otkrytie tsarskikh vrat izobrazhaiut otverstvie liudiam nebesnogo tsarstva." See Konstantin Nikol'skii, *Posobie k izucheniiu ustava* (St. Petersburg, 1900), 21, 22.

9. *Velikii sbornik*, 814.

10. As the Israelites are "baptized into Moses" and physically saved by crossing the Red Sea, so, in Christian tradition, catechumens are spiritually saved by passing into life with Christ through baptism. See

Archpriest Mikhail Kheraskov, *Rukovodstvo k izucheniiu Sviashchennogo Pisaniia Vetkhago Zaveta* (Vladimir, 1897), 112–14.

11. *Velikii sbornik*, 804.

12. Ieronim compares Nikolai's voice with that of Christ: "What a bright mind . . . what harmonious and sweet language." And then he adds, citing a verse from the Easter canon that refers to Christ: "Exactly as one will sing at matins: 'O beloved one! O you with the sweetest voice!'" Ieronim claims that for Nikolai there is no "sweeter" writing than the Resurrection canon. In addition, Ieronim quotes from "the Akathistos to our Sweetest Lord Jesus Christ."

13. *Velikii sbornik*, 851.

Eschatology and Entombment in "Ionych"

1. All quotations from "Ionych" are from the David Magarshack translation of A. P. Chekhov, *Lady with Lapdog and Other Stories* (Baltimore, 1964). The Russian text referred to is from the Academy edition: A. P. Chekhov, *Polnoe sobranie sochinenii i pisem*, 30 vols. (Moscow, 1974–83), *Sochineniia*, vol. 10.

2. Representative of the older Soviet view are the following: Z. S. Papernyi, "Probuzhdenie geroia," *Voprosy literatury*, no. 1 (1960):80–96; idem., "Ispytanie geroia: O povesti A. P. Chekhova 'Ionych,'" in D. Ustiuzhanin, ed., *Russkaia klassicheskaia literatura: Razbory i analizy* (Moscow, 1969), 389–405; V. V. Golubkov, *Masterstvo A. P. Chekhova* (Moscow, 1958), 113–14.

For a similar, non-Soviet perspective, see Rufus Mathewson, "Intimations of Mortality in Four Chekhov Short Stories," in *American Contributions to the Sixth International Congress of Slavists*, vol. 2, *Literary Contributions* (The Hague, 1968), 272–75.

3. "Voznesenie Gospodne," in *Entsiklopedicheskii slovar'*, vol. 12, ed. F. A. Brockhaus and I. A. Efron (St. Petersburg, 1892), 898. See also K. T. Nikolskii, *Posobie ustava bogosluzheniia pravoslavnoi tserkvi* (St. Petersburg, 1900), 648.

4. This ambiguity of *nastoiashchii* is also played upon in "Man in a Case," where Belikov is said to be possessed by a horror of it (*otvrashchenie k nastoiashchemu*). In describing Belikov's perennially layered clothing, Chekhov makes eminently clear that he disregards time and the seasons as well as the reality of human relations.

5. Golubkov, 117. A. Chudakov makes note of the combined importance in this story of music and the reiterative structure of the lyrical passages; "Stil' i iazyk rasskaza Chekhova 'Ionych,'" *Russkii iazyk v shkole*, no. 1 (1958):69.

6. Chekhov refers to the song by name. Magarshack leaves out the name of the song, translating it simply as "a folk song."

7. *Russkie narodnye pesni: Melodii i teksty* (Moscow, 1986), 75.

8. Chekhov, *Sochineniia* 10:367–68.

9. One summary of this account can be found in the Brockhaus and Efron encyclopedia entry for the holiday: "Vozdvizhenie Kresta Gospodnia," p. 869.

10. John Meyendorff, *St. Gregory Palamas and Orthodox Spirituality* (Crestwood, N.Y., 1974), 116–17.

11. Timothy Ware, *The Orthodox Church* (Baltimore, 1963), 238.

12. Magarshack has "idol" for *iazycheskii bog*. I have substituted the term "pagan god" for a more accurate translation.

13. See *Butler's Lives of the Saints*, vol. 3, ed. D. Attwater and H. Thurston (New York, 1956), 192–93. A Russian account, contemporary with Chekhov, of this saint is given in Brockhaus and Efron: "Panteleimon," *Entsiklopedicheskii slovar'*, vol. 40, ed. F. A. Brockhaus and I. A. Efron (St. Petersburg, 1897), 705.

14. Iu. K. Shcheglov, "Iz poètiki Chèkhova: 'Ionych,'" *Russian Literature* 20 (1986):226–27.

15. N. A. Petrovskii, *Slovar' lichnykh imën* (Moscow, 1966), 97.

16. In his unabridged version of *The Golden Bough*, J. G. Frazer mentions September and October as harvesting months especially dedicated to the memory of Demeter; *The Golden Bough: A Study in Magic and Religion*, part 5, *Spirits of Corn and the Wild*, vol. 1, 3d ed. (London, 1912), 47–48.

17. Shcheglov also notes the parallel between Startsev and Chichikov, particularly in regard to their relations with their coachmen (226).

18. Vladimir Nabokov, *Nikolai Gogol* (New York, 1966), 72–73.

19. Petrovskii, 122.

20. T. S. Eliot, *Selected Poems* (New York, 1964), 78.

Life beyond Text

1. Avreliia Groman to A. P. Chekhov, February 16, 1899, Gosudarstvennaia biblioteka imeni Lenina, Otdel rukopisei, Fond 331, 41:33. A research grant from the International Research and Exchanges Board (IREX) in 1991 afforded me the opportunity to locate material used in this article.

2. Quoted in A. P. Chekhov, *Polnoe sobranie sochinenii i pisem*, 30 vols. (Moscow, 1974–83), *Sochineniia* 8:512.

3. All translations are my own.

4. Letter to A. S. Suvorin, November 12, 1889, in Chekhov, *Pis'ma* 3:284.

5. I explicate the cultural ramifications of the Marian paradigm and analyze its functions in fifteen Chekhov stories in my dissertation, "Chekhov's Two Marias: Artistic Functions of the Christian Paradigm of the Virgin and the Harlot," Cornell University, 1992.

6. This holds true for the works of Pushkin, Turgenev, Dostoevsky, and Leo Tolstoy. Boris Kisin's examples from twentieth-century Russian literature bear out this observation as well: see Kisin, *Bogoroditsa v russkoi literature* (Moscow, 1929).

7. *Akafist Bozhiei Materi* (Acathist to the Mother of God) (Brussels, 1954), 16.

8. Critics have discussed this piece of fabric at some length. A. P. Chudakov cites it as an illustration of a detail extraneous to the resolution of the scene, in *Poètika Chekhova* (Moscow, 1971), 152. Z. Papernyi interprets the fabric as an emblem of *poshlost'* in *Zapisnye knizhki Chekhova* (Moscow, 1976), 113–15. L. M. Tsilevich, in *Siuzhet chekhovskogo rasskaza* (Riga, 1976), 121–23, agrees with Papernyi.

9. John Baggley, *Doors of Perception* (Crestwood, N.Y., 1988), 128.

10. Savely Senderovich demonstrates the means by which Chekhov distributes formal features delineating a cultural complex between different characters. See Senderovich, "Chudo Georgiia o zmie: Istoriia oderzhimosti Chekhova odnim obrazom," *Russian Language Journal* 39 (1985):135–226.

11. D. S. Likhachev, *Poètika drevnerusskoi literatury* (Moscow, 1979), 163.

12. The phenomenon of polarized thinking is played out in the story through a rich layer of black and white imagery. Chekhov displaces the conventional values associated with this color opposition to suggest the inviability of dichotomized understandings.

13. In "Peasants," Chekhov foregrounds a similar context by weaving into one scene the themes of milk, a small child, the fast of the Virgin's Dormition, and a character named Maria. Chekhov may well have been familiar with the Orthodox *Maria Lactans* icon, which made a highly publicized journey through Russian from 1893 to 1896, coincident with the writing of this story. *Skazaniia o chudotvornykh ikonakh Bozhiei Materi imenuemoi "Mlekopitatel'nitsa"* (Legends of the Miracleworking "Milk-provider" Icons of the Mother of God) (Odessa, 1900).

14. *Akafist*, 20.

15. Thomas Winner notes this link. See Winner, *Chekhov and His Prose* (New York, 1966), 128.

16. Boris Gasparov asserts that Natalya Petrovna "represents (in the most ironic way) the syncretic image of 'Russia' and 'Madonna' (*Bogoroditsa*)." This is a suggestive addition to my argument. See Gasparov, "The Apocalyptic Theme in Pushkin's 'Count Nulin,'" in *Text and Con-*

text: Essays to Honor Nils Åke Nilsson, ed. P. A. Jensen et al. (Stockholm, 1987), 19.

17. Robert Louis Jackson explicates Chekhov's concern with the questions of fate, illusion, freedom, and responsibility in both prose and drama. See Jackson, "Chekhov's *Seagull*: The Empty Well, the Dry Lake, and the Cold Cave," in *Chekhov's Great Plays: A Critical Anthology*, ed. with an introduction by Jean-Pierre Barricelli (New York, 1981), 3–17.

Chekhov's "The Student"

1. A. A. Bogolepov, *Rozhdestvo, Strastnaia i Paskha v pravoslavnom bogosluzhenii* (New York, 1973), 53.

2. I use Constance Garnett's translation of "The Student." For stylistic purposes I have amended the translation in places.

3. "O liubvi k narodu: Neobkhodimyi kontrakt s narodom," in F. M. Dostoevsky, *Polnoe sobranie sochinenii*, 30 vols. (Leningrad, 1972–90), 22:43.

4. In Russian—*ispustil dukh*—he breathed his last, or, literally, let out the spirit.

5. Bogolepov, 60.

6. See Ivan Bunin, *Sobranie sochinenii*, vol. 9 (Moscow, 1967), 186.

7. See Dostoevsky's letter to N. D. Vonvizina on his release from prison in 1854. Dostoevsky, vol. 28, bk. 1, p. 176.

8. Chekov's story first appeared in *Russkie vedomosti* in 1894 under the title "Vecherom" (In the Evening). It was later included in a collection, *Povesti i rasskazy* (1894), under the title "Student." On Chekhov's possible reason for his choice of the original title, "Vecherom," see R. A. Klostermann's note on the kinship between the words *vecherom* and *vechernja* ("vespers," also "supper," as in *Tainaia vechernja*, "Last Supper") in "Die Novelle 'Der Student': Ein Diskussionsbeitrag," in *Anton Čechov, 1860–1960: Some Essays*, ed. T. Eekman (Leiden, 1960), 104–5.

9. See my discussion of this idea in my essay, "Chekhov's *Seagull*: The Empty Well, the Dry Lake, and the Cold Cave," in *Chekhov's Great Plays: A Critical Anthology*, ed. with an introduction by Jean-Pierre Barricelli (New York, 1981), 15–16.

"In Exile" and Russian Fatalism

1. In a letter to Suvorin of March 5, 1889, Chekhov writes: "I bought Dostoevsky in your shop and am now reading him. It's good,

but it's very long-winded and immoderate. It makes great claims." See A. P. Chekhov, *Polnoe sobranie sochinenii i pisem*, 30 vols. (Moscow, 1974–83), *Pis'ma* 3:169. For Chekhov's "Literary Table of Ranks," see *Sochineniia* 3:143. See also *Pis'ma* 3:201–2, 203, 421.

2. See I. A. Goncharov, *Sobranie sochinenii*, 6 vols. (Moscow, 1959–60), 4:396.

3. See Chekhov, *Pis'ma* 4:31–32. Cf. F. M. Dostoevsky, *Polnoe sobranie sochinenii*, 30 vols. (Leningrad, 1972–90), 15:31.

4. See Chekhov, *Pis'ma* 4:26. See also the commentary of M. L. Semanova in Chekhov, *Sochineniia* 14–15:783 (for allusions to Dostoevsky, see 26, 64, 65, 135, 137, 241, 320, 324, 351, 424, 653, 818–19, 829; and on Goncharov, 34, 647, 889). Chekhov appears to have thought highly of *The Frigate Pallas*. See *Pis'ma* 1:29; 9:19.

5. In *The Island of Sakhalin* the description of the prison hospital may be related to the conditions described in "Ward Six." See Chekhov, *Sochineniia* 14–15:114, 370, 372. Details here of the prisoner abandoned by both his wife and his daughter may have furnished the story of Vasily Sergeich in "In Exile." In its first version Vasily Sergeich's daughter also left him. Cf. Chekhov, *Sochineniia* 18:355–57.

6. See Chekhov, *Pis'ma* 4:84.

7. Goncharov, 4:8.

8. See Dostoevsky, 4:51–54 (cf. also the figure of Nurra, p. 50).

9. Cf. the words of Dmitry Karamazov on Siberia: "No, life is full; there is life even under the earth." Dostoevsky, 15:31. See also the introduction to *Notes from the House of the Dead:* "Generally speaking, Siberia is a snug berth in spite of the cold. . . . not only from the standpoint of the civil servant, but even from many other points of view Siberia can be a place of blissful contentment." (4:5).

10. "Behind the door of every contented, happy man somebody should stand with a little hammer constantly to give a reminder with a knock that there are unhappy people." Chekhov, *Sochineniia* 10:62. Cf. the words of Dmitry Karamazov (Dostoevsky, 15:31). There is also a comment in *The Island of Sakhalin* on the exceptional arduousness of underground work. Chekhov, *Sochineniia* 14–15:389.

11. Chekhov, *Sochineniia* 8:73–74. Cf. the figure of Isai Fomich (Dostoevsky, 4:55, 92–104), and the category of "beggars from birth" (*ot prirody nishchie*) (49).

12. See Chekhov, *Sochineniia* 8:86.

13. Ibid., 7:330, 337. The confrontation of *smirennik* and *protestant* has been seen as a possible response to a similar confrontation in Garshin's story "Signal" (see 683).

14. Zosima's image, however, seems more geographic than historical: "For everything is like an ocean, everything is flowing and blend-

ing, a touch in one place sets up movement at the other end of the earth"; "Ibo vse kak okean, vsë techet i soprikasaetsia, v odnom meste tronesh', v drugom kontse mira otdaetsia." Dostoevsky, 14:290.

Fear and Pity in "Ward Six"

1. Translations of "Ward Six" are from A. P. Chekhov, *Ward Six and Other Stories*, trans. Ann Dunnigan (New York, 1965). Translations of Chekhov's letters are from A. P. Chekhov, *Letters*, trans. Michael Henry Heim with Simon Karlinsky (New York, 1973), except where letters quoted are not found in this collection. Other translations are my own. References to the Russian edition (A. P. Chekhov, *Polnoe sobranie sochinenii i pisem*, 30 vols. [Moscow, 1974–83]), which has separate numbering of the volumes of works and volumes of letters, are given here as *Sochineniia* (works) and *Pis'ma* (letters).

2. Chekhov wrote to V. M. Lavrov on October 25, 1892, when the story was already about to come out: "In fact, the 'Ward' should be refurbished or it will stink of the hospital and the mortuary. I'm not a fan of such stories" (quoted in Chekhov, *Sochineniia* 8:451). Some of the aspects that may have made Chekhov consider the story uncharacteristic are its lack of a "love interest" and its "liberal orientation" (letter to Suvorin, March 31, 1892). For more on this, see the notes in Chekhov, *Sochineniia* 8:451.

3. One critic, A. Roskin, has suggested that "Ward Six" can be seen as a story "dictated by Sakhalin"; *A. P. Chekhov: Stat'i i ocherki* (Moscow, 1959), 215–16, also cited in Chekhov, *Sochineniia* 8:449. See also N. N. Sukhikh, "*Ostrov Sakhalin* v tvorchestve Chekhova," *Russkaia literatura*, no. 3 (1985):72–84.

4. Chekhov, *Letters*, 160; Chekhov, *Pis'ma* 4:32.

5. One of Chekhov's contemporary readers, S. I. Smirnova-Sazonova, placed "Ward Six" within a corpus or Russian works that acquaint readers with places that in real life they would tend to shun. She writes (in a letter to Suvorin, November 25, 1892, as quoted in Chekhov, *Pis'ma* 5:429): "And above all he wants unfortunates such as myself not to sleep at night because of his works; he wants through the brilliance of his palette and the depth of his thought to shed light on the dark corners of our life. Ostrovsky found such corners on the Taganka, Dostoevsky in prison camp. Chekhov went farther; we went down a few more steps to the insane ward, to the most horrifying extreme, where we are are loathe to peek."

6. Chekhov, *Letters*, 159; Chekhov, *Pis'ma* 4:32.

7. As critics have noted, Chekhov's motivation for the trip to Sakhalin was complex. He was dissatisfied with the state of literary affairs

in Russia at the time, he wanted to pay back his debt to science, and he felt a social responsibility to learn more about and to publicize the plight of the convicts in Sakhalin. For more on this subject, see Karlinsky's notes in Chekhov, *Letters*, 152–53.

8. Chekhov, *Letters*, 159–60; Chekhov, *Pis'ma* 4:32.

9. V. I. *Lenin o literature i iskusstve* (Moscow, 1976), 609 (as quoted in Chekhov, *Sochineniia* 8:463).

10. A. P. *Chekhov v vospominaniiakh sovremennikov* (Moscow, 1947), 316 (as quoted in Chekhov, *Sochineniia* 8:458).

11. Aristotle, "Poetics," in *On Poetry and Style*, trans. S. M. A. Grube (Indianapolis, 1958), 24 (1453a).

12. S. H. Butcher, *Aristotle's Theory of Poetry and Fine Art*, 4th ed. (New York, 1951), 265.

13. D. W. Lucas, "Pity, Fear, and Katharsis," Appendix II of Aristotle, *Poetics*, ed. D.W. Lucas (Oxford, 1968), 274.

14. Butcher, 263.

15. Sophocles, *Tragedies I*, trans. Robert Fitzgerald (Chicago, 1954), 90 (l. 245).

16. Homer, *The Iliad*, trans. Richmond Lattimore (Chicago, 1951), 488 (bk. 24, ll. 503–8).

17. Chekhov, *Sochineniia* 7:365.

18. *Ostrov Sakhalin*, in Chekhov, *Sochineniia* 14–15:324.

19. Aristotle, "Poetics," 24 (1453a).

20. Evidence within the story suggests that the doctor was not by nature insensitive. On the contrary, it seems that his callousness may mask an extreme sensitivity. We are told that the sight of blood upset him and that "when he has to open a baby's mouth to look at his throat and the child cries and defends himself with his little fists, the noise makes his head spin and tears come to his eyes. He hastily writes a prescription and motions the mother to take the child away."

21. Aristotle, "Rhetoric," *On Poetry and Style*, 93 (1412a).

22. This passage occurs in the chapter "Fugitives on Sakhalin" (Chekhov, *Sochineniia* 14–15:343), which Chekhov had completed before he began work on "Ward Six." The possible relevance of this passage to Dr. Ragin's attitudes is pointed out in the notes to Chekhov's works (*Sochineniia* 8:449–50).

23. See the notes to Chekhov's works (*Sochineniia* 8:447–48). Marcus Aurelius, *Meditations*, trans. Maxwell Staniforth (Harmondsworth, Eng., 1964), 91 (6.2).

24. Chekhov, *Letters*, 261; Chekhov, *Pis'ma* 5:283. In this same letter (written to Suvorin on March 27, 1894), Chekhov describes his disenchantment with Tolstoyan philosophy. His argument seems to be that love for one's fellow man should express itself actively, through the

elimination of physical suffering and the improvement of material conditions.

25. Chekhov defends materialism in a letter written to Suvorin on May 7, 1889, in which he writes that "outside of matter there is no experience, no knowledge, and hence no truth either" (Chekhov, *Pis'ma* 3:208). Chekhov's stance on materialism is discussed by John Tulloch in *Chekhov: A Structuralist Study* (New York, 1980), especially in "Chekhov the Doctor" (47–97).

26. Andrew Ortony discusses the absurd consequences of asserting that everything is literally like everything else and uses the term *tautology* to apply to this context; "Similarity in Similes and Metaphors," in *Metaphor and Thought*, ed. Andrew Ortony (Cambridge, Eng., 1979), 192.

27. Ragin's behavior illustrates the truth of Butcher's observation about Aristotelian fear and pity: "Those who are incapable of fear are incapable also of pity" (265).

28. *King Lear* III.iv.26–36, in *The Riverside Shakespeare* (Boston, 1974), 1276. When Cordelia returns to find her father a broken man, she appeals to a doctor, saying: "What can man's wisdom / In the restoring his bereaved sense?" (IV.iv.8–9). At her request, her father is given new clothes and made physically more comfortable. While these acts cannot, as it turns out, save his life, as she herself seems to realize, she refuses to adopt a passive, defeatist attitude to suffering. In this sense, she embodies some of the principles Chekhov held sacred.

29. Butcher, 265.

30. Chekhov, *Letters*, 160; Chekhov, *Pis'ma* 4:32.

31. Richard Janko, *Aristotle on Comedy: Towards a Reconstruction of Poetics II* (Berkeley, 1984), 141. For centuries, scholars of Aristotle speculated about what Aristotle meant by the term *catharsis*. Since the last century it has become accepted to hold that Aristotle in using the term was actually drawing an analogy to medicine, where health is restored by purging potentially debilitating substances from the organism. This interpretation was presented by Jacob Bernays in 1857.

On the role played by medicine in Aristotle's worldview, Bernays writes: "The son of a royal doctor and himself a practicing physician in his youth, Aristotle profited from the medical gifts he had inherited not only in the rigorously scientific parts of his philosophy: his moral and psychological works, despite all the links that bind them to the *Metaphysics*, constantly reveal a lively concern for the physical side of things and a rejection not only of asceticism but also of any ethereal spirituality—a rejection common among doctors and working scientists, but rare among philosophers, even in Greece, once they have ascended into the heaven of idea"; "Aristotle on the Effect of Tragedy," *Articles on Aristotle,* vol. 4, ed. Jonathan Barnes et al. (New York, 1978), 159. The view presented here suggests a possible affinity between Aristotle and Chekhov, who both used medical knowledge to understand human nature. For example, Chekhov wrote: "Psychic phenomena are so strikingly similar to physical ones that you cannot determine where the former begin and the latter end." He continued, "If you know how great the similarity is between physical and mental illnesses, and when you know that the same medicines cure both types of illness, then willy-nilly you will want not to separate the soul from the body" (Chekhov, *Pis'ma* 3:208).

32. Hannah Arendt, in discussing the understanding of metaphor presented by Kant in his *Critique of Judgment; The Life of the Mind,* vol. 1, *Thinking* (New York, 1971), 59.

33. The technique Chekhov employs to force his readers to identify with the characters bears some resemblance to the method of acting developed by Stanislavsky, with some input from Chekhov. Stanislavsky encourages the actor to identify with the character he plays by recognizing a "kinship" with him. Stanislavsky writes: "To achieve this kinship between the actor and the person he is portraying, add some concrete detail which will fill out the play, giving it point and absorbing action. The circumstances which are predicated on IF are taken from sources near to your own feeling, and they have a powerful influence on the inner life of an actor. Once you have established this contact between your life and your part, you will feel that inner push or stimulus. Add a whole series of contingencies based on your own experience in life, and you will see how easy it will be"; *An Actor Prepares,* trans. Elizabeth Reynolds Hapgood (New York, 1936), 46.

34. Chekhov, *Letters,* 160; Chekhov, *Pis'ma* 4:32.

Chekhov's "Volodya"

Research and preparation of this study was aided by University of Kansas General Research Fund grant no. 3724-0038 (July 1988).

1. For a summary of Russian critical assessment of Turgenev's influence on Chekhov, see S. E. Shatalov, "Cherty poètiki: Chekhov i Turgenev," in *V tvorcheskoi laboratorii Chekhova* (Moscow, 1974), 296–309; M. O. Gabel', *Voprosy izucheniia tvorchestva I. S. Turgeneva* (Kharkov, 1959), 46–50; and Nicholas G. Žekulin, "Chekhov and Turgenev: The Case of Nature Description," *Opera Slavica,* n. s., 18 (1990):688–713.

2. Turgenev's story is not without its own literary precedent: see Pushkin's fragment "The Guests Gathered at the Dacha" (Gosti s"ezhalis' na dachu, written between 1828 and 1830). The first line of Turgenev's

text suggests Pushkin's work: "Gosti davno raz"ekhalis'." It is brief, as were many of Pushkin's introductions, and it somewhat echoes his wording. But there are many more important correspondences between the two stories: Pushkin's Zinaida Volskaya (Turgenev's Zinaida has a phonetically similar married name: Dolskaya) is young and beautiful and is despised by other women. She has an entourage of men, including a certain Minsky, who pretends to be indifferent to society's norms; by criticizing her admirers, he becomes her confidant, much as Woldemar's firmly independent father is disdainful of Zinaida's gentlemen friends and becomes her lover. For further details, see Peter Brang, *I. S. Turgenev: Sein Leben und sein Werk* (Wiesbaden, 1976), 136–40.

3. The definitive text is found in I. S. Turgenev, *Polnoe sobranie sochinenii i pisem*, 30 vols. (Moscow, 1960–68), *Sochineniia*, 9:62. An almost acceptable English translation is that of David Magarshack, in *Ivan Turgenev: First Love and Other Tales* (New York, 1960). But Magarshack changed Turgenev's Volodya to Vladimir in both instances. To distinguish between Turgenev's young protagonist and that of Chekhov, I will use Woldemar for the the former and Volodya for the latter.

4. Chekhov's heroine shares each of these qualities: she does indeed "enchant" Volodya, she treats him imperiously as her plaything, and she encourages him to caress her. Then she mocks him, and yet he imagines her as his beloved.

5. An important leitmotiv accompanying Zinaida is her smile; the usual translation of *lukavyi* is "sly" or "mocking." In Russian folklore this epithet (or its adverbial form) is commonly applied to the devil, a spirit that may appear to a man as an attractive young woman, the better to tempt him. It has been suggested that both Woldemar's father and Zinaida display characteristics of the devil; see Walter Koschmal, *Vom Realismus zum Symbolismus: Zu Genese und Morphologie der Symbolsprache in den späten Werken I. S. Turgenevs*, Studies in Slavic Literature and Poetics 5 (Amsterdam, 1984), 14–16. Whether or not Turgenev intended any such connection, the frequency of *lukavyi* to modify Zinaida's smile seems unusual.

But there is a second meaning, that is, "playful" (or "teasing"), which is perhaps more current among educated speakers of Russian. This would seem to be Turgenev's intention, and I have translated it accordingly.

6. In addition to those already identified, other corresponding details link these stories: the leitmotivs of the white kerchief or scarf worn by each heroine and their mocking smiles; the surnames Zasekina and Shumikhina, which are both quatrosyllabic and have the accent on the second syllable; and the names of the card games played in the two stories, *fanty* and *vint*, respectively, which are phonetically similar.

7. A. P. Chekhov, *Polnoe sobranie sochinenii i pisem*, 30 vols. (Moscow, 1974–83), *Sochineniia* 6:529. All citations will be from this edition and refer either to Chekhov's final version of "Volodya," pp. 197–209, or to Chekhov's first version of the story, "Ego pervaia liubov'," (His first love), pp. 529–536. Translations of Chekhov's text are my own.

8. Woldemar had experienced a similar sensation of shame upon first seeing Zinaida: "My heart took such a leap; I was very ashamed and happy: I felt a heretofore unknown excitement." After his game of forfeits, Woldemar had "sat on his chair, like one enchanted." And Vladimir Petrovich tells us: "What I felt was so new and so sweet."

9. In perhaps his most important, although somewhat later, commentary on Turgenev, Chekhov admitted (in a letter of February 24, 1893) to A. S. Suvorin that he admired a few of Turgenev's works (but did not mention "First Love") and then complained that "Turgenev's women and maidens are insufferable in their artificiality and . . . falseness. . . . When you remember Tolstoy's Anna Karenina, all these Turgenevian noble maidens with their enticing shoulders can go to the devil!" *Pis'ma* 5:174.

10. From his early stories on Chekhov purposely used names as a device for effect in characterization. See L. I. Kolokolova, *Imena sobstvennye v rannem tvorchestve A. P. Chekhova* (*Literaturno-khudozhestvennaia antroponimika*) (Kiev, 1961); and N. V. Surova, "Stilisticheskoe naznachenie lichnykh imen i familii v rannikh rasskazakh A. P. Chekhova," in *Sbornik statei i materialov*, vyp. 4 (Rostov, 1967), 258–70.

11. During his first game of forfeits with Zinaida and her retinue of admirers, Woldemar was so excited that he "began to laugh and chatter louder than the others" (*stal khokhotat' i boltat' gromche drugikh*).

12. Just before Volodya recognizes who is coming toward him, we read that "something white flashed at the gate." Niuta's white kerchief (*platok*) and sheet may foreshadow Volodya's end, for white (as well as black) is associated with death in Slavic folklore, and the adjective *mokhnatyi* ("furry," "hairy," "mossy," but here "fluffy") is a second epithet for the devil among the Russian people. Might Chekhov have applied these details intentionally to echo Turgenev's use of *lukavyi* and Zinaida's white scarf (variously termed *platok*, *platochek*, and *sharf*) in "First Love," as an indication that Niuta is even more tempting, and fatal, for young Volodya?

13. Turgenev, too, was disturbed by that disparity, but his concern tends to be reflected in philosophical exclamations at or near the end of his works. For example, we read in "First Love": "O Youth! O Youth! You don't care for anything, you seem to own all the treasures of the

world; even sorrow amuses you, even grief becomes you; you are so self-confident and insolent; you say, 'I alone am alive—look at me!' even while your days pass and vanish without trace and without number." The very early Chekhov might write in this vein, but only in parody.

14. In the final text Lushin admonishes Woldemar: "Let that be a lesson to you, young man. The whole trick is that people don't know how to part in time, how to break the net. . . . Watch out, don't get caught again." It is a pity that Chekhov's Volodya had no one to give him this sound advice. Be that as it may, many of Turgenev's later stories, such as "The Unhappy One" (Neschastnaia, 1869) and "Knock . . . Knock . . . Knock!" (Stuk... stuk... stuk...! 1871), his novelette *Torrents of Spring* (Veshnie vody, 1872), and the unfinished tale "Klara Milich" (1883) treat the unfortunate ends of despairing protagonists by their own hands. Given Chekhov's interest in Turgenev's works, it is almost certain that he read them.

15. The name is German and signifies humility. Is this an instance of Turgenev's sympathetic irony, suggesting that the once haughty Zinaida is now in a state of penitence?

16. Because of censorious criticism (following the tale's first publication) for his having written of adultery, Turgenev for the French edition added yet another death, the brief story of an old woman who, as she lay dying, pleaded: "Oh Lord, absolve me of my sins" (*Gospodi, otpusti mne grekhi moi*). The last line of "First Love" unites the deceased Zinaida, Woldemar's father, and the narrator himself, as Vladimir Petrovich confesses: "I became terribly afraid for Zinaida, and I wanted to pray for her, for my father—and for myself."

Allusion and Dialogue in "The Duel"

1. Zvonnikova, "Skvernaia bolezn' (K nravstvenno-filosofskoi problematike 'Dueli')," *Voprosy literatury*, no. 3 (1985):160. The term *cacophony of egos* is also Zvonnikova's.

2. Chekhov quotes Leskov as using the second-person singular form, *ty*, indicating either closeness or, in this context, a certain mock solemnity. Chekhov himself does not use a second-person form to Leskov. I have retained Chekhov's shift to historical present, which renders action more vividly and is common in standard literary Russian.

3. A. P. Chekhov, *Polnoe sobranie sochinenii i pisem*, 30 vols. (Moscow, 1974–83), *Pis'ma* 1:88. All translations are my own.

4. Ibid., 4:269.

5. N. S. Leskov, "Legenda o sovestnom Danile," in N. S. Leskov,

Polnoe sobranie sochinenii, vol. 30 (St. Petersburg, 1903), 3–19. All translations are my own.

6. "The Duel" appears in Chekhov, *Sochineniia* 7. All translations are my own.

The Black Monk

1. See Joan Delaney Grossman, "Blok, Briusov, and the *Prekrasnaia Dama*," in *Aleksandr Blok Centennial Conference*, ed. Walter N. Vickery (Columbus, Ohio, 1982), 160.

2. The question of Chekhov's attitude to symbolism has been discussed to some extent by V. I. Kuleshov in "Realizm Chekhova v sootnoshenii s naturalizmom i simvolizmom v russkoi literature kontsa XIX i nachala XX veka," in *Chekhovskie chteniia v Ialte* (Moscow, 1973), 21–37.

3. Nikolai Minsky, *Pri svete sovesti: Mysli i mechty o tseli zhizni* (St. Petersburg, 1890).

4. Bernice Rosenthal, *Dmitri Sergeevich Merezhkovsky and the Silver Age: The Development of a Revolutionary Mentality* (The Hague, 1975), 57–79.

5. The translations from Chekhov are mine. A Chekhovian critique of Schopenhauer has been suggested by E. I. Kulikova in her article "Ob ideinom smysle i polemicheskoi napravlennosti povesti Chekhova 'Chernyi monakh,'" *Metod i masterstvo*, vyp. 1, *Russkaia literatura*, no. 1, ed. V. V. Gur (Vologda, 1970), 272–81.

In Chekhov's correspondence we do not find a reference to Nietzsche until after the publication date of "The Black Monk," but it is likely that he had learned about the German philosopher's ideas from the press, especially from V. P. Preobrazhenskii's essay "Friedrich Nietzsche: Kritika morali al'truizma," *Voprosy filosofii i psykhologii* 15 (1892):115–60. For more detail about Nietzsche's early reception in Russia, see Edith W. Clowes, *The Revolution of Moral Consciousness: Nietzsche in Russian Literature, 1890–1914* (DeKalb, Ill., 1988), 43–66.

6. Dmitry Merezhkovsky, *Polnoe sobranie sochinenii*, 17 vols. (St. Petersburg, 1911–13), 13:13.

7. "Staryi vopros po povodu novogo talanta," *Severny vestnik* 11 (1888):77–99.

8. For details about the two men's relationship, see S. Povartsov, "'Liudi raznikh mechtanii' (Chekhov i Merezhkovskii)," *Voprosy literatury* 6 (1988):153–83.

9. *Chekhov i ego sreda* (Leningrad, 1930), 359–60.

10. "O prichinakh upadka i o novykh techeniiakh sovremennoi russkoi literatury," in Merezhkovsky, *Polnoe sobranie sochinenii* 14:304.

11. Merezhkovsky, *Polnoe sobranie sochinenii* 14:214. The probability that Chekhov was alluding to Merezhkovsky's brochure has been mentioned by M. Gushchin in *Tvorchestvo A. P. Chekhova* (Kharkov, 1954), 126–31. Gushchin's argument is that Chekhov was satirizing Merezhkovsky in an attempt to defend a Chernyshevskian aesthetic.

12. See Samuel D. Cioran, *Vladimir Solovyov and the Knighthood of the Divine Sophia* (Waterloo, Ont., 1977), 13, 40.

13. L. I. Ianzhul, "Vospominaniia," *Russkaia starina* 3 (1910):481.

14. Chekhov's letters of October 12, 1891, to N. A. Leykin and of November 18, 1891, to A. S. Suvorin show that he considered the philosopher a well-known person.

15. See, e.g., Evgenii Trubetskoi, "Lichnost' V. S. Solov'eva," in *Sbornik pervyi: O Vladimire Solov'eve* (Moscow, 1911), 45–74.

16. Vladimir Solovyov, *Sobranie sochinenii*, 12 vols. (St. Petersburg, 1911–14; Brussels, 1966–70), 12:14, 8, 33.

17. Ibid., 8.

18. Ibid., 7:55.

19. Ibid., 46.

20. Ibid., 23, 53.

21. Ibid., 44.

22. Ibid., 49.

23. Chekhov also alludes, of course, to Gaetano Braga's "Walachian Legend," sung by Tanya, as a source of Kovrin's hallucination.

24. See also M. P. Chekhov, *Vokrug Chekhova: Vstrechi i vpechatleniia* (Moscow, 1960), 251.

25. See Leonid Grossman, "The Naturalism of Chekhov," in *Chekhov: A Collection of Critical Essays*, ed. Robert Louis Jackson (Englewood Cliffs, N.J., 1967), 32–48 (originally in *Vestnik Evropy* 7 [1914]:218–47); and Phillip A. Duncan, "Chekhov's 'An Attack of Nerves' as 'Experimental' Narrative," in *Chekhov's Art of Writing: A Collection of Critical Essays*, ed. Paul Debreczeny and Thomas Eekman (Columbus, Ohio, 1977), 112–22.

26. V. B. Kataev, *Proza Chekhova: Problemy interpretatsii* (Moscow, 1979), 196.

27. Merezhkovsky, *Polnoe sobranie sochinenii* 15:248.

28. Joseph Conrad, "Vestiges of Romantic Gardens and Folklore Devils in Chekhov's 'Verochka,' 'The Kiss,' and 'The Black Monk,'" in *Critical Essays on Anton Chekhov*, ed. Thomas Eekman (Boston, 1989), 87.

29. For an analysis of natural archetypes in "The Black Monk," see Ruth Ellen Porter, "Language, Myth, and Art in the Poetic Process of Edith Wharton and Anton Chekhov," Ph.D. diss., University of North Carolina, 1990, pp. 106–41.

30. *Novosti i birzhevaia gazeta* 48 (February 17, 1894), p. 2, col. 4.

31. *Russkoe bogatstvo* 4 (1900):132–33.

32. A. P. Chudakov, *Mir Chekhova* (Moscow, 1986), 173.

33. I am paraphrasing Bernice Rosenthal's summary of the symbolist method. See her *Merezhkovsky*, 15.

34. Merezhkovsky, *Polnoe sobranie sochinenii* 15:249.

"The Darling"

1. A. S. Melkova, "Tvorcheskaia sud'ba rasskaz 'Dushechka,'" in *V tvorcheskoi laboratorii Chekhova* (Moscow, 1974), 81, 79.

2. M. Gorky, "A. P. Chekhov," in *Sobranie sochinenii*, vol. 18 (Moscow, 1963), 14.

3. See Leo Tolstoy, "An Afterword, by Tolstoy, to Chekhov's Story, 'Darling,'" in *What Is Art? and Essays on Art*, trans. Aylmer Maude (London, 1938), 325.

4. An analysis of Tolstoy's reproduction of Chekhov's "Darling" in *Krug chteniia* can be found in V. Lakshin, "Liubimyi rasskaz Tolstogo," in *Tolstoi i Chekhov* (Moscow, 1975), 95–97.

5. Melkova, 78.

6. Poggioli's interpretation of the "darling" as "one of the Russian equivalents of the Greek Psyche" is elaborated upon by Thomas Winner who points to the "ironic implications of the parallel with the myth." See Renato Poggioli, "Storytelling in a Double Key," in *The Phoenix and the Spider* (Cambridge, Mass., 1957), 130; and Thomas Winner *Chekhov and His Prose* (New York, 1966), 215.

7. All translations of "The Darling" and "Gooseberries" are mine based on A. P. Chekhov, *Polnoe sobranie sochinenii i pisem*, 30 vols (Moscow, 1974–83), *Sochineniia*, vol. 10, pp. 102–13, 55–65.

8. Tolstoy, 326.

9. Ibid.

10. J. Hollander, *The Figure of Echo* (Berkeley, 1984), 11.

11. See Z. Papernyi, *Zapisnye knizhki Chekhova* (Moscow, 1976) 331.

12. Tolstoy, 324.

13. Ibid., 327.

14. J. Kristeva, *Tales of Love* (New York, 1987), 103.

Offenbach and Chekhov

1. David Rissin, *Offenbach ou le rire en musique* (Paris, 1980), 84 87. Unless otherwise noted, all translations are my own.

2. Friedrich Nietzsche, *Die Willie zu Macht*, quoted in *Jacques Offenbach*, ed. Heinz-Klaus Metzger and Rainer Riehn, *Musik-Konzepte* 13 (May 1980):4.

3. A. I. Vol'f, *Khronika peterburgskikh teatrov s kontsa 1855 do nachala 1881 goda* (St. Petersburg, 1884), 75, 79–80, gives 128 performances; the number is corrected in Institut istorii iskusstv Ministerstva kul'tury SSSR, *Istoriia russkogo dramaticheskogo teatra v semi tomakh*, vol. 5, *1862–1881* (Moscow, 1980), 61. The situation was the same in the provinces: in Novocherkassk in 1870–71 six performances of *La belle Hélène* and *Orphée aux enfers* brought in 4,685 rubles, while Ostrovsky's *Paddle Your Own Canoe* (Ne v svoei sani ne sadis') earned only 118. I. Petrovskaia, *Teatr i zritel' provintsialnoi Rossii vtoraia polovina XIX veka* (Leningrad, 1979), 180.

4. "Kogda 'Prekrasnaia Elena' / Predstanet vdrug... / Vse zabyvaetsia vokrug: / Katkov, tarify i izmeny / I goloda nedug." Quoted in Iu. A. Dmitriev, *Mikhail Lentovskii* (Moscow, 1978), 56. M. N. Katkov was a reactionary editor who opposed the sociopolitical reforms of the times.

5. M. Yankovsky, *Operetta: Vozniknovenie i razvitie zhanra na zapade i v SSSR* (Leningrad, 1937), 221–22. A picture of the stage and the audience during a Russian production of *Orphée aux enfers* is given in V. Vsevolodsky-Gerngross, *Istoriia russkogo teatra*, ed. B. V. Alpers (Leningrad, 1929), 2:153, 459.

6. August Strindberg, *The Son of a Servant*, trans. Evert Sprinchorn (New York, 1966), 199–203. The interrelationship between Offenbach and the Second Empire *demi-monde* is dealt with in Siegfried Kracauer, *Jacques Offenbach und das Paris seiner Zeit* (1937), ed. Karsten Witte (Frankfurt, 1976).

7. Institut, 62. Ostrovsky's animadversions on operettas and *féeries* were summed up in his proposal for a national theater: "Zapiska o polozhenii dramaticheskogo iskusstva v Rossii v nastoiashchee vremia (1881)," in *Polnoe sobranie sochinenii*, 12 vols. (Moscow, 1973–80), 10:126–42.

8. Institut, 63; Yankovsky, 248–50.

9. N. Shchedrin (M. E. Saltykov), *Gospoda Golovëvy* (Moscow, 1968), 354, 438. A more urbane commentary on French operetta on the Russian stage can be found in K. Skalkovsky, *V teatral'nom mire: Nabliudeniia, vospominaniia i rassuzhdeniia* (St. Petersburg, 1899).

10. Yankovsky, 265–66.

11. I. P. Chekhov, "O Chekhove," in *Chekhov i teatr: Pis'ma, feletony, sovremenniki o Chekhove*, ed. E. D. Surkov (Moscow, 1961), 99.

12. V. F. Tretyakov, ed., *Ocherki istorii Taganrogskogo teatra* (Ta-

ganrog, [1928]), 59–61. His attendance is attested to by his brother Mikhail in M. P. Chekhov, *Anton Chekhov i ego siuzhety* (Moscow, 1923) and *Vokrug Chekhov: Vstrechi i vpechatlenniia* (Moscow, 1964).

13. Institut, 276.

14. P. A. Markov, *Iz istorii russkogo i sovetskogo teatra* (Moscow, 1974), 179.

15. "Iz zapisnoi knizhki Ivana Ivanycha," in A. P. Chekhov, *Polnoe sobranie sochinenii i pisem*, 30 vols. (Moscow, 1974–83), *Sochineniia* 10:236.

16. Letter to N. A. Leykin, August 21 and 24, 1883, in Chekhov, *Pis'ma* 1:81–82. See also 2:257; 4:159.

17. "Oskolki moskovskoi zhizni" 16, in Chekhov, *Sochineniia* 18: 253–54.

18. Chekhov, *Sochineniia* 16:128.

19. Letter to A. S. Suvorin, September 11 [23], 1897, in Chekhov, *Pis'ma* 7:49.

20. Ronald Hingley, in *Short Plays*, by A. P. Chekhov (London, 1969), 142, says: "Though Chekhov does not state the name of the play in which his hero has been acting, this was presumably Shakespeare's *Troilus and Cressida*, the dramatis personae of which include: 'Calchas, a Trojan priest taking part with the Greeks.'" Vera Gottlieb, in her *Chekhov and the Vaudeville* (Cambridge, Eng., 1982), 122–23, works hard to figure out the implications of this "Shakespearean" allusion. Curiously enough, one contemporary journalist did draw a parallel between *La belle Hélène* and *Troilus and Cressida:* S. I. Sychevsky, "Shekspir i Offenbakh," *Odesskii vestnik* 95 (May 31, 1873). It is unlikely, however, that the thirteen-year-old Chekhov read the article.

21. Rissin, 135.

22. Henri Meilhac and Ludovic Halévy, *La belle Hélène: Opéra bouffe en trois actes*, musique de Jacques Offenbach (Paris, 1960), 8 (act I). This text differs somewhat from that provided in the recording issued in the Everest Opera Series S-458/2. I have conflated them to create a master text.

23. "Nous naissons toutes soucieuses / De garder l'honneur de l'époux, / Mais de circonstances fâcheuses / Nous font mal tourner malgré nous... / Témoin l'exemple de ma mère! / Quand elle vit le cygne altier / Qui, chacun le sait, fut mon père, / Pouvait-elle se méfier? / Dis-moi, Vénus, quel plaisir trouves-tu / A faire ainsi cascader la vertu?

"Ah! malheureuse que nous sommes!... / Beauté, fatal présent des dieux! / Il faut lutter contre les hommes / Il faut lutter contre les dieux!... / Avec vaillance, moi, je lutte / Je lutte et ça ne sert à rien... / Car si l'Olympe veut ma chute, / Un jour ou l'autre il faudra bien."

24. Rissin, 150–52, 162.

Uncle Vanya as Prosaic Metadrama

1. Chekhov's belief in the prosaic virtues and skepticism of the grandiose and dramatic, in which he detected falsity, is often expressed explicitly in his correspondence. Consider, for instance, his famous letter of March 1886 to his wayward and talented brother Nikolai. "In my opinion," Chekhov wrote, "people of culture must fulfill the following conditions":

> 1. They respect the human personality and are therefore forbearing, gentle, courteous, and compliant. They don't rise up in arms over a misplaced hammer or a lost rubber band. They do not consider it a favor to a person if they live with him, and when they leave, they do not say: "It is impossible to live with you!"
>
> 2. They are sympathetic not only to beggars and cats. . . .
>
> 3. They respect the property of others and therefore pay their debts.
>
> 4. They are pure of heart and fear lying like fire. They do not lie even in small matters. . . . They don't pose. . . .
>
> 5. They do not humble themselves in order to arouse sympathy in others. They do not play upon the heartstrings in order to excite pity. . . . They don't say, "I'm misunderstood!". . .
>
> 8. They develop an aesthetic taste. They cannot bring themselves to fall asleep in their clothes, look with unconcern at a crack in the wall with bedbugs in it, breathe foul air, walk across a floor that has been spat on, or feed themselves off a kerosene stove. . . . What they, and especially artists, need in women is freshness, charm, human feeling, and that capacity to be not a . . . [whore] but a mother. . . .
>
> . . . Such are cultured people. It is not enough to have read only *Pickwick Papers* and to have memorized a monologue from *Faust*. . . .
>
> What you need is constant work. (Ernest J. Simmons, *Chekhov: A Biography* [Boston, 1962], 111–13).

2. Simmons, 111.

3. For a more extensive discussion of "generic refugees," see Gary Saul Morson, "Genre and Hero / *Fathers and Sons:* Inter-generic Dialogues, Generic Refugees, and the Hidden Prosaic," in *Literature, Culture, and Society in the Modern Age*, ed. Edward J. Brown, Lazar Fleishman, Gregory Freidin, and Richard Schupbach, Stanford Slavic Studies 4.1 (Stanford Calif., 1991), 336–81.

4. Letter to Leontiev-Shcheglov, May 3, 1888, Simmons, 165.

5. I have discussed the concept of "prosaics" in a number of articles, including "Prosaics: An Approach to the Humanities," *The American Scholar* (Autumn 1988):515–28; "Prosaics and *Anna Karenina*," *Tolstoy Studies Journal* 1 (1988):1–12; "Prosaics, Criticism, and Ethics,"

Formations 5, no. 2 (Summer-Fall 1989):77–95; and "The Potentials and Hazards of Prosaics," *Tolstoy Studies Journal* 2 (1989):15–40. The concept is also mentioned in my book *Hidden in Plain View: Narrative and Creative Potentials in "War and Peace"* (Stanford, Calif., 1987). It is central to the argument of the book I coauthored with Caryl Emerson, *Mikhail Bakhtin: Creation of a Prosaics* (Stanford, Calif., 1990).

6. Citations from Chekhov's plays are from *Chekhov: The Major Plays*, trans. Ann Dunnigan (New York, 1964).

7. Milton Ehre, ed., *The Theater and Plays of Nikolay Gogol: Plays and Selected Writings*, trans. Milton Ehre and Fruma Gottschalk (Chicago, 1980), 104.

Notes on Contributors

Anton Pavlovich Chekhov (1860–1904) is one of the world's greatest short-story writers and dramatists.

Ivan A. Bunin (1870–1953), a major Russian prose writer, was awarded the Nobel Prize in 1933.

Marena Senderovich, Assistant Professor of Russian Language and Literature at Ithaca College, has written on Chekhov, Pushkin, Baratynsky and Blok. She is co-author with Savely Senderovich of a collection of essays, *Penaty.*

Michael C. Finke, Assistant Professor of Russian Language and Literature at Washington University, St. Louis, has written on Chekhov and Pushkin.

Robert Louis Jackson, B.E. Bensinger Professor of Slavic Languages and Literatures at Yale University, and President of the International Chekhov Society, is author of *Dialogues with Dostoevsky: The Overwhelming Questions,* as well as of studies on Dostoevsky, Chekhov, Turgenev, Tolstoy, Gogol, Vyacheslav Ivanov, Pasternak, and other writers.

Vladimir Golstein, Assistant Professor of Russian Language and Literature at Yale University, has written on Pushkin and Lermontov.

Nils Åke Nilsson, Emeritus Professor of Slavic Languages and Literatures at the University of Stockholm, Sweden, and author of *Studies in Cechov's Narrative Technique: "The Steppe" and "The Bishop,"* has written extensively on Russian literature and culture (seventeenth-century Russian literature, Russian romanticism, Gogol, the Russian imagists, Osip Mandel'shtam, Pasternak, Ibsen in Russia, etc.).

257

Willa Chamberlain Axelrod received her doctorate in Slavic Languages and Literatures at Yale University and has taught Russian at Harvard University and M.I.T.

Alexandar Mihailovic, Assistant Professor of Russian Literature at Hofstra University, has written on Skovoroda, Gogol, and Bakhtin. He is also a translator of Russian literature.

Julie W. de Sherbinin, Assistant Professor of Russian Language and Literature at Colby College, has written on Chekhov, Dostoevsky, and Russian sectarianism.

Richard Peace, Professor of Russian Language and Literature and Head of the Department of Russian Studies at the University of Hull, England, is the author of *Chekhov: A Study of the Four Major Plays* and of works on Dostoevsky, Goncharov, and Gogol.

Liza Knapp, Assistant Professor of Slavic Languages and Literatures at the University of California, Berkeley, has written on Dostoevsky, Tolstoy, and Marina Tsvetaeva.

Joseph L. Conrad, Professor of Slavic Languages and Literatures at the University of Kansas, has written on Chekhov and Turgenev, among other Russian writers. He has also written on South Slavic folklore.

Paul Debreczeny, Professor of Slavic Languages and Literatures at the University of North Carolina (Chapel Hill), is the author of *The Other Pushkin: A Study of Alexander Pushkin's Prose Fiction* and has written on Gogol, Chekhov, Dostoevsky, and other Russian writers.

Svetlana Evdokimova, Assistant Professor of Russian literature at Brown University, has written on Pushkin and Chekhov.

Andrew R. Durkin, Fletcher Professor of Drama at Tufts University, is the author of *Anton Chekhov, Russian Dramatic Theory from Pushkin to the Symbolists*, and other studies.

Gary Saul Morson, Frances Hooper Professor of the Arts and Humanities and Professor of Slavic Languages at Northwestern University, is the author of *Hidden in Plain View: Narrative and Creative Potentials in "War and Peace"* and of other works on Dostoevsky, Tolstoy, Turgenev, and Chekhov. Co-author with Caryl Emerson of *Mikhail Bakhtin: Creation of a Prosaics*, he writes widely on Bakhtin and literary theory.